BUSINESS IN THE RAIN FORESTS

Corporations, Deforestation and Sustainability

Conrad B. MacKerron

Douglas G. Cogan
EDITOR

Investor Responsibility Research Center

Washington, D.C.

The Investor Responsibility Research Center compiles and impartially analyzes information on the activities of business in society, on the activities of institutional investors, on efforts to influence such activities, and on related public policies. IRRC's publications and other services are available by subscription or individually. IRRC's work is financed primarily by annual subscription fees paid by some 400 investing institutions for the Environmental Information Service, the Social Issues Service, the Corporate Governance Service, the South Africa Review Service and the Global Shareholder Service. This report is a publication of the Environmental Information Service. The Center was founded in 1972 as an independent, not-for-profit corporation. It is governed by a 21-member board of directors.

Executive Director: Margaret Carroll
Director, Environmental Information Service: Scott Fenn

ISBN 1-879775-08-5

Cover photo credits:
   Landsat image of deforestation in Rondonia, Brazil; Goddard Space Flight Center.
   Oil rig in Ecuadoran rain forest, courtesy of Maxus Energy Corp.
   Medicine man and ethnobotanist, courtesy of Shaman Pharmaceuticals.

Table of Contents

Tables

Figures

Acknowledgements

The Investor Responsibility Research Center is indebted to the Rockefeller Foundation and the John Merck Fund for generous grants that made this study possible. The Rockefeller Foundation grant was intended to support the Center's studies of corporations as they affect the global environment and the ways in which the environment and environment-related policies affect corporations in turn. The Merck Fund grant made possible the author's field studies in Brazil and Costa Rica, which provided an element of fresh, on-site research.

The author would like to thank Dr. Gerardo Budowski, professor of forestry at the University for Peace, San Jose, Costa Rica, who reviewed draft portions of the text and provided valuable insights that helped shape the study. Dr. Budowski is a former president of the International Union for the Conservation of Nature. The author also wishes to acknowledge Dr. William Burch, Hixon professor of natural resources management at Yale University's School of Forestry and Environmental Studies, and William Bentley, a senior research scientist at Yale and a senior program officer for Winrock International, who read draft portions of the text.

Research for this study involved contact with representatives of more than 100 multinational companies as well as scores of human rights, environmental, government and industry officials from around the world. Gabriel Sanchez provided invaluable assistance by contacting Latin American environmental groups that alerted us to a number of the multinational companies operating in their countries. Miguel Guevara and Leonardo Lacerda served as translators and guides during the author's site visits to Costa Rica and Brazil, respectively. Their understanding of their respective cultures enriched the experience and provided unique insights into the problems of tropical deforestation.

The author is also grateful for the spirit of cooperation that many companies showed in discussing their tropical forest operations. Summaries of these discussions, which appear throughout the book, generally reflect the degree to which company officials were forthcoming with information. Secondary sources also were used to provide additional information on companies' tropical forest operations; some of these sources are highly critical of the companies' operations. Readers are advised to consider the sources of information provided. (Footnotes indicating the sources of information appear throughout the book.) Because circumstances are constantly changing, readers may wish to seek information on developments that may have occurred since this research was performed.

The author would like to thank many others who provided insights and access to credible sources of information. I would like to extend special thanks to Wendy Baer of the International Hardwood Products Association; Diane Jukovsky, Chris Wille and Ivan Ussach of the Rainforest Alliance; Stephan Schwartzman of the Environmental Defense Fund; and Pam Wellner of the Rainforest Action Network.

At IRRC, I would like to thank Margaret Carroll, Scott Fenn, Carolyn Mathiasen and Teresa Opheim for internal review and comments on drafts of the report. Heidi Asbjornsen contributed valuable preliminary material. Shirley Carpenter produced this report for publication, and Susan Williams assisted in production of the report. I owe a special debt of gratitude to Douglas Cogan, Manager of Global Issues for IRRC's Environmental Information Service, for proposing this project and serving as an unfailing source of insight and support and as a superb editor.

Finally, thanks to my wife, Karen Arndt, for her personal support and belief in this project through difficult times.

Conrad B. MacKerron
Berkeley, California
July 1993

About the Author . . .

Conrad B. MacKerron served as a senior analyst for IRRC's Environmental Information Service while researching and writing this study. Before joining IRRC, Mr. MacKerron worked for more than a decade as a distinguished environmental journalist. He was Washington Bureau Chief for *Chemical Week*, with a specialization in environmental matters, and senior editor and reporter for the Bureau of National Affairs' *Environment Reporter*, where he co-authored the publication "Superfund II: A New Mandate." Mr. MacKerron is also former editor of *Critical Mass Energy Journal*, published by Public Citizen Inc. He holds a B.A. in Humanities from New College of the University of South Florida and an M.A. in Journalism and Public Affairs from The American University. He is currently Director of Social Research for Progressive Asset Management Inc., an Oakland, Calif., brokerage firm specializing in socially responsible investing.

Introduction and Summary

To many people, it is the latest environmental fad....Save the rain forests! Conservation groups have calculated how many acres of tropical forest will burn before you finish reading this sentence. Senators from the United States have gone to the Amazon and delivered paternalistic messages about the dangers of felling trees. Rock stars like Madonna, Sting and the Grateful Dead have even given benefit concerts. American consumers have been urged to boycott fast food restaurants because the hamburger meat might come from cattle raised on denuded rain forest land. Yet these same consumers are urged to eat fat-laden ice cream laced with equally fattening Brazil nuts because the practice ostensibly promotes the health of the forests. American food and timber companies insist, meanwhile, that *they* are not the ones deforesting the tropics, yet some readily admit to importing products from other companies that are.

Saving the rain forests sounds like a simple idea but it is not. And while it may seem like a passing environmental fad to some, saving the rain forests is an urgent global priority.

Rain forests and moist tropical forests (collectively known as humid tropical forests) cover only one-sixteenth of the earth's land surface, yet they are home to fully half of the planet's species. With about 1 percent of the world's humid tropical forests disappearing every year, perhaps 50,000 species are vanishing along with them. Four hundred million people also live in or near humid tropical forests. They, too, are endangered. As indigenous tribes struggle to maintain their traditional way of life, migrants seeking a "better" life often clear the forested land. Finding ways to preserve the rain forest *and* promote the development of the people who live there poses a tremendous challenge. It is one of the reasons why this book was written: to highlight practices that promote sustainable development—and others that do not.

Tropical deforestation often is regarded as an environmental problem, but at its root it is a social and economic problem. Developing countries are converting their forests largely in response to poverty, overpopulation and development problems. Often in alliance with multinational industries, they seek riches from the forests to build a stronger economic base—just as countries in Europe and North America have done before them. Only now the developed countries want to see tropical forests protected, requiring new forms of technical assistance and financial incentives to come forward. Some of the private sector initiatives featured in this book exemplify new thinking about the development process.

Consumers and investors also have a vital role to play in saving the rain forests. Environmentally conscious consumers are becoming more selective in their purchase of products from tropical nations. Yet they still find it difficult—if not impossible—to determine which products meet the test of "environmental sustainability." Investors face a similar dilemma. They cannot easily rule out investments in multinational companies simply because they are engaged in timber, agricultural, oil or mining activities in tropical nations. Yet some investors are trying anyway to make distinctions about the extent to which these activities are harming or benefitting the forests, and they are investing accordingly.

The primary objective of this book is to enable investors and consumers to learn more about products that come from tropical forest areas and the environmental practices of the companies bringing these products to market. Some of the book's major findings are as follows:

Timber

- About 10 percent of the world's tropical deforestation can be attributed directly to commercial logging. Timber interests make much greater damage possible, however, by building logging roads that provide migrants access to previously remote forest areas. Typically, these migrants slash and burn the remaining trees in selectively cut forests to grow crops, then move on to new land in two or three years when soil nutrients are depleted.

- No major U.S. forest products companies have large land holdings in rain forests today. Yet about $4 billion worth of tropical timber products are imported annually into the United States and sold by small- and medium-sized companies. Some large U.S. forest products companies continue to purchase tropical hardwood from these importers or buy it directly from loggers in tropical countries for resale in the United States.

- Japan is the world's largest tropical timber importer by far. Japanese trading companies such as **Dai-Ichi Kangyo**, **Fuyo** (Fuji), **Mitsubishi** and **Sumitomo** have major logging operations in Southeast Asia. Most U.S. forest products companies sold their timber concessions in the region as governments banned the export of unprocessed logs. **Georgia-Pacific** and **Weyerhaeuser** sold large concessions in Indonesia, Malaysia and the Philippines in the early 1980s, for instance, but they retain ties to some of the operations they helped establish.

- Pressure from environmental groups may have been a factor in some companies' recent decisions not to go forward with projects in tropical countries. **Scott Paper** scuttled a controversial plan for a major new operation in Indonesia in 1990, for example. **Stone Container's** bid to develop a huge plantation on virgin pine forest in Honduras also met opposition and was rejected by the Honduran government in 1992.

- **Scott Paper** and **Stone Container** continue to operate small plantation forests for pulp in degraded forest areas of Costa Rica, but no primary forest is being cut. **Champion International** operates a similar plantation in Brazil.

- U.S. tropical timber importers support a goal of sustainable forestry practices by their overseas suppliers by the year 2000, but they admit they have limited influence over forestry practices in developing countries. Efforts under way to set standards for sustainably grown wood include the Rainforest Alliance's Smart Wood Project, the Green Cross Certification program and the Forestry Stewardship Council, which hopes to serve as an international accreditation body for forest products certification systems in both tropical and temperate forests.

- Two home improvement chains, **B&Q** of the United Kingdom and **The Home Depot** of the United States, have expressed interest in purchasing tropical timber exclusively from sustainably grown sources by 1995. The current market for "green wood" represents only 2 to 3 percent of all tropical hardwood imported into North America and Europe. But the market could boom if consumers thought that retailers' "green" claims were credible.

Major companies profiled in the timber chapter include: **C. Itoh, Karl Danzer, Georgia-Pacific, Honshu Paper, Marubeni, Mitsubishi, Mitsui, Robinson Lumber, Scott Paper, Russell Stadelman, Stone Container** and **Weyerhaeuser**.

Petroleum

- The petroleum industry has the largest investment among U.S. multinationals operating in rain forest areas. American investment in oil and gas exploration and development totals billions of dollars in Southeast Asia, West Africa and Latin America.

- Oil production can be especially disruptive to rain forest communities when new roads and pipelines penetrate deep into the forest; a number of rain forest communities have been transformed forever. Production wastes infused with petroleum and other chemicals can leak into rivers when not properly contained, killing fish and contaminating food and drinking water supplies. Forest dwellers living near some oil projects reportedly have become sick or died because they drank or bathed in contaminated water.

- The Oil Industry Exploration and Production Forum has issued a set of voluntary guidelines for operations in rain forest areas. **Conoco** proposed a "model" oil development plan in Ecuador but withdrew from the project in 1991. **Maxus Energy** now is leading a multi-company effort in Ecuador and has pledged to follow through with Conoco's environmentally sensitive plan. **Chevron** has a similar model program under way in Papua New Guinea.

- **Texaco** and **Petroecuador** are conducting an environmental audit of their joint operations in Ecuador, which date back to the 1960s. Results of the audit (expected later this year) should shed light on past oil industry practices in tropical areas as well as the evolution of regulations in developing countries to protect rain forests and rain forest dwellers.

Major companies profiled in the petroleum chapter include: **Atlantic Richfield, British Petroleum, Chevron, Elf-Aquitaine, Exxon, Maxus Energy, Mobil, Occidental Petroleum, Royal Dutch Shell, Texaco** and **Texas Crude Petroleum**.

Mining

- When performed responsibly, mining does less damage to rain forests than many other commercial activities. Mining generally encompasses much smaller areas than commercial timber and agricultural operations; reforestation can occur after mining has ceased. Surface and groundwater contamination from mine tailings and cyanide solutions remains a serious threat to the environment, however, and inadequate restorative measures can leave a permanent blight on the landscape.

- Huge mining conglomerates in Brazil such as **Mineracao Rio do Norte** and **Companhia Vale do Rio Doce** (in which North American mining companies like **Alcan** and **Alcoa** have interests) have spawned a giant export industry for Brazil and created major social and environmental problems within the Amazon. Pig-iron blast furnaces—fueled by charcoal wood—have consumed millions of acres of rain forest. Disputes between miners, cattle ranchers and forest dwellers have led to more than 1,000 murders since 1980. Tens of thousands of forest dwellers have been displaced from their homes.

- Illegal gold mining by prospectors is pervasive in much of Latin America. Rivers poisoned by mercury during processing of mining ore has contaminated the food and water supplies of many forest communities. The Brazilian government has taken recent steps to demarcate Indian lands in the Amazon and evacuate "garimpeiros" who have mined indiscriminately there.

- The International Water Tribunal (an ad hoc adjudicatory body) ruled in 1992 that the huge Ok Tedi mine in Papua New Guinea, partly owned by **Amoco**, has severely polluted rivers and disrupted area ecosystems. Human rights groups in Brazil have criticized **Alcoa** for proposing a new bauxite mine in a rain forest area claimed by descendants of freed black slaves. **Freeport McMoRan** has been accused of pollution and human rights abuses at its huge copper and gold mine in Irian Jaya, Indonesia. A wave of protests and a sabotage campaign led to the closure of the giant Bougainville mine (partly owned by **RTZ**) off the coast of Papua New Guinea in 1989.

Major companies profiled in the mining chapter include: **Alcan, Alcoa, Amoco, Billiton, Brascan, CRA Ltd., Freeport McMoRan, Placer Dome and RTZ**.

Agriculture

- The extent of damage to rain forest ecosystems from corporate agriculture depends largely on the crops grown on denuded lands. The use of heavy equipment and farm chemicals in some instances degrades rain forest environments more severely than traditional slash-and-burn farming methods. Cattle ranching is the most destructive farming activity in former rain forests, although recent evidence suggests that most abandoned pasturelands recover well over time.

- Beef exports to the United States do not appear to be a major source of tropical deforestation. No major U.S. fast food company admits to such imports; **Burger King** halted a practice of buying rain forest beef in 1987. While tremendous acreage has been cut for cattle grazing, available data suggest that most of the beef raised on denuded rain forest land is consumed domestically in tropical countries. American laws that allow beef importers to relabel their product as domestic beef make imports hard to track, however.

- Banana companies—principally **Chiquita, Del Monte** and **Dole**—have cut large tracts of rain forest in Central and South America and are still expanding their plantations. Adjoining rain forest areas are polluted when pesticide runoff enters rivers and streams. Offshore coral reefs and sea animals (such as leatherback turtles) also are harmed by banana operations. The Rainforest Alliance is working with banana growers to improve their environmental practices and bring "eco-friendly bananas" to market.

- The tobacco industry has been a chief contributor to tropical deforestation in the south Atlantic coast of Brazil, where destruction of the rain forest is nearly complete. **Philip Morris** and **RJR Nabisco** are among the largest tobacco companies operating in Brazil, which is the world's third largest tobacco producer. Most major tobacco companies do not grow and cure their own tobacco, however; rather, they purchase it through contractual arrangements with farmers or local companies. Tobacco curing with charcoal wood is a larger source of deforestation than tobacco growing itself.

Major companies profiled in the agriculture chapter include: **BAT Industries, Chiquita Brands, Coca-Cola, Dole Food, Del Monte, Geest, Goodyear, McDonalds, Metropolitan Foods, Philip Morris, RJR Nabisco** and **Unilever**.

Innovative Investment Opportunities

- The rate of tropical deforestation will not diminish significantly until the underlying social, economic and political problems that contribute to it— poverty, overpopulation, inequitable land distribution and government corruption—are effectively addressed. Nevertheless, tropical forests offer intriguing, new investment opportunities.

- Pharmaceutical companies like **Merck**, **Eli Lilly** and **Shaman Pharmaceuticals** are investing millions of dollars in an effort to develop new drugs from native species in tropical forests. Other commercial products extracted from the rain forests include fruits, nuts, fiber, resins and latex rubber. Further development of the trade in nontimber forest product markets, if done responsibly, may hold a key to preserving large tracts of rain forest—and provide higher returns on investment than traditional logging or slash-and-burn agricultural practices.

- So-called "debt-for-nature" swaps have emerged as another innovative way for the financial community to help preserve tropical forests. In these complicated transactions, a developing country is able to retire a portion of its foreign debt by agreeing to take certain measures to protect its tropical forests. Critics say that developing countries are trading away national sovereignty in order to reduce their debt burdens, but proponents maintain that the swaps have provided vital, sustainable sources of funding for conservation organizations and indigenous groups in forested regions.

- Power companies like **AES Corp.** and **New England Electric System** are planting and preserving millions of trees in tropical countries to offset carbon dioxide emissions from fossil-fueled power plants. (Carbon dioxide is a greenhouse gas; its buildup in the atmosphere may contribute to global warming.) The efficacy of these offset programs is yet to be determined, however. Tree seedlings can perish if neglected after planting, and preservation of certain forests can put added harvesting pressure on neighboring forests. Also, in the case of an AES plant in Hawaii, coal is being provided from a coal strip mine owned by **British Petroleum** and **RTZ Corp.** The mine is in a degraded rain forest area of Indonesia.

New means of economic development are critical to the preservation of the rain forests. This book identifies ways that investors can invest in such development. A sampler of innovative rain forest projects appears at the end of Chapter 8. New sources of international funding, local lending projects and venture capital partnerships also are discussed. While such investments often carry high risk, they offer investors a way to help reduce the rate of tropical deforestation while improving the quality of life for people who live in or near rain forests areas.

Conclusions

Efforts to tame the world's tropical forests have been underway for more than a century. The rubber boom in the Amazon brought the first wave of commercial development. Visionary businessmen like Henry Ford (and later Daniel Ludwig) failed to see the complexities of establishing commercial ventures in this wild land; they lost millions. Other commercial enterprises have been more successful. Profitable or not, such ventures have forever altered the nature of tropical forests. Nations have sparred over land once regarded as inaccessible and inconsequential. Local tribes have suffered indignities and disease from an influx of immigrants. Questions still remain as to who has sovereign rights over tropical forests, its peoples and resources.

Despite these vexing issues, the riches of tropical forests are simply too tantalizing to ignore. Pursuit of their precious resources has opened up vast tracts of land and spawned large domestic industries. The scale of deforestation has increased with the construction of new roads, the damming of rivers, the creation of new towns and the felling of millions of acres of trees for food, fuel and shelter.

Survival of the remaining tropical forests will depend on better-planned and -managed development schemes that give value to the forest, provide indigenous peoples with the means to make a living and still preserve enough of the forest to allow it to perform its essential ecological function. Yet with an estimated 1 percent or less of tropical forests now managed in a "sustainable" fashion, the challenge facing foresters and governments in tropical countries—which own 80 percent of the world's tropical forests—is indeed formidable.

Unless and until the governments of the world come together on a rescue plan, responsibility to save the rain forests will remain in the hands of those who occupy the forests, those who consume their resources and those who invest in or manage the enterprises that operate there. The best hope may be to improve the environmental management practices of timber, oil, mining and agricultural industries that are operating in rain forest areas already. Also important will be the effort to develop new markets for nontimber forest products—including foods, fibers and pharmaceuticals—and to stimulate innovative investment policies—such as debt-for-nature swaps and carbon offset programs—that give greater value to the forests, provide a livelihood for its peoples and limit the destruction of one of the world's most precious natural resources.

Each enterprise engaged in tropical forest activities leaves its own particular footprint on the land. This report offers a detailed examination of companies engaged in timber, oil, mining and agricultural activities—and their impacts— on tropical forests around the world. Readers may wish to evaluate whether these companies should carry on with their existing plans, amend their plans to make them more culturally and ecologically amenable or withdraw from tropical forest activities altogether. Given the global reach of tropical forest products and the global importance of tropical forest ecosystems, the choice is for investors and consumers as well as for the companies themselves to make.

Chapter 1
Tropical Forests in Trouble

$\mathbf{T}$ he earth's tropical forests are disappearing just as the world is waking up to their enormous value. These magnificent yet fragile lands are caught in a whipsaw of human need and economic aspiration that will change them forever, if they survive at all. Half of the world's tropical forests have vanished in this century—10 percent of them in the 1980s alone. If the trend is not reversed, most remaining virgin tropical forests will be wiped out in the next century.

Tropical forests are at the mercy of complex forces: a burgeoning world population in need of more room to grow, political systems that discourage land reform, and economic systems that undervalue forest resources and exploit them primarily for short-term gain. At the same time, tropical forests are crucial to life on earth in many ways. Approximately 400 million people depend on them for fuelwood, food and shelter—including more than 50 million indigenous forest dwellers. Tropical forests also provide habitat for life-saving medicinal plants and many strange and wonderful creatures. Covering a mere 4 percent of the planet's surface, tropical forests are home to perhaps as many species as the rest of the world combined.

Altogether, about 14 billion acres, or roughly one-third of the earth's *land* surface, is forested. Tropical forests account for a third of this forested acreage and grow in more than 80 countries. Between 2 billion and 2.5 billion acres of tropical forest is considered moist forest or rain forest—with mean annual temperatures exceeding 75 degrees Fahrenheit and rainfall totals ranging from 80 inches to more than 300 inches a year. Canopies in these humid tropical forests are so thick that little sunlight penetrates to the forest floor, with the consequence that much of the wildlife lives in the trees themselves. The understory and forest floor are a mosaic of unique and colorful shrubs, plants and vines—all competing for light, nutrients and water. Another 2.5 billion acres of tropical forests consists of open woodlands and fallow areas. These dry tropical forests have rainfall totals of less than 80 inches a year.[1]

While tropical forests look lush and fertile, their appearance is deceiving. Less than 10 percent are rooted in deep soils; most have poor-quality topsoil only a few inches deep. (By contrast, temperate forests often have seven feet or more of rich topsoil). In some areas, humid tropical forests grow on white sandy soil that resembles desert soil. The lateritic clay that underlies most tropical soils is an especially poor retainer of moisture. Rain forest trees compensate by developing enormous buttress-like root systems that spread out laterally to provide stability and tap sufficient moisture.[2]

Sixty to 75 percent of the rain that falls on humid tropical forests condenses back into clouds and falls again. Such abundant rainfall helps to maintain the lush vegetation and the local hydrologic cycle. Biomass decay from the vegetation supplies the organic carbon, nitrogen and other nutrients necessary to nourish the trees. (In a temperate forest, most nutrients come directly from the soil.) Countless varieties of insects and fungi speed up the process of biomass decay in this humid climate, facilitating the rapid growth of rain forest trees.

Like other forests, tropical forests perform an important earthly function by stabililizing the soil to control erosion and flooding. But tropical forests exert a powerful influence over the atmosphere as well. Like a human lung operating in reverse, tropical forests "breathe in" vast amounts of carbon dioxide from the atmosphere and "exhale" vast amounts of oxygen. Acre for acre, tropical forests harbor five to ten times as much carbon as temperate forests—a result of their higher rate of photosynthesis. When they are cut and burned, tropical forests return this carbon to the atmosphere as carbon dioxide, the primary gas linked to global warming. As a result, tropical deforestation contributes about 15 to 20 percent as much carbon dioxide to the atmosphere as the burning of fossil fuels. Brazil, in fact, now is one of the world's largest emitters of carbon dioxide, principally because it is felling more acres of tropical forest than any other nation. (For more on efforts to sequester carbon in tropical forests, see Chapter 7.)

Location of Tropical Forests

Nearly all tropical forests are in the warm climes between the Tropic of Cancer and the Tropic of Capricorn. Rain forests tend to grow in coastal areas or close to the equator, where temperatures are relatively steady and annual rainfall exceeds 80 inches. Moist tropical deciduous forests, or monsoon forests, grow on the edges of rain forests, where rainfall is more seasonal and does not sustain leaf growth year-round. Like temperate deciduous forests, monsoon forests shed their leaves to conserve stored food and energy. In most other respects, however, they are similar to tropical rain forests. Together, tropical rain forests and moist deciduous tropical forests are known for purposes of this book as humid tropical forests.

Half of the world's humid tropical forests are found in the Americas. Such forests extend as far north as Mexico and spread southward through Central and South America to the northern tip of Argentina. Brazil alone has approximately 883 million acres of humid tropical forest—30 percent of the world's total and more than the next two highest countries combined (Indonesia with 281 million acres and Zaire with 261 million acres). The United States has humid tropical forests in the state of Hawaii and the commonwealth of Puerto Rico.

In Africa, an area as large as Western Europe is partially covered with humid tropical forests. The forests spread across equatorial Africa, from Senegal in the

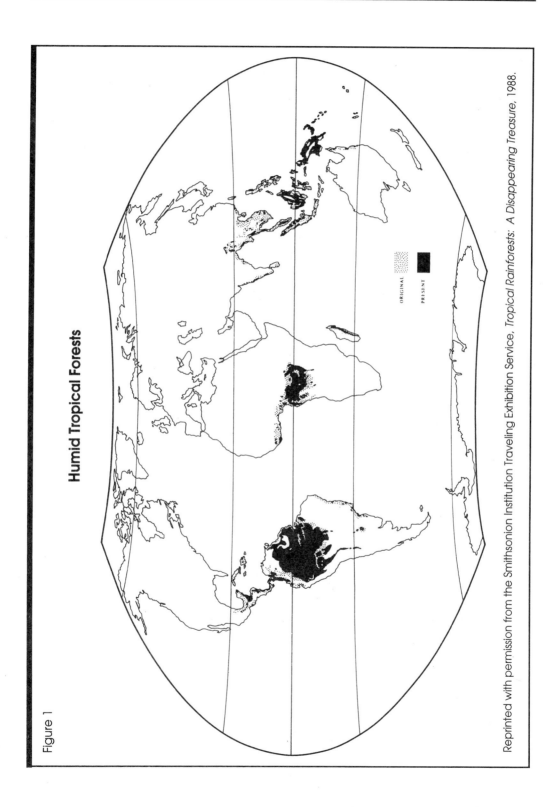

Figure 1

Humid Tropical Forests

ORIGINAL
PRESENT

Reprinted with permission from the Smithsonian Institution Traveling Exhibition Service, *Tropical Rainforests: A Disappearing Treasure*, 1988.

west through the Horn of Africa to the south and east. The forests continue inland from Cameroon, Gabon and The Congo through Zaire. Zaire alone harbors one-eighth of the world's rain forests—and half of all of Africa's. Madagascar, off the east coast of Africa, is renowned for many unique rain forest species. Separated from the continent for 150 million years, Madagascar hosts 8,500 types of plants—75 percent of which exist nowhere else—although 90 percent of the land in Madagascar has been denuded for cattle raising and agriculture.

In Asia, the tropical forests still cling to parts of India, Bangladesh, Burma (now called Myanmar by its military government), Laos, Thailand, Cambodia and Vietnam. Large tracts of humid tropical forest once were found in the Pacific islands of the Philippines, Malaysia, Indonesia and Papua New Guinea, although many are being rapidly depleted now.

Some nations have lost their virgin tropical forests forever. All primary tropical forests are gone or nearly gone in Bangladesh, Benin, El Salvador, Haiti, Sierra Leone, Sri Lanka and Togo. In the next decade, virgin tropical forests are likely to disappear in Burma, China, Côte d'Ivoire, Ghana, Laos, Nigeria, the Philippines and Vietnam. In many of these countries, however, secondary forests have sprung up to replace the virgin forests, and some governments have created large forest plantations. Accordingly, while primary tropical forests are being lost at an estimated rate of 42 million acres a year, secondary forests and forest plantations are expanding at a rate of more than 21 million acres a year.

Biodiversity of Tropical Forests

Tropical forests possess at least half and perhaps far more of the world's plant and animal species. While the total number of species inhabiting the planet is far from certain, estimates range from 6 million to 100 million species. Only 1.4 million species have been catalogued and named thus far.

The most studied species are large creatures living outside the tropics, such as birds and mammals. Probably twice as many species of birds and mammals live inside the tropics as outside, although no one knows for sure. If the same ratio applies to tropical insects, there may be two yet unnamed species of tropical insects for each named temperate or boreal one.[3] Scientists do know that more types of insects live in the tropics than anywhere else; the question is whether there are 3 million insect species or perhaps as many as 30 million.

Harvard University biologist Edward O. Wilson estimates that as many as 27,000 tropical forest species are going extinct each year. Wilson once retrieved 43 species of ants from just one tree in Peru. That is about as many ant species as live in all of the British Isles.[4] Smithsonian Institution biologist Terry Erwin once counted 1,200 species of beetles residing in the canopies of tropical trees in Panama. Extrapolating from his count, Erwin calculates that as many as 600 insect species may inhabit each variety of tropical tree. Multiplying that figure by 50,000 species of known tropical trees, possibly 30 million species of insects may reside in tropical forests.[5]

Tropical forests support about two-thirds of the world's 250,000 known

Table 1

Countries with Threatened Humid Tropical Forests

Country	Closed forest area thousands of acres	Annual deforestation rate thousands of acres	% loss
Latin America and the Caribbean			
Bolivia	108,705	215	0.2
Brazil	882,976	4,415	0.5
Colombia	114,608	2,025	1.8
Ecuador	35,197	840	2.4
Peru	172,110	688	0.4
Venezuela	78,720	309	0.4
Sub-Saharan Africa			
Cameroon	40,755	247	0.6
Congo	52,710	54	0.1
Côte d'Ivoire	11,011	716	6.5
Gabon	50,635	37	0.1
Madagascar	25,441	370	1.5
Zaire	261,203	450	0.2
Asia and the Pacific			
Burma	78,894	1,672	2.1
India	90,254	3,705	4.1
Indonesia	281,321	2,223	0.8
Malaysia	51,860	630	1.2
Papua New Guinea	84,548	54	0.1
Philippines	23,490	353	1.5

SOURCE: World Resources Institute, *World Resources 1992-93.*

species of vascular plants—including 86,000 in the Americas, 30,000 in Africa and 45,000 in Asia. One Harvard biologist in Kalimantan, Indonesia, has identified more than 700 species of trees in just 10 one-hectare (2.47-acre) plots. That equals the number of tree species found in all of North America.[6]

Thirty percent of all bird species are thought to be dependent on tropical forests—about 1,300 in the Americas, 400 in Africa and 900 in Asia.[7] While much evidence of rain forest destruction seems remote outside the tropics, in the United States one tangible sign is a recent dramatic decline in the number of migrating songbirds, whose wintering habitat is being diminished.[8]

Slash-and-burn agriculture and other forms of development upset the precarious balance that sustains the tropical forests. In effect, such fragmented forests become less than the sum of their parts. In one pioneering experiment outside of Manaus, Brazil, researchers from the World Wildlife Fund found that the number of species declined dramatically when only patches of the original forest remained. In plots of less than 25 acres (10 hectares), for example, colonies of army ants no longer survived, prompting birds who feed on them to vanish as well. The 25 acre plots also became too small for larger mammals like wild pigs. And predators such as jaguars need much larger plots—perhaps 1,000 times the size—to accommodate their wide-ranging territorial needs. The ability of these animals to roam has an important indirect effect on the forest, because their droppings are prime agents for seed dispersal that assures new growth.[9]

Therefore, concerns about biodiversity mount as the humid tropical forests fall. As a rule of thumb, the number of species eventually falls by half when a patch of habitat shrinks by 90 percent. Based on these calculations, Wilson of Harvard University figures that 10 to 22 percent of rain forest species will be lost in the next 30 years if current trends in habitat destruction are not reversed. Over the next 50 years, more than a quarter of the planet's species could be eliminated.[10]

In June 1993, President Bill Clinton signed an international convention aimed at preserving biodiversity. (For more on the biodiversity convention, see

Figure 2

Biodiversity 'Hot Spots'

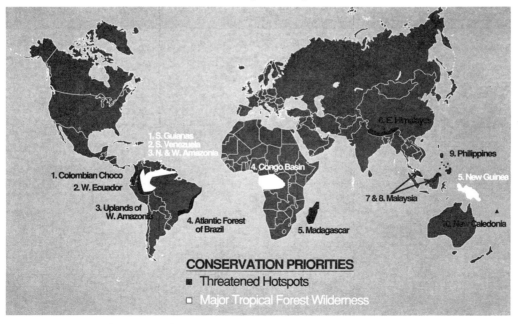

The rate at which tropical forests are being lost creates an urgent need to protect remaining areas of prime biodiversity. Conservation International, a group dedicated to tropical forest preservation, has identified 10 such biodiversity "hot spots."

Chapter 7.) President George Bush had refused to sign the biodiversity treaty during his visit to the United Nations Conference on Environment and Development, popularly known as the Earth Summit, in Rio de Janeiro, Brazil, in June 1992. In one of his last official acts as president, however, Bush did order the establishment of a national center for biodiversity studies. The center—to be housed at the Smithsonian Institution—will assemble information on plant and animal diversity in the United States and will serve as part of a United Nations worldwide monitoring program. The center is expected to become operational in early 1994 and is likely to be headed by Thomas Lovejoy, an eminent biologist with the Smithsonian Institution, who is presently on loan to the Clinton administration.

Food from Tropical Forests

Destruction of tropical forests and the associated loss of species is not just a scientific and political concern. Tropical forests contain a wealth of animal and plant material that is of economic value to society as well. Food and medicine are principal among these. Food crops that supply the bulk of the world's diet, such as wheat and corn, have wild ancestors found only in tropical forests. Such wild strains can be bred to increase the productivity of food crops and offer natural forms of protection from insects and diseases.

Many staples in kitchens around the world—rice, potatoes, tomatoes, sugar, citrus, peanuts, pepper, coffee, chocolate and vanilla—originated in tropical countries. An estimated 98 percent of U.S. crop production, in fact, has come from outside American borders. "If we had to live on plants that originated in the United States, our diet would consist of pecans, sunflower seeds, cranberries, blueberries, grapes, wild rice, pumpkins, squashes and jerusalem artichokes," writes ethnobotanist Mark Plotkin, who studies indigenous peoples and their use of tropical plants.[11]

Of the thousands of species of plants known to be edible, only about 150 have entered into world commerce. Today, fewer than 20 plant species produce most of the world's foods. The four major carbohydrate crop species—wheat, corn, rice and potatoes—feed more people than the next 26 most prominent crops combined. The tropics offer a promising place to look for new crops to reduce heavy reliance on such a small number of species. Some of the more interesting candidates to enter the food trade include:

- **acai**, a palm tree grown in many parts of Brazil whose fruits can be eaten separately or pulped into wine and ice cream; its palm hearts are considered delicacies in salads, and oil from the trees is used for cooking;

- **amaranth**, a grain grown in Latin America since pre-Columbian times; it is already sold as a cereal in American health food stores and can take the place of wheat in a number of applications;

- **babassu palm**, whose oil is nearly identical to olive oil in its chemical and physical properties and can be refined into a cooking oil or used to make detergents and plastics; a single tree may produce up to a half-ton of the oil-laden fruit;

—Photo by Conrad MacKerron.

Guanabana is an example of a potentially marketable, nontimber rain forest product. Beneath its prickly skin is a tasty fruit that can be eaten raw or pulped into a juice.

- **camu-camu**, a fruit with 30 times more vitamin C than orange juice;

- **guanabana**, a fruit native to the neotropics that can be eaten raw or made into a fruit drink or yogurt;

- **lulo**, a yellow-orange fruit made into a refreshing drink, already marketed as frozen concentrate in Panama, Costa Rica and Guatemala; and

- **peach palm**, or pupunha, which yields bunches of fruit that can produce more carbohydrates per acre than corn.

While the potential economic value of foods such as these remains undetermined, one study by Charles Peters of the Institute of Economic Botany at the New York Botanical Garden has yielded some promising preliminary results. Peters examined 12 forest products from a village in northeastern Peru that are, or could be, sold in markets. Peters found that harvesting edible fruits, rubber, oils and cocoa would generate nearly twice as much revenues as harvesting timber or grazing cattle on the same land. Critics of Peters' study maintain that he selected unusually bountiful plots and that market prices for the products would drop as significantly larger quantities were gathered and sold. Nevertheless, Peters estimates that tropical forest products from one acre of land could generate $2,563 in revenues over the next 50 years, with the products sold in local markets and the cost of harvesting deducted from the market price. If the same land were used as a timber plantation, Peters estimates that only $1,289 in revenues would be generated per acre, and only $1,198 if converted to cattle pasture.[12] (For more on sustainably grown nontimber forest products, see Chapter 7.)

Medicines from Tropical Forests

Another largely untapped market in the tropical forests are medicinal plants that indigenous tribes have used for thousands of years to treat ailments and ward off disease. In India alone, more than 2,500 plant species have been officially recognized for their medicinal value, although 85 percent of the world's plants to date have not been screened for their therapeutic potential.

Despite a lack of screening, tropical plants already have made impressive contributions to modern medicine. More than 120 clinically useful prescription drugs now on the market are derived from higher plant species. Of these species, 39 originated in tropical forests, resulting in 47 marketed drugs.[13] Perhaps the most striking examples are vincristine and vinblastine, alkaloids isolated from the rosy periwinkle, found originally in the forests of Madagascar. The drugs have been used to treat childhood leukemia and Hodgkin's disease, turning an 80 percent mortality rate around to an 80 percent survival rate. Sales of the drugs are estimated at $100 million a year.

Another prominent drug is the plant extract curare—used originally by South American tribes as a poison for the tips of darts and arrows. Western scientists found that curare could be used safely as a relaxant to control muscle spasms. Other rain forest-derived drugs include quinine to fight malaria, reserpine (from the rauwolfia plant) for hypertension, ipecac as an emetic, quinidine (from the cinchona tree) as an antiarrhythmic for heart problems, and pilocarpine (from the jaborandi tree) to treat rheumatism and glaucoma. Even the birth control pill was derived originally from the wild Mexican yam. The Mexican yam produces chemicals from which oral contraceptives and sex hormones are synthesized. These same chemicals can be used in the production of other steroid drugs, including those used to treat skin diseases and various forms of arthritis.[14]

Of course, tropical forests also have been the source of some prominent illegal drugs. Coca, the plant from which cocaine is derived, provides a multi-billion-dollar export market for Colombia that dwarfs that country's largest legal export—coffee. But a coca derivative, lidocaine, also is used in the prevention and treatment of one of the most common causes of death from heart attack—irregularities of the electrical rhythm of the heart known as ventricular fibrillation.

Altogether, the cross-counter value of plant-derived pharmaceuticals exceeds $40 billion a year. Yet the vast majority of pharmaceutical companies have not expressed much interest in prospecting the rain forest for new drugs, because in a sense it is like looking for needles in a haystack. As millions more forested acres are cleared each year, however, ethnobotanists fear that other potentially life-saving plants may vanish along with them. One fledgling U.S. company, **Shaman Pharmaceuticals**, is making a serious effort to study the folklore and contact the native healers of tropical forests to identify promising new drugs. In 1992, **Eli Lilly** made a $4 million equity investment in Shaman to further its efforts.

Before then, **Merck** had been the only major pharmaceutical company that routinely screened hundreds of tropical plants a year, in an arrangement with the New York Botanical Garden.[15] Merck also struck a deal with a private Costa Rican research organization in 1991 in which Merck agreed to pay $1.1 million over two years for rights to explore for rain forest plants with possible medicinal value. Largely because of such enterprises, Costa Rican biologists have managed to catalogue more species in the last three years than in the previous 120 years combined.[16] (For more on medicines derived from tropical forests, see Chapter 7.)

Causes of Rain Forest Destruction

Despite many compelling reasons for saving the rain forests—species preservation, carbon sequestration, food production, medicinal products and more—the forests continue to fall at alarming rates. Past estimates of the loss have been hampered by a lack of reliable data. In 1980, the United Nations Food and Agricultural Organization estimated that 28.1 million acres of tropical forest were being cleared annually, based on data gathered in the 1970s. Ten years later, the World Resources Institute released an analysis of nine critical tropical forested nations which concluded that deforestation is occurring at a much higher rate—somewhere in a range of 40 million to 50 million acres a year during the 1980s. That amount of forest loss is equal to all the land in the state of Washington and represents about a 1 percent yearly loss of the world's remaining humid tropical forests.[17]

The 1990 data indicate that the rate of deforestation is much higher than previously thought in Brazil, Burma, Cameroon, Costa Rica, India, Indonesia, the Philippines, Thailand and Vietnam. The top loss leaders are Brazil, which lost up to 7.5 million acres a year during the 1980s (although recent figures indicate that Brazil's deforestation rate has slowed considerably since 1987); India, which lost nearly 4 million acres a year during the 1980s; and Indonesia, with more than 2 million acres in annual losses. Rates of deforestation also rose dramatically in Colombia, Côte d'Ivoire, Laos, Nigeria and Thailand during the 1980s.

Forest loss is most acute in land-scarce countries with little room for a burgeoning population and a growing economy. Costa Rica, for instance, lost more than a million acres of forest during the 1980s, equal to 25 percent of the country's remaining forested land area. This small Central American country has now put a greater percentage of its land area under protected status than virtually any other nation in the world, but most unprotected places in Costa Rica already have been deforested. While Costa Rica is committed to a program of massive reforestation, it, like many other tropical countries, will likely be importing wood from other countries before the end of the century.

The root causes of deforestation are complex and vary by region. In Central and South America, the most widely cited causes are poverty and population pressures. Transient rural poor commonly practice unsustainable agriculture and harvest tropical wood for fuel and temporary shelter. But in Costa Rica, according to a 1990 report by two World Bank economists, "preliminary information indicates, contrary to our expectations, [that] most of the deforestation at present is not being done by squatters, but driven by profit and asset

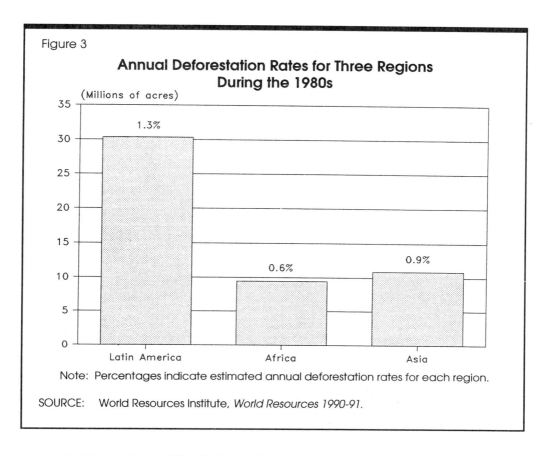

Figure 3

Annual Deforestation Rates for Three Regions During the 1980s

(Millions of acres)

Note: Percentages indicate estimated annual deforestation rates for each region.

SOURCE: World Resources Institute, *World Resources 1990-91.*

maximization motives of the timber industry, banana companies and large cattle ranchers."[18]

Similarly, in parts of Central Africa and Southeast Asia, the tropical timber industry is considered a primary cause of rain forest destruction.[19] In some locations, mineral and oil extraction is to blame. In many forested areas, however, the complex interaction between modern commercial activities and traditional slash-and-burn agriculture makes it difficult, if not impossible, to assign clear responsibility for the loss of tropical forested land.

One common problem is that roads opened up for commercial activities generally lead landless poor people to settle in the newly cleared areas. More than 600 million rural poor in the developing world are without land or long-term title to land. Indonesia and Brazil—the two countries with the largest tropical rain forest areas—have especially high percentages of landless citizens. About 85 percent of the households on the main island of Java in Indonesia are landless. In Brazil, 4.5 percent of the landowners control 81 percent of the nation's agricultural land.

While slash-and-burn agriculture is commonly the greatest source of tropical deforestation, the destruction process often begins when loggers open up the forests. Loggers may take only a few commercially valuable trees per acre and leave the forest's soil system essentially intact, but they open up as much as 40 to 60 percent of the forest canopy through road-building and damage to non-commercial trees during the extraction process. When the harvest is over, leftover logging roads become a path for landless peasants to follow.

The landless peasants usually settle in harvested areas to which the government holds title—claiming plots adjacent to the logging roads. They slash and burn any remaining trees to grow subsistence crops. The ash from these fires usually puts enough nutrients into the soil to support crops for a couple of years. But as the soil's nutrients are depleted, the migrant farmers are forced to move on to other patches of forest, where the process is repeated. In their wake, ranchers often convert the denuded land to pasture for cattle grazing. But even the ranchers eventually have to move on as the cattle trample the rain forest soils.

Some agronomists believe rural people would have greater success with crops in the rain forests if they adopted some of the ancient cropping methods still used by indigenous peoples. Native Indians, for example, clear small circular plots in the forest to plant yams, potatoes, manioc and other tubers between felled trees. When the trees are burned, the tuber roots keep the soil from washing away. Ash from the pyre falls at the edge of the circular plots and provides nutrients. Crops are then planted in rings, according to their particular needs for food and light.

Regardless of the agricultural methods used, however, tropical deforestation is likely to continue as long as root problems with poverty, rising population and inequitable distribution of income and resources remain. "The underlying causes [of deforestation] are perverse incentives of greed and unattractive land tenure," maintains Robert Goodland, a tropical forestry expert with the World Bank.[20] While commercial logging and requisite logging roads often trigger the deforestation process, short-sighted government and economic policies set the stage for the process to begin. Governments own or control nearly 80 percent of the world's tropical forests.

In a seminal study of forestry economic policies, researchers Robert Repetto and Malcolm Gillis documented how government policies affecting taxation, credit, timber concessions and public investment have contributed to deforestation in 10 countries, mostly in tropical areas. The ventures examined in a series of case studies were intrinsically uneconomic yet supported by generous public subsidies. The result: forests were "sacrificed to make quick profits."[21]

Similarly, World Bank economists have found that a combination of generous tax and investment credits, land allocation rules and low overall taxes on agricultural income in Brazil accounted for perhaps 30 percent or more of the deforestation in Brazil's Amazon basin during the 1980s. In some instances, government subsidies covered three-quarters of the cost of opening a ranch in the Brazilian Amazon. The government also offered property to any who could demonstrate that they had "improved" the land by clearing it.

A fiscal crisis in Brazil has depleted government subsidy programs, and now Amazonian farmers are required to leave 50 percent of their land forested. "While reducing perverse economic incentives for deforestation will slow down the destruction of the Amazon forest, incentive policies alone are not enough," writes

World Bank economist Hans Binswanger. "A coherent system of land use planning that sets aside more marginal lands in forest reserves and establishes biological reserves is also required."[22] In Brazil, as many as 121 million acres have recently become or are in the process of being designated as reserves for indigenous peoples.[23]

Despite considerable economic strides in recent years, wealth rarely has trickled down to the poorest members of society in developing countries. In heavily deforested El Salvador, for example, annual per capita income was $430 in 1980, with the poorest 20 percent of the population earning only $46 a year.[24] Similarly, in Venezuela, the poorest 70 percent of the population owns only 4 percent of the land, while the richest 3 percent owns 80 percent of the land.[25] Such inequity has fueled social tensions and led to the invasion of farm and forest areas by frustrated landless poor.

Saving Indigenous Cultures

Perhaps a more intractible problem than tropical deforestation itself is the dissolution of indigenous rain forest cultures. One of the greatest controversies surrounding rain forest development, in fact, is the effect on native tribes, which become victims of death, disease, displacement and cultural assimilation. In Brazil, about 45 native Indian groups survive in the Amazon basin; but their numbers have dwindled from about 4 million at the time when Europeans first arrived in Brazil in 1500 to only 220,000 today.

Brazil's Yanomami

One of the recent embattled Indian groups is the Yanomami—numbering only 9,000—who live on both sides of Brazil's border with Venezuela. Gold was discovered recently on their land, prompting a gold rush of 45,000 gold prospectors, or garimpeiros, into Yanomami territory since the late 1980s. About 15 percent of the Yanomami have since died, mostly victims of tuberculosis and rampant venereal disease against which the Indians have no defense. The miners also have contaminated the Yanomami's food and water supply by disposing of mercury (used in the refining process) in rivers.

Brazil's attorney general brought charges of genocide against the national Indian welfare agency, Funai, in 1990 for failure to stop the killing of the Yanomami by garimpeiros. Brazilian President Jose Sarney had once vowed to evict the miners, but he subsequently acceded to many of their requests—including reducing Yanomami territory from 5,600 to only 800 square miles. Fernando Collor de Mello, who replaced Sarney as president of Brazil in 1990, ordered the army to dynamite landing strips that the garimpeiros use to fly into the remote area. And in 1991, he granted the Yanomami permanent rights over 36,000 square miles of rain forest territory in the northern state of Roraima.

"We can't separate the Indians' rights from the miners' rights," Collor once remarked. "We are all Brazilians and we will have to find solutions with

(continued on p. 16)

Box 1A

Colonizing the Rain Forests

The governments of some tropical forested nations have encouraged wholesale migrations of their peasant populations into rain forest areas—and received aid from international lending institutions like the World Bank to do so. Two such migration projects, the Polonoreste project in Brazil and the transmigration program of Indonesia, are described below.

Brazil's Polonoreste Project

A concerted effort to develop the Amazon rain forest in the 1960s by the then-military government in Brazil started a chain reaction, resulting in massive deforestation in the 1970s and 1980s. One of the government's goals was to populate areas near Brazil's borders to quell fears of a foreign invasion. Another goal was to develop a road system that eventually would be linked to the Pacific Ocean. With funding support from the World Bank, the Brazilian government built its first road through the Amazon, BR-364, through the western part of the state of Mato Grosso and through neighboring Rondonia. Completed in 1972, the road opened up vast tracts of land, which the government offered at nominal rates to settlers willing to clear the forest.

Many poor Brazilians from the southern state of Parana were eager to accept the government's offer. Tens of thousands of agricultural workers had lost their jobs there in the late 1960s and early 1970s as coffee-growing areas were converted to soybean cultivation—which required larger farms, more mechanization and fewer workers. Altogether, 2.5 million people left Parana during the 1970s, and about one-quarter of them entered Rondonia via BR-364, enticed by the prospect of owning their own land.

The Amazon land generally was of poor quality, however, and few migrants knew how to work with the soil to grow crops, nor could they afford fertilizer to enrich the soil. At the same time, the government was offering generous tax credits to wealthy landowners, who cleared vast swaths of forest for cattle ranches. By 1989, the World Bank discovered that the rate of deforestation "was truly astonishing," with an estimated 13 percent of the state of Rondonia cleared of trees.[1a]

More recent analysis of satellite photographs, which excludes natural savannah and water bodies from the total, suggests that only 10 percent of Rondonia has been deforested. Yet the network of roads branching off from BR-364 at 2.5-mile intervals has created a "fishbone" pattern of colonization covering some 30,000 square miles in the heavily forested state. "If you want to maximize the habitat fragmentation of the forest, this is the best way to do it," warns Compton Tucker, a NASA scientist who conducted the recent satellite analysis with University of New Hampshire scientist David Skole. Compton and Skole estimate that the total area of biological disturbance in the Brazilian Amazon has increased from 80,000 square miles in 1978 to 227,000 square miles in 1988, equal to about 15 percent of the region's total forest area.[2a]

Beyond the problems of forest and habitat loss, the Brazilian government has been unable to accommodate the huge number of migrants, which reached 1.2 million settlers in Rondonia alone by 1987. Promised health and social services have been slow in coming, and malaria and other diseases have reached epidemic proportions. Many farmers have given up their livelihood as their lands failed and settled into hastily created slums in frontier jungle towns.

The World Bank halted funding for an extension of BR-364 through the state of Acre, northwest of Rondonia, in 1985, because the Brazilian government had failed to disburse $26 million to protect Indian lands and forest preserves.

The Inter-American Development Bank cut off funding in 1987, after several U.S. senators threatened to suspend American contributions to the bank. Brazilian President Fernando Collor de Mello finally called for an end to construction of BR-364 in 1990.

As part of the "Our Nature" program begun under President Jose Sarney in 1989, Brazil's civilian government suspended tax incentives for ranching and logging projects in the rain forest and began levying fines against violators of new rain forest protection laws. Combined with a public information campaign, a sharp decline in the Brazilian economy and heavy rains during the traditional burning season, the deforestation rate in Brazil has slowed dramatically in recent years. Analysis of Landsat 5 satellite images by researchers from Brazil's National Institute for Space Research finds that annual deforestation in the Amazon appears to have dropped from a peak of about 7.5 million acres in 1985 to about 2.75 million acres in a one-year period ending in August 1991, a decline of 63 percent. Given that the Brazilian Amazon covers 1.9 million square miles, the rain forest would not disappear for another 330 years at the recent rate of deforestation.[3a]

Indonesian Transmigration Project

In Indonesia, another government effort to relocate landless people has devastated the rain forests. More than 100 million of Indonesia's 185 million citizens are crammed onto the small but remarkably fertile island of Java. The rest of the population is spread thinly over thousands of other islands in the archipelago. During this century, the Indonesian government has relocated about 1 million families to the outer islands. Migrants usually receive five acres of land, and get title to the land if they remain for five years.

Many families were put on land with poor soil quality, however, and have not been able to grow enough food on five acres to survive. As a result, many have expanded their plots or moved on to new ones, destroying millions of acres of rain forest in the process. Others have abandoned their land altogether and moved back to the slums of the capital city of Jakarta. A decline in government oil revenues forced Indonesia to cut back on its transmigration program in 1986. Even so, a rain forest area the size of Massachusetts was expected to fall over the ensuing five years.[4a]

Despite many difficulties, Indonesia has had better success than Brazil in providing housing and health services for migrating families. In addition, some forms of social forestry are beginning to take hold in densely settled areas, enabling rural people to grow subsistence crops without clearing entire forests. The Social Forestry Project—with funding support from The Ford Foundation and technical support from the government—is providing landless farmers with long-term leases on degraded state lands and encouraging them to use agroforestry techniques to make the lands more productive. (For more on the Social Forestry Project, see Chapter 7.)

intelligence and good will." Once demarcated, however, the Yanomami can place their new territory off limits to outside developers.[26] (For more on the Yanomami, see Chapter 5.)

Brazil's Kayapo

The Kayapo of Brazil are engaged in a similar struggle to get the government to demarcate a portion of their lands and protect it from development. The Kayapo control 25 million acres in northern Brazil, a region the size of Ontario, Canada. In 1988, a planned hydroelectric dam on the Xingu River would have flooded 18 million acres of Brazilian rain forest—much on Kayapo land. That project has since been canceled, but other areas claimed by the Kayapo have not been granted official protection. (The Sarney government had said it did not have the necessary funds to map the area.) The British rock star, Sting, has taken a strong interest in the plight of the Kayapo and raised $1.1 million to pay for the government's costs to survey a 19,000 square mile area. The new reserve, if approved, would link protected Kayapo lands to form a 44,000 square mile reserve—an area almost as big as New York state. Like many indigenous cultures, however, the Kayapo do not speak with one voice. Some of the Kayapo have expressed interest in promoting ecotourism and marketing valuable medicinal plants that grow on their land to pharmaceutical companies. Others have opted to sell mahogany wood and mining rights, much to the lament of environmentalists.[27]

Ecuador's Huaorani

In northeastern Ecuador, oil development rather than hydro development has threatened an indigenous Indian tribe. Nomadic Huaonari are on the verge of extinction; their numbers have plummeted from 20,000 in 1970 to fewer than 1,500 today. (Thousands of other Huaorani have settled in a more densely populated protectorate.) With the government's blessing, a major oil consortium led by **Maxus Energy** plans to drill for oil in Yasuni National Park, a prime rain forest area and hunting ground for the nomadic Huaorani. Environmental groups critical of the project assert that roads used to transport the oil will invite outside colonization of the area and decimate the Huaorani. Maxus has pledged to abide by a development plan created previously by **Conoco** to minimize such impacts. Conoco has withdrawn from the project. (For more on the Huaorani, see Chapter 4.)

Malaysia's Penan

The Penan, a tribe of 7,500 traditional hunters and gatherers, are the last known nomadic tribe of Sarawak—the Malaysian portion of the island of Borneo. Nearly 50 percent of Sarawak's land is held in government logging concessions that overlap three-quarters of the Penan's homeland. Logging in Sarawak has intensified in recent years. Sarawak now supplies 35 percent of the world's raw tropical timber exports. More than a third of Sarawak's forests are gone, and if the pace continues, all valuable timber will be felled by shortly after the turn of the century.

Many Penan have been pushed into settlement camps by the bulldozers and chainsaws leveling the surrounding forest. But some of the Penan have surprised the government by fighting back. About 1,000 Penan blocked logging trails and temporarily shut down operations at 23 sites in 1987. The Malaysian government has blamed much of the Penan's resistance on a young Swiss activist named Bruno Manser, who lived with the Penan for five years and taught them direct action methods. Manser was denounced in this Islamic nation as a "subversive Zionist and communist." Several logging companies even placed a $30,000 price on his head. Yet Manser escaped the country in 1990 and has traveled widely in developed countries since then to criticize Malaysian logging policies.[28]

Even some timber associations have criticized the breakneck pace of forest clearing on Sarawak. The International Tropical Timber Organization (ITTO), an intergovernmental group that promotes the use of tropical timber, issued a report in August 1990 that concluded the forest in Sarawak could by depleted by 2001. Such rapid deforestation would significantly decrease wildlife, create massive environmental and sedimentation problems in rivers, and diminish nontimber resources that local people depend on for their livelihood, the report said. The report recommended a 30 percent reduction in logging activities. (Environmental groups have sought a 60 percent reduction.) The Malaysian government has concurred with the findings of the ITTO report but has not announced any commitment to reduce the rate of logging. Meanwhile, logging companies have moved on to hilly parts of the island, where soil erosion problems are greater. Many rivers and streams have become so silty that the Penan can no longer use them for drinking or fishing.[29] (For more on the Penan and logging on Sarawak, see Chapter 3.)

Brazil's Rubber Tappers

While they are not an indigenous people, Brazil's rubber tappers also have become well-known for their struggle to maintain their livelihood in rain forest areas. Instead of felling trees, rubber tappers collect latex resins from trees as well as a variety of edible and decorative nuts. Many North Americans came to learn about Amazonian deforestation in the 1980s through the widely publicized efforts of Francisco Alves "Chico" Mendes Filho, chief of a rural rubber tappers' union. Mendes led a campaign of popular resistance to fend off illegal encroachment by wealthy cattle ranchers. After more than a half-dozen attempts on his life, Mendes was murdered by ranchers in the western Brazilian state of Acre in December 1988. (For more on Mendes and Brazil's rubber tappers, see Chapter 7.)

Rubber tappers and indigenous peoples have since forged a political alliance to save tropical forests from destruction. The Alliance of Forest Peoples is using modern tools of coalition building—and the media—to lobby for protection of their lands. In addition, the Coordinating Body for Indigenous People's Organizations of the Amazon Basin (Coica), based in Lima, Peru, now represents 1.2 million Indian people in Bolivia, Brazil, Colombia, Ecuador and Peru. Coica's president, Peruvian Evaristo Nugkuag, travels around the world to promote their cause. Nugkuag wants the World Bank to adopt tougher loan policies to curb rain forest exploitation, and he has urged the United Nations to endorse a universal declaration of indigenous rights to compel Amazon basin governments to recognize Indian rights. Coica representatives also met with U.S. environmental groups in 1990 and criticized them for sometimes appearing more concerned with saving trees, plants and animals than the people who live in the rain forests.[30]

International Efforts to Save the Rain Forests

Several environmental groups have made rain forest protection one of their top priorities. But the Natural Resources Defense Council, for one, ran into controversy when it became involved in negotiations with **Conoco** in 1991 over the development of oil fields in the rain forests of Ecuador. Some accused the environmental group of proposing terms of a deal with Conoco without fully involving the Indian people on whose land the drilling would take place. (For more on this controversy, see Chapter 4.)

Other environmental groups have become embroiled in Indian land disputes as well. The Environmental Defense Fund was instrumental in bringing Chico Mendes to the United States to meet with representatives of multilateral development banks that had been funding construction of BR-364, the main road through the Brazilian rain forest. The fund's Stephen Schwartzman later lobbied the Brazilian government to set aside extractive reserves in the rain forest for rubber tappers, after Mendes was assassinated.

The World Wildlife Fund is another environmental group that has worked directly with people of the rain forest—in this case promoting sustainable forestry principles. World Wildlife Fund forester Gary Hartshorn has been a key figure in developing the Yanesha Forestry Cooperative in Peru, probably the first instance where native peoples own and operate a timber operation dedicated to sustainable forest management. (For more on this operation, see Chapters 3 and 8.) World Wildlife Fund affiliates around the world also are participating in projects in Asia, Africa and other parts of Latin America. The fund has also advised corporations on how to minimize the ecological impacts of their operations on tropical forests.

Some environmental groups have taken a more confrontational approach in defense of the rain forest and its dwellers. Greenpeace and the Sierra Club have challenged U.S. tropical wood importers to take a stronger stand against unsustainable logging practices in Sarawak, Malaysia, that are destroying homelands of the Penan Indians. Rainforest Action Network has urged outright boycotts of companies thought to be contributing to tropical deforestation (see box). Greenpeace, Rainforest Action and Earth First! also have taken direct action in some instances, such as hanging banners across company display advertising and blocking ships carrying tropical timber into U.S. ports.

Environmental organizations are by no means the only groups working to save the rain forests, however. Several international organizations, including the

Box 1B

Rainforest Action Network

The environmental group considered most active and confrontational in defense of tropical forests is the Rainforest Action Network (RAN), based in San Francisco. Founded in 1985, the group now has 35,000 members and an annual budget of $2 million. RAN first gained national attention when it called for a boycott of **Burger King** restaurants (then owned by **Pillsbury**) after the company admitted that some of its beef had been imported from cattle ranches in Central America. Burger King subsequently canceled $35 million in beef contracts with Central American beef processors.

After the Burger King boycott, RAN rallied its troops to oppose a planned timber plantation by **Scott Paper** in Indonesia, a planned citrus plantation by **Coca-Cola** in Belize and a planned oil development project by **Conoco** in Ecuador. Each of these companies subsequently withdrew its plans, citing better investment opportunities elsewhere. Now RAN is calling for boycotts of **Georgia-Pacific** and **Mitsubishi**, which import tropical timber from Southeast Asia.

Director Randall Hayes acknowledges that RAN has focused heavily on the negative impacts of rain forest destruction in the past, instead of offering constructive alternatives. "We're not against economic activity in rain forests," Hayes says, "but we want the people who live there to be able to decide what and how much development will occur."[1b] RAN does approve of the development of extractive reserves to provide income for rain forest people, for example, and it has endorsed the use of portable saws by native peoples in Papua New Guinea for selective timber harvesting purposes.

But RAN is still best known for its denunciation of companies that it believes are destroying the rain forests. Hayes says: "I'm proud we take a hard line against transnational corporations because they are really out of control. No one effectively provides a check on their activities. The United Nations' Center on Transnational Corporations and Environment Program are a sad joke. **Chevron's** budget is bigger than that of most nations. We need an Environmental Protection Agency for the planet. When you don't have control over companies, any time you can push them around a little it helps your cause, because it shows you have more influence."

RAN is not averse to working with companies willing to phase out their rain forest operations over time. "I'll go into partnership with the sleaziest multinational around if I feel they are serious and sincere about addressing the problem of deforestation," Hayes vows. But his group pushes hardest when companies ignore or try to hide their activities in the rain forests. "Burger King was secretive," Hayes maintains. "They gave us the corporate cold shoulder. We had few choices but to blow the whistle on them."

RAN's tactics may cause the environmental group to lose some leverage by forcing U.S. companies out of rain forest areas. In the case of **Scott Paper** in Indonesia, a local company took over the project and wanted to expand it. Hayes acknowledges that, "In negotiations with Scott, the company said 'We have no doubt you can stop us but if we abandon the project someone worse will come in.' We chose to proceed against them anyway." Hayes says that while a confrontational approach does not always stop projects from going forward, each withdrawal represents an important step forward in a worldwide campaign. In RAN's battle with Scott, Hayes insists, "It was a victory because we showed we could flex some muscle."

United Nations and the World Bank, became formally involved in 1985, when they helped to devise a wide-ranging Tropical Forestry Action Plan. The tropical forests also took center stage at the June 1992 Earth Summit in Rio de Janeiro, where scores of nations signed a biodiversity treaty and endorsed a statement of forestry principles. Even so, the difficulty in reaching and implementing these agreements suggests that much work remains to be done to save the rain forests—and those who inhabit them.

Tropical Forestry Action Plan

The Tropical Forestry Action Plan marked the beginning of a worldwide effort to halt the destruction of tropical forests. The World Resources Institute, an internationally funded research group based in Washington, D.C., organized a task force in 1985 that called for $8 billion in public and private investment to promote forest conservation and sustainable development activities. Cosponsors of the action plan include the World Bank and the United Nations Development Program. The lead organization in administering the plan is the UN Food and Agricultural Organization, based in Rome.

The Tropical Forestry Action Plan seeks to educate people in tropical countries about sustainable management of forest resources, while increasing the flow of technical assistance and investment through bilateral and multilateral sources. The plan has five priorities for action: integrating forestry into agricultural systems, promoting appropriate forest-based industries, restoring depleted fuelwood supplies, reserving areas for conservation purposes, and strengthening government forestry agencies to monitor and administer such policies.[31]

To implement the plan, each participating country has been asked to write a paper summarizing the demands being made on its tropical forests and the obstacles toward achieving sustainable development goals. Significantly, nongovernmental organizations and residents of tropical forests were encouraged to participate in the drafting of these papers. As of 1990, however, only nine countries had completed their papers out of 75 that had become participants in the plan, and many of the papers were criticized for failing to involve nongovernmental organizations and indigenous peoples in a meaningful way.

"Worse," says Bruce Rich, an attorney with the Environmental Defense Fund, the Tropical Forestry Action Plan has emerged as a way "to promote traditional, export-oriented timber industry investments camouflaged by small components for environmental purposes." Rich, who was among the chief proponents of recent World Bank lending reforms, says that environmental groups in developing countries are "particularly outraged because the plan seemed to blame the poor for the destruction of tropical forests while promoting investments to open up large areas of pristine forest for exploitation, rebaptizing such projects as 'sustainable forestry.'"[32]

Of the nine country forest action plans analyzed by the World Rainforest Movement, an environmental group based in Malaysia, the plans for Cameroon, Guyana and Peru would massively increase logging, according to Marcus Colchester, who directs the group's forest peoples program. Colchester says these countries' plans fail to address the very reasons why rural farmers clear forests in the first place—lack of "land security for rural people both inside and outside the forests." Colchester believes that instead of marginalizing the concerns of forest peoples, the process must be restructured so that indigenous groups can help "set the agenda."[33]

The independent Thailand Development Research Institute has found similar shortcomings with the Tropical Forestry Action Plan. Commercial logging, as now sanctioned, "does not alleviate poverty since it fails to redistribute the benefits of the enterprise to the local populations," the institute says. "Nor does it recognize traditional rights or any interest or capability on the part of local communities to manage resources around them."[34] Thailand's action plan, in particular, "is totally biased in favor of the commercial and industrial sector," claims Thai activist Witoon Permongasacharoen. "It ignores the root cause of forest destruction," he continues, "which is the economic development policies of the government, the multilateral lending institutions, and international aid agencies."[35]

It now appears that the Tropical Forestry Action Plan was so ambitious in scope—and the causes of tropical deforestation so complex—that it was destined to fall short of its lofty goals. Lacking specific policy recommendations, the plan ran into an array of policy, planning and funding problems soon after it was announced. In addition, governments in tropical countries remained more concerned with obtaining economic aid for their development programs than with devising schemes to preserve their rain forests.

The Earth Summit

The dichotomy of interests in protecting the rain forests also was evident in events leading up to the Earth Summit in Rio de Janeiro in June 1992. The world's seven richest nations had stated at a G7 meeting in July 1990 that they regarded rain forest preservation as one of the world's most urgent environmental concerns. Chancellor Helmut Kohl of Germany announced that his country would make $100 million available to Brazil unilaterally to protect the Amazon, and he urged his fellow G7 leaders to provide $1.6 billion in funding support—through the World Bank's Global Environment Facility—for the Amazon overall.

While the other G7 nations did not come up with the amount of funds sought by Kohl, American President George Bush was persuaded to make rain forest protection his top priority at the Earth Summit. While refusing to sign the biodiversity convention, Bush pledged to add $150 million in yearly assistance from the United States to help tropical nations preserve their forests. He also urged leaders from other industrialized countries to double their collective aid for tropical forest preservation from $1.35 billion to $2.7 billion a year. (In fiscal year 1992, the United States contributed $368.3 million for such assistance, including $120 million in bilateral aid.)

Bush's proposal got a cool reception from other leaders attending the Earth Summit, however. While the American delegation stressed the biodiversity of tropical forests and their ability to store vast amounts of carbon as vital reasons for protecting them, it remained steadfast in its opposition to signing the biodiversity convention and to committing to a timetable for reducing U.S. carbon dioxide emissions. Environmental groups were quick to point out the irony. The same Landsat 5 satellite that took dramatic photographs of deforestation from road building and slash-and-burn agriculture in the Amazon revealed a crazy-quilt of clearcuts and logging roads in photographs of the western United States—with as little as 10 percent of the original communities of Douglas fir, western red cedar, hemlock and other old-growth species remaining. The Amazonian rain forest, by comparison, looked relatively undisturbed. In the end, leaders from developing nations at the Earth Summit resisted calls for changes in their own forestry practices when leaders from industrialized nations rebuffed suggestions that they, too, place limits on domestic timber cutting. During the 1980s, the United States had been harvesting its remaining old growth forests at a faster rate than most tropical nations were cutting theirs.

In preparatory meetings leading up to the Earth Summit, industrialized nations had expressed a desire for an international forestry convention to be signed at Rio. But the parties eventually had to settle for a Statement of Forestry Principles, a non-binding document that calls on each signatory to assess the impacts of economic development on its forests and to identify steps to minimize further damage. Despite a call for sustainable management of timberlands, the document sets no standards for measuring compliance and offers no deadline for action. Given this, the Statement of Forestry Principles may meet the same fate as the Tropical Forestry Action Plan.

Some important progress was made at the Earth Summit, nevertheless. Lengthy preparatory reports submitted by conference participants on the environmental problems they face have assembled more information in one place than ever before. In addition, 8,000 journalists and 10,000 environmentalists were in Rio for the Earth Summit and the associated Global Forum, an unprecedented meeting of non-governmental organizations. Perhaps the information exchanged by these groups and the stories generated by journalists attending the conference will have the most tangible long-term impact on the debate over tropical deforestation.

The new U.S. administration of President Bill Clinton and Vice President Albert Gore also could breathe new life into the negotiating process. Clinton has committed the United States to reducing its carbon dioxide emissions to 1990 levels by the end of the decade, under a "joint implementation" plan that allows it to invest in further reductions of greenhouse gas emissions in other nations for lesser reductions at home. Clinton has also signed the biodiversity convention, with the addition of an interpretive statement regarding U.S. intellectual property rights—the sticking point that deterred Bush from supporting the treaty.

While a consensus has emerged that the world's tropical forests are in trouble, world leaders clearly are not yet in agreement about how best to save them. The problems of the rain forests are so complex and so enmeshed in political forces that the best-laid plans of conservationists and foresters may not come to pass. A natural tension exists between industrialized nations seeking restrictions on tropical forest activities and developing nations insisting on their rights to sovereignty. The root causes of the destruction—such as the clearing of the land for agriculture and cutting trees for fuel and timber sales—were not addressed at Rio. Instead, there was rancorous debate over who should profit from the exploitation of the rain forests and who should pay in an effort to conserve them. Altogether, the Earth Summit raised pledges in excess of $6 billion a year for a variety of environmental causes. But that contribution remains far less than the $70 billion in additional funding aid that conference organizer Maurice Strong had sought (an amount that would bring the total environmental aid contribution to $125 billion a year).

Unless and until the governments of the world come together on a rescue plan, the responsibility to save the tropical forests will remain largely in the hands of those who occupy the forests, those who consume their resources and those who invest in or manage the enterprises that operate there. The remainder of this book focuses on the major industries at work in tropical forests—starting with a history of past development efforts, followed by in-depth examinations of the timber, oil, mining and agricultural industries. The book concludes with two chapters concerning the development of new markets for nontimber forest products, such as foods and pharmaceuticals, and innovative investment policies, such as debt-for-nature swaps and carbon offset programs, that give greater value to the forests, provide a livelihood for its peoples and limit the destruction of one of the world's most precious natural resources.

Chapter 2
Early Efforts to Tame the Rain Forests

For generations, the riches of the jungle have lured enterprising businessmen into wild tropical forests. Many have learned the hard way that these forests are not easily tamed. Henry Ford, the founder of **Ford Motor**, sank a fortune into Brazil's Amazon forest in a futile effort to tap a seemingly endless supply of rubber. Years later, reclusive billionaire Daniel K. Ludwig set his sights on pulp and timber, which also turned out to be a chimera.

Some rain forest enterprises have been more successful, however. In a number of cases, the multinational corporations undertaking these ventures have played a key role in the economic development of tropical forested nations. In Brazil, for example, **U.S. Steel** found huge deposits of bauxite in the eastern Amazon, opening up a vast area of mineral wealth. In Ecuador, **Texaco** and **Gulf** discovered large quantities of oil beneath the rain forest and worked in partnership with **Petroecuador** and other multinational oil companies to extract more than 1.5 billion barrels of oil there. In Indonesia and the Philippines, timber giants **Weyerhaeuser** and **Georgia-Pacific** established joint ventures with local companies to log tropical hardwoods, furthering the development of a huge logging industry in Southeast Asia. And in Central America, United Fruit Co. (now **Chiquita Brands**) gave meaning to the phrase "banana republics" after it was formed in 1899 to export bananas to America.

These ventures (unlike Ford's and Ludwig's) paid off for investors and provided desperately needed income and jobs for people in host countries. Consumers around the world also benefitted from the affordably priced products and materials brought out of the rain forests. But these enterprises shared one adversity as well: the inevitable destruction of pristine tropical forest areas and indelible changes for the people who live there.

Now a new era of environmental consciousness has emerged. Scientists have released alarming statistics about the rate at which tropical forests are disappearing. Conservationists and biologists warn that tampering with the rain forest's delicate ecosystem could lay waste to the cleared land and possibly even change the climate. Multinational companies, while still welcome in many host countries, face greater challenges at home from a newly energized environmental movement.

For these and other reasons, some multinational companies have scaled back their presence in rain forest areas of the world in recent years. **Weyerhaeuser** and **Georgia-Pacific** sold their South Pacific joint ventures in the early 1980s after host countries placed restrictions on the export of unprocessed tropical timber. **Burger King** (then owned by **Pillsbury**) stopped purchasing beef from Central American ranchers (whose cattle grazed on previously forested land) after a consumer boycott got underway in 1987. **Coca-Cola** shelved a plan in 1988 to plant citrus trees in the subtropical forests of Belize. And in 1989, **Scott Paper** canceled plans for a huge plantation of fast-growing trees in the tropical forests of Indonesia.

Despite the recent retrenchment, multinational companies are by no means about to withdraw from rain forest areas altogether, nor would some consider such an outcome desirable. The current emphasis on sustainable, environmentally sound business practices suggests, in fact, that the scope of multinational activities in the tropics may expand once again. This chapter reviews some of the prominent ventures of the past—in rubber, timber, mining and agriculture—and seeks out lessons for projects of the future.

The Rubber Boom

In 1839, Charles Goodyear patented the process of vulcanization, which increases the strength and durability of rubber so that it can be used in numerous industrial applications. Europeans had known since the mid-1700s that rubber trees grow in the Amazon, but it was not until Goodyear's invention that investors took an interest in acquiring rubber in large quantities. The 1888 invention of the pneumatic tire for the emerging U.S. auto industry increased demand for rubber still further. Soon a land grab was underway in the Amazon forest.[1]

The rubber boom lasted from 1890 to 1912. At the time, a dispute was brewing between Bolivia and Brazil over the territory of Acre in the western Amazon. Bolivia occupied the region, but Brazil had longstanding claims there. Both wanted the land because it contains some of the richest rubber-producing forests in the world. At one point, now-defunct **U.S. Rubber** and powerful U.S. banking and insurance interests (including **Metropolitan Life Insurance**) intervened on behalf of the Bolivians, joining a Bolivian colonial charter company known as the **Bolivian Syndicate**. The syndicate sought to administer Acre for 30 years, giving Bolivia 60 percent of the rubber profits and pocketing the remainder for itself.[2]

A major problem with the syndicate's scheme was that transporting rubber to Bolivia was practically impossible; more than 200 miles of the Abuna River that borders the territory is unnavigable. Consequently, the syndicate sought to internationalize the Amazon River, allowing rubber-laden boats to travel east through Brazil to the Atlantic Ocean. But a brief guerrilla war by residents of Acre sent the Bolivian army into retreat. Bolivia subsequently signed a peace treaty, ceding Acre to Brazil for $2 million in 1903.

While the Bolivian Syndicate's plans were dashed, the idea of internationalizing the Amazon River sowed fears of foreign domination among the Brazilian population. Those fears grew as foreigners like Ford and Ludwig came to develop large tracts of the jungle later in the 20th century. This legacy partly explains Brazil's longstanding determination to colonize remote regions of the Amazon basin and the indignation of some Brazilians toward recent efforts by U.S. and European politicians and environmental groups to preserve the Amazon forest in its primitive state.[3]

The effect of the rubber boom on the Amazon region was more socioeconomic than physical, because rubber trees are scarred and tapped—not felled—in a very labor-intensive process. With rubber trees widely dispersed throughout the forest, workers must cover large areas to ensure a steady supply of latex drippings. Thousands of new workers entered the Amazon forest during the rubber boom, and often they fell victim to "debt peonage." Rubber wholesalers—backed by British and American capital—paid the workers the equivalent of only one-half cent for a pound of rubber, which sold on the open market for 20 cents a pound. At the same time, they charged the workers exorbitant prices for food, supplies and transportation, and those who attempted to flee without paying their debts often were severely punished.[4]

In his book, *Assault on the Amazon*, Richard Bourne recounts how one "tyrannical" rubber baron, Julio Arana, registered his Peruvian Amazon Rubber Co. in London. Visitors to Arana's holdings returned to England with harrowing accounts of murder, rape, floggings and warfare, which eventually led the House of Commons to liquidate his company. Bourne writes that "though the Arana empire was probably the worst, it was not unique, and it was only the fact that it had a registered office in London, and was using British subjects to support its despotism, that allowed it to become an international scandal."[5]

In the early 1900s, the successful establishment of rubber plantations in Malaysia, where rubber was more plentiful, brought the rubber boom in the Amazon basin to an end. While rubber tapping took a great toll in human misery, it did not inflict serious damage on the forest itself. That was about to change, however, as post-boom Brazilians sought to emulate the Asian plantation model that had eclipsed their own monopoly on the rubber market. They cleared large areas of forest for rubber plantations, only to find that South American rubber trees that thrived in the wild became vulnerable to a variety of diseases when grown in plantations. Undaunted, some entrepreneurs doggedly pursued their projects. One of them was automobile pioneer Henry Ford.

Fordlandia: Not a Better Idea

Henry Ford, the founder of **Ford Motor**, was lured into the Amazon rain forest by the attractive notion that rubber for his Detroit auto plants could be supplied more cheaply from Brazil than from distant Asia. Ford purchased 2.5 million acres of Amazon land in 1927 and named it "Fordlandia." Trying to carve a slice of middle America out of the jungle, Ford ordered the construction of a plantation headquarters that would resemble an auto factory town in Michigan—complete with school, hospital, church and power plant. By Amazon standards, Fordlandia was luxurious. Streets and sidewalks were paved; there were even park benches and street lights.

But the 7,000 acre patch of forest that was cleared and planted with 800,000 rubber trees did not fare so well. The hilly terrain and sandy soils were not well-suited for plantation growth. The worst problem was a blight known as South American leaf disease that struck in 1932 and destroyed nearly all the newly planted trees on the estate.[6]

After several unsuccessful attempts to conquer the blight, Ford sold part of his Fordlandia acreage for another plantation site called "Belterra," about 60 miles south of the original plantation. Ford planted 2 million rubber trees there, but the blight struck again. Disease-resistant grafts were brought in from Asia and Africa but they, too, succumbed to the disease. After an investment of nearly $10 million, Ford sold off his plantation interests to the Brazilian government in 1945 for only $500,000.[7]

Timber: Ludwig's Bungle in the Jungle

The next American who thought he could tame the Amazon for a massive tree plantation was Daniel K. Ludwig, a multibillionaire who made his fortune building oil supertankers. Ludwig's dream was ambitious on an epic scale. In the 1960s, he chose to gamble what had been one of the largest fortunes ever amassed in the United States on possibly the largest project ever embarked on by a private citizen.

Ludwig was convinced that the world would face a wood fiber shortage by the end of the 20th century. To overcome the shortage, Ludwig believed the Amazon could be turned into a supertree factory, even though the area had no history of commercial forestry. Key to his plan was translocation of the gmelina tree, originally grown in Burma and India. Gmelina is one of the fastest growing trees in the world, shooting up as rapidly as one foot a month in tropical climes.

In 1967, Ludwig spent $1 per acre for a 3 million acre tract of land bordering the Jari and Amazon Rivers—an area the size of Connecticut. He announced grandiose plans for a huge commercial forestry operation (for both timber and pulp), the world's largest rice plantation as well as projects in mining and cattle ranching.

Ludwig's first mistake was allowing heavy bulldozers into the forest to knock down hundreds of thousands of trees, uprooting the thin layer of topsoil that sustained the lush tropical flora. Thus, when the gmelina seedlings were planted, most of them promptly died. Ludwig then switched from bulldozers to chain saws to stanch the loss of topsoil. But the sudden need for 2,000 laborers sharply increased site-preparation costs.[8] Road building added to the level of deforestation and further increased maintenance costs. The vast network of roads cut through Jari now measures nearly 2,500 miles. By comparison, the total length of the Trans-Amazon Highway within Amazonia is only 2,100 miles.[9]

Just as Henry Ford's rubber trees were cursed by leaf disease, Ludwig's gmelina were attacked by a variety of larvae and fungi—although not to the extent that doomed Fordlandia. The Jari plantation had other problems, however. While the gmelina fared well on clay soils, most had been planted on sandy soils and grew only half as rapidly as expected. Under ideal conditions, gmelina can be harvested for pulp after six years and for timber after 10 years. But the slower rate of growth of the tree in Jari caused the gmelina wood to begin to deteriorate after only seven years.

Rather than experimenting with a variety of other trees, Ludwig stuck stubbornly with gmelina, convinced his vision would someday pay off. But as years passed and growth levels still lagged, Ludwig abandoned his plan to produce high-quality timber and focused on the pulp market instead. He hired the same Japanese firm that had built his supertankers to construct a huge $260 million pulp mill. Amid much hoopla, components of the mill were shipped across two oceans from Japan and then by barge up the Amazon and Jari Rivers. For the mill to operate efficiently, 1.6 acres of trees would have to be felled every day. But with the yield of gmelina trees still too low to supply the mill adequately, Ludwig reluctantly started planting Caribbean pine. Caribbean pine grows better than the gmelina in sandy soils—but not as fast.

By 1979, costs of the Jari project had soared to $780 million, compared with earlier estimates of $300 million to $500 million. Brazil's military government continued to support the project, but many Brazilian citizens viewed it with increasing suspicion. Tight security around the project area fueled old fears that outsiders were trying to steal the wealth of the Amazon.

Having diversified into Caribbean pine, the Jari project started to produce usable pulp, but still not enough for the mill to run profitably. Ludwig then ordered a second mill to produce newsprint for the Brazilian market. But he had depleted his own savings to the point where he was forced to turn to outside investors for help. None found the risks attractive.

Ludwig's managers finally concluded that the Jari project would never attract investors unless it was pared back even further and began to turn a profit. With gmelina falling short of growth-rate targets by 40 to 75 percent (depending on the soils where it was planted), Ludwig finally turned to native species like imbauba and parapara. "This move, after a decade spent burning most of the native forest and spending millions on an imported species, surpasses irony," one *Fortune* magazine article observed.[10]

By 1982, the cost of the Jari project had soared beyond $1 billion and Ludwig bailed out. A consortium of 27 companies, backed by the Brazilian government, bought the project for $280 million. While the consortium appears to have eliminated the project's operating losses, this "cannot be interpreted as meaning that large scale silvicultural plantations are now an economically viable development mode in Amazonia," maintains Philip Fearnside, an Amazonian forest ecologist.[11] The Jari project appears to have climbed into the black only because of a profitable clay mine that offset continuing losses from the forestry operation. As of 1988, the mill was still short of wood, and a significant amount of native forest wood was being hauled in from other project areas to make up the difference. Fearnside calculated in 1988 that the Jari plantation area would have to expand by another 21 percent to meet the capacity of its mills.

As for the wood-fiber shortage Ludwig predicted, it has yet to materialize. Pulp prices today are barely more than half what Ludwig had projected when the Jari project began.

Mining: Another Rush to Open the Amazon

While the Jari project hardly can be considered a model of success, the Brazilian military government used it as a model to attract both foreign and domestic investors into the Amazon. As historian Shelton Davis observed in 1977, "A new partnership has emerged in Brazil between international lending institutions, multinational corporations and the Brazilian military regime. The strength of this partnership [over the last decade] has been a primary factor in the rapid opening up of the Brazilian Amazon."[12]

The Inter-American Development Bank and the World Bank paved the way for development of the Amazon basin by funding major road construction. Between 1968 and 1972, Brazil received $400 million in highway loans, constituting the largest World Bank loans ever made to a country for that purpose. Then in 1974 the Brazilian government created the Program of Agricultural, Livestock, and Mineral Poles in Amazonia (Polamazonia), a government agency to provide fiscal and credit incentives for investment in the region. The new government agency granted lumber, ranching and mining concessions to tap the Amazon's previously inaccessible natural resources. Such concessions provided desperately needed foreign exchange for Brazil's soaring foreign debt.

Of all the resources of the Amazon, minerals offered the greatest investment potential. A handful of multinational mining companies began to stake their claims in the 1960s. Ferusa, a subsidiary of the Billiton International unit of **Royal Dutch Shell**, had invested more than $3 million in Rondonia tin deposits by 1967. Other early entrants included **Molybdenum Corp. of America**, **Grace Ore and Mining** (a subsidiary of **W.R. Grace**) and **NL Industries**.[13] By 1972, more than 50 multinational corporations were mining in the Amazon basin, according to the *Engineering and Mining Journal*. The companies included **Alcan, Bethlehem Steel, International Nickel, Kaiser Aluminum, Reynolds Metals, Rio Tinto Zinc, Union Carbide** and **U.S. Steel**.

The Carajás Project

U.S. Steel started a large prospecting program in Brazil in 1967, after a subsidiary of **Union Carbide** discovered trace deposits of manganese ore in the Sereno Range in the northern state of Para. Soon it became apparent that the Carajás region had vast reserves of manganese, tin ore, nickel, bauxite, copper and gold, making it one of the richest mineral areas of the world.

U.S. Steel and the **Companhia Vale do Rio Doce (CVRD)**, a Brazilian state-owned company, then set up a partnership, **Amazonia Mineracao S.A.**, to organize and operate a Carajás iron ore extraction project. CVRD's concessions totaled nearly 3,000 square miles. CVRD held 51 percent of the shares in the partnership, and U.S. Steel 49 percent. In 1977, however, U.S. Steel sold its shares in the mining project to CVRD for $55 million.

Other financial backing came from the World Bank. Since no infrastructure existed to carry iron from the remote Carajás region to the Atlantic Ocean, the World Bank lent CVRD $304 million in 1982 for construction of a railroad

Figure 4

Location of CVRD Project

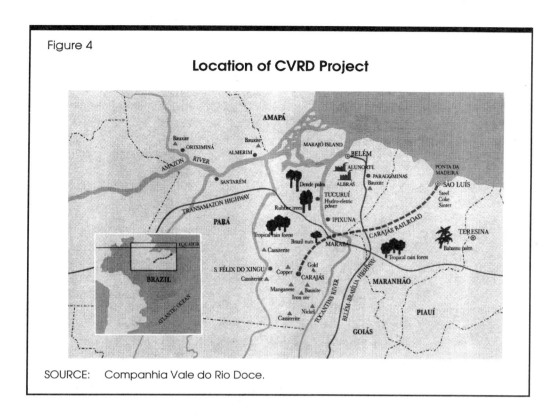

SOURCE: Companhia Vale do Rio Doce.

through the rain forest to the port of Sao Luis. The loan agreement also provided for co-financing of other elements of the project, including an iron ore mine, an ore processing plant, marine terminal and a village to house the mine workers. Altogether, CVRD raised $3.6 billion in capital investments, including $600 million from the European Economic Community.

As the mining project took shape, the Carajás area saw a huge influx of migrants. Between 1980 and 1985, the population more than doubled, from 60,000 to 134,000. Squatters by the thousands set up shantytowns on the fringes of the project. Some of the rain forests around Carajás had been degraded previously when cattle ranchers moved to the area, following completion of a highway through the city of Maraba. The growth spurt in the early 1980s accelerated the deforestation trend and spawned violent conflicts over land rights.

The greatest cause of deforestation around Carajás, however, came from the use of charcoal-fired smelters to refine ore into pig iron and manganese. Fifteen such smelters were approved for operation as of 1987, each of which was capable of consuming between 216,000 and 480,000 acres of trees a year to yield 1.2 million tons of charcoal.[14] One study indicated that the only way for the operation to show a profit—given the low market price for pig iron—was to set the value of the forest destroyed at zero.[15]

The CVRD did not overlook environmental considerations completely, however. Before operations began, the state-owned company performed baseline studies on the climate, ecology and botany of areas proposed for mining. And between 1981 and 1985, it spent $54 million on environmental activities such as land reclamation, creation of protected reserves, topsoil stockpiling and erosion control.[16] Nevertheless, by 1986 between 4 million and 7 million acres of land had been deforested in the Carajás region.

In 1990, Brazilian President Fernando Collor de Mello placed a moratorium on the construction of new smelters in Carajás and announced a plan to reforest 2.2 million acres in the region. According to Gustavo Bessa, CVRD's General Manager for Forestry, the state-owned company is planting 1.7 million acres of eucalyptus and pine plantations to feed the pig iron smelters, while leaving 740,000 acres of natural forest undisturbed. The company also is experimenting with 250 species of exotic and native trees and plants to see which are best adapted to the area's soil and climate. CVRD has signed contracts with companies in Japan, Norway and Finland to carry out portions of the reforestation.

Citrus: Do Trees Grow Better with Coke?

Corporate efforts to tame the rain forests have occurred in parts of the world other than Brazil, of course, and in recent years some of these efforts have met considerable opposition. In the Central American country of Belize, **Coca-Cola** purchased 196,000 acres of land in partnership with two Texas ranchers in 1985. Coca-Cola, maker of Minute Maid orange juice, wanted to plant citrus trees on the former estate of the **Belize Estate and Produce Co.** (a United Kingdom-registered company) to supplement its supply of oranges after a series of devastating winter freezes had struck its Florida groves.

According to Coca-Cola, the purchased land was classified as a transitional forest between subtropical moist and tropical dry forest and had been logged for more than 100 years. Coke wanted to plant citrus trees on 25,000 to 30,000 acres of the land and construct a citrus processing plant. Its ranching partners planned to clear about 5,000 acres to raise cattle.

Despite Coca-Cola's insistence that it would not be denuding a tropical rain forest per se, Friends of the Earth and other environmental groups denounced the project and urged a boycott of the soft drink in Europe. Several Belizean groups also expressed concern about the sale of the land. Coca-Cola executives now acknowledge that a slow response to the environmentalists' concerns appears to have aggravated the situation. "We could have done a much better job about getting information out in a proactive way—which we didn't do," remarked Michelle Beale, Coca-Cola's senior vice president for human resources and public affairs.[17]

Coca-Cola subsequently shelved the Belizean project in 1988, citing opposition from environmentalists, an inability to obtain political risk insurance and a recovery in the world market price for orange juice. "Our concern was that the most important asset Coke has is its name, its trademark. If that is in jeopardy, we have to decide that the project is not worth it," Beale said.

To shore up its corporate image, Coca-Cola donated 42,000 acres of the 196,000 acre parcel to the Programme for Belize, a Belizean conservation group, for use as a nature preserve. It also contributed $50,000 to the group to further its efforts to buy additional parcels of land. Coca-Cola has retained ownership of 55,000 acres of the Belizean land, however, and it does not rule out the possibility of planting citrus trees there in the future. The remaining 90,000 acres has been sold to Belizean commercial interests: 30,000 acres to **New River Enterprises**, a Belizean logging company, and 60,000 to a group of Mennonites, who reportedly have deforested significant portions of their parcel for the development of farms and settlements.

Ironically, less deforestation might have occurred had the entire parcel remained under Coca-Cola's control.

From Timber to Tissue: Scott in Indonesia

A proposal by **Scott Paper** to establish a eucalyptus plantation for a pulp and paper mill in Indonesia has met a similar fate. Scott announced in 1988 that it was forming a partnership with an Indonesian logging company to meet growing demand for toilet paper and facial tissues in Asia. Scott's partner in the project was **Astra International**, Indonesia's second largest company. Together, they formed **P.T. Astra Scott Cellulosa** to operate the $635 million venture; Scott's share was 60 percent, and Astra's was 40 percent.

The partnership held a concession of more than 2 million acres on Irian Jaya, the Indonesian portion of the island of New Guinea. Rain forest land was to be cleared to make way for the eucalyptus trees, although Scott said it would plant trees on no more than 384,000 acres of the concession. Scott said much of the area had been cut or burned previously and now contained many brush and bamboo thickets.

As the partnership started a test nursery on 150 acres (to see if high-quality eucalyptus would grow in the required volume of wood per acre), opposition to the project was already mounting. Environmental and human rights organizations said the project would destroy virgin rain forest and threaten the livelihood of 15,000 to 25,000 native inhabitants of the area, most of whom are hunters and gatherers. (According to one account, at least four tribes would be pushed off their lands.) The groups also objected to the planting of eucalyptus, because such plantations consume large amounts of water and sometimes lead to erosion.

Scott promised to perform environmental and sociological impact studies before proceeding with the project, and it said it would encourage "public participation and feedback, especially from the local people who are most directly affected by the potential project."[18] The company planned to hold a public hearing in Irian Jaya to obtain the views of all interested parties, including those of U.S. and Indonesian environmental groups.

But in a surprise move, Scott backed out of the project in October 1989. Internal company studies found that its fiber needs could be met from other sources. "Our studies concluded that although eucalyptus kraft pulp continues to be part of our long-term material needs, it no longer plays the leading role we once thought...and we have higher and more urgent priorities," said J. Richard

Leaman, president of Scott Worldwide.[19] Scott reportedly is making greater use of recycled and high-yield fibers. Some industry observers think environmental pressure contributed to Scott's decision to withdraw from the Indonesian project, however, and environmental groups were quick to take credit.

Whatever the case may be, the opposition of environmental groups may backfire, similar to Coca-Cola's experience in Belize. Scott's partner in the Indonesian project, **Astra International**, has sought to expand the project rather than abandon it. When Scott withdrew, Astra took on a new partner, **Inhutani II**, an Indonesian state forestry corporation. Under a new plan, Astra and Inhutani II planned to cut 741,000 acres—double the size proposed in the Scott joint venture. Rainforest Action Network reported that the projected price of the project also rose to $1 billion, of which about 35 percent of funds would be provided by the Indonesian government's Reforestation Fund.[20]

In August 1992, however, Astra shelved its plans for the giant pulp and paper project, citing financial difficulties. Indonesia's Forestry Minister, Hasrul Harahap, vowed to find new investors and continue the project. In November 1992, **Barito Pacific Timber Group** purchased $400 million of Astra's shares, making it the controlling shareholder with 44 percent ownership. Barito Pacific, which once engaged in logging operations only, has diversified into industrial tree plantations for pulp and paper production in recent years. Barito Pacific's controlling interest in Astra may signal a revival of Astra's Irian Jaya project.[21]

Environmental groups acknowledge that while they may have had a measure of influence over a large multinational company like Scott, which wants to protect its international image, Astra and its new partners may be less likely to respond to the concerns of outside environmental groups. One lever of outside influence remains the **International Finance Corp.**, a private investment arm of the World Bank, which has a small equity stake in Astra's parent company. Indonesian and U.S. human rights and environmental groups are trying to demonstrate that the project violates the World Bank's new "green" lending policies and would displace tribal people from their lands.[22]

A final hurdle is silvicultural. Just as Daniel Ludwig hoped to transplant the gmelina tree in Brazil, Astra still must prove that eucalyptus will attain sufficient harvest yields in Indonesia. Trees growing on the 150 acre nursery established by Scott Paper still have more than a year to grow before a determination can be made to move forward with the project.

Chapter 3
The Tropical Timber Industry

$\mathbf{T}$ he tropical timber industry is at the center of the controversy over tropical deforestation. Environmental groups assert that multinational timber companies are to blame for a significant amount of tropical forest loss. Timber companies counter that they provide jobs and valuable exports for developing countries and are moving toward sustainable forestry practices. Yet questions remain as to what "sustainable forestry" is and how it will be carried out in chronically poor regions where rapid economic development is an urgent priority. In fact, logging and socio-economic development in tropical countries often are inseparably linked, making responsibility for forest loss difficult to assign. The United Nations Food and Agricultural Organization estimates that commercial logging directly accounts for 10 percent of tropical deforestation.[1]

With 80 percent of tropical forests owned or controlled by governments, mainly in developing countries, funds for sustainable forestry management are scarce. Private parties generally receive timber concessions—often through patronage and at low fees—to carry out harvests over five to 25 years, even though most logged tropical forests require at least 60 years to regenerate. Concessionaires usually complete the harvest of old-growth trees quickly, since standing mature timber does not earn a return on their investment. Governments, in turn, usually invest timber proceeds in unrelated public services or in promotion of other private industries as part of their national economic growth plans. Thus, a nation's timber boom can easily go bust once the old-growth trees are felled.

A boom-and-bust timber export pattern emerged in West Africa in the 1950s and 1960s. As the timber trade expanded in the 1970s and 1980s, the pattern became more prevalent, spreading to Southeast Asia. In Thailand and the Philippines, the timber industries have now gone bust, and the boom is cresting in most remaining countries of the region. Only South America has enough tropical forest intact to sustain another timber boom.[2]

This chapter provides an overview of tropical timber operations in Asia, Africa and Latin America, with a special focus on selected countries in each region: the Philippines, Malaysia and Indonesia in Asia, Cameroon, Gabon and Zaire in Africa, and Brazil and Costa Rica in Latin America. Recent efforts by timber

Table 2

Forest Concessions, Domestic Consumption and Timber Exports

	Area of Productive Natural Closed Broadleaved Forest (acres)	Area under Concession (acres)	Domestic Forest Product Consumption 1989 (1,000 M³)	Volume Growth in Domestic Forest Product Consumption 1979-1989 (%)	Forest Product Exports 1989 (1,000 M³)	Volume Growth in Forest Product Exports 1979-1989 (%)
Brazil	742,556,100	31,119,164[a]	3,571	60	1,262	37
Colombia	97,565,000	3,858,140[a]	3,359	(20)	--	--
Indonesia	159,076,890	131,833,780	46,457	353	11,734	(44)
Malaysia	36,519,197	23,378,463	24,454	56	27,638	33
Papua New Guinea	37,050,000	5,969,990	1,383	116	1,408	113
Peru	107,000,400	3,591,380	1,687	(24)	--	--
Zaire	148,200,000	54,340,000	2,821	32	144	54

[a] This area is "Production Forest Estate" or natural forests designated by the government for logging.

SOURCE: World Resources Institute, *Surviving the Cut*, 1993.

producing countries and wood industry groups to establish more sustainable forestry practices are examined in detail. Finally, the operations of key multinational timber companies in each of these tropical regions are documented in an appendix.

Overview of the Tropical Timber Market

The tropical timber trade dates back to the time of the early European colonial empires. The Portuguese extracted Brazilwood from coastal forests in Latin America as early as the 1500s, and the English imported teak from India and African oak for shipbuilding in the early 1800s. Until the 20th century, however, tropical timber was regarded mainly as a luxury. The market grew rapidly after World War II, as population increases in tropical countries coincided with shrinking supplies of some hardwood species in temperate countries, especially in Europe.

The world tropical timber trade surged from 4.4 million cubic meters in 1950 to 61.2 million cubic meters in 1980.[3] Commercial logging ventures sprung up in West Africa and throughout the Pacific Rim. Today, the largest trade in tropical logs and plywood is within the Pacific Rim—mainly shipments from Southeast Asia to East Asia. Japan alone imports 40 percent of the tropical timber sold abroad. Eighty percent of all tropical timber is consumed in the countries that produce it, however.[4]

Advances in technology have boosted the tropical timber trade. As development of mechanized logging with chainsaws has replaced felling trees with axes alone, larger areas can be cut much more rapidly. Bulldozers have cut roads through areas that previously were jungle trails, speeding the transportation of wood to ports for shipping. Improvements in pulping technologies have permitted several types of tropical hardwoods to be pulped into a single mixture, making them attractive to pulp and paper producers. Still other technological advances have made it less costly to produce veneer and plywood from tropical woods like mahogany and meranti. As these production costs fall, tropical timber is better able to compete on the world market with other utility grade construction materials.[5]

The tropical timber industry now concentrates mainly on wood for construction purposes and for furniture. The greatest exports of tropical timber are four types of wood products: hardwood logs, hardwood sawnwood, veneer sheets and plywood. Tropical sawnwood is used in joinery products (mainly in Europe) and for decorative pieces. Plywood is used in concrete forms and for structural purposes (mainly in Asia). A small but lucrative luxury market also exists for prized woods like rosewood, mahogany and teak used in musical instruments and solid hardwood furniture.

Prices for tropical timber have been held down by competition from temperate species. Temperate softwoods and gypsum board are potential substitutes in the plywood market. Temperate softwoods and hardwoods are potential substitutes in the sawnwood market.

The export value of tropical hardwoods peaked in 1980, with $8 billion in sales. At the time, the export market was as large as that of cotton, twice that

Table 3

Imports of Tropical Timber by Major Consuming Countries

	Cubic Meters of Roundwood Equivalents 1989
Japan	23,939,512
South Korea	6,027,300
Taiwan	4,209,625[a]
United States	3,605,848[b]
United Kingdom	2,586,634
Netherlands	2,350,914
France	2,249,956
Italy	1,860,012
Germany	1,738,320
Spain	1,165,400

[a] Figure represents logs only, much of which is converted into furniture and resold abroad.
[b] Figure does not include imports of furniture.

SOURCE: Yoichi Kuroda, Japan Tropical Forestry Action Network, 1992. Figures derived from the 1990 Annual Review by the International Tropical Timber Association.

of rubber and three times that of cocoa. By 1990, however, receipts had dropped to $6 billion annually, and were projected to decline to $2 billion by 2000.[6]

Japan is the world's largest importer of tropical hardwoods by far. Practically all of the wood used in Japan is imported, even though 68 percent of the country is forested. Japan imported 23.9 million cubic meters (in roundwood equivalents) of tropical hardwoods in 1989, about 30 percent of the world total. The Japanese go through 25 billion pairs of waribashi chopsticks each year and spend $2 billion a year on tropical hardwood plywood forms for concrete, which typically are discarded after only a couple of uses. South Korea was the second largest importer of tropical timber in 1989, followed by Taiwan, the United States and the United Kingdom.

While the United States is not the top tropical timber importer in terms of volume, its imports are equal in value to those of Japan and Western Europe because it imports more highly valued finished goods, such as furniture and veneer, and fewer unfinished logs. In 1984, the United States imported more than $1.5 billion in wood furniture, whereas Japan imported only $220 million, and the EC nations imported $120 million.

Restrictions on the export of unfinished logs by many exporting countries have contributed to market and price distortions in recent years. As tropical timber-producing nations export fewer unfinished logs and more manufactured products, one result may be that the U.S. market will rely more on domestic timber producers. In 1989, nearly two-thirds of all U.S. hardwood imports into the United States were from tropical countries, according to U.S. Department of Commerce statistics analyzed by the Sierra Club.[7]

Tropical timber markets remain in flux. In 1991, the tropical timber industry faced increasing competition from temperate timber products and declining sales because of an economic recession. In the United States, import volumes of tropical wood products (excluding furniture) fell from $454 million in 1990 to

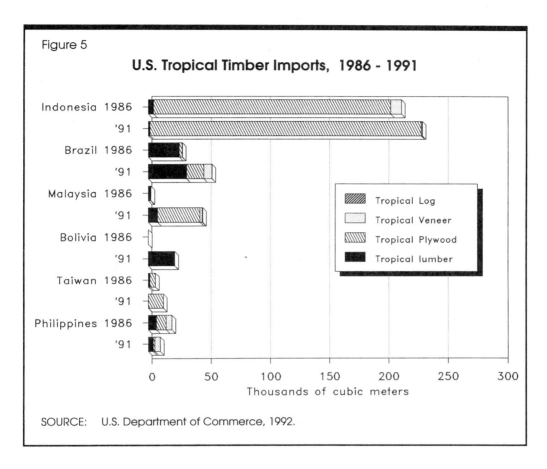

Figure 5

U.S. Tropical Timber Imports, 1986 - 1991

Legend:
- Tropical Log
- Tropical Veneer
- Tropical Plywood
- Tropical lumber

Countries/years (top to bottom): Indonesia 1986, '91; Brazil 1986, '91; Malaysia 1986, '91; Bolivia 1986, '91; Taiwan 1986, '91; Philippines 1986, '91

X-axis: 0, 50, 100, 150, 200, 250, 300
Thousands of cubic meters

SOURCE: U.S. Department of Commerce, 1992.

$410 million in 1991, even as product prices rose. The rise in prices was largely at the hands of Indonesian producers, who control three-quarters of the world's hardwood plywood market and account for 60 percent of tropical hardwood sales into the United States.[8]

Several political and economic factors have contributed to unsustainable logging practices. Log-export restrictions in places like Indonesia and peninsular Malaysia have boosted domestic processing capacity and created jobs, but the costs have been high, as these countries do not enjoy a comparative advantage in processing the natural resource. The resulting rise in export prices has reduced foreign demand and depressed the stumpage price of logs in turn. Such a fall in prices sends an erroneous signal to producers that tropical wood is in abundant supply, when in fact it is not.

Timber concessions that are not renewable or transferable have also given private timber interests an incentive to harvest as much volume as they can while the land is under their control. As Malcolm Gillis of Duke University points out, "licenses of such short duration clearly create no incentives for logging firms to undertake yield-sustaining measures or actively preserve the forest's productive and protective functions."[9]

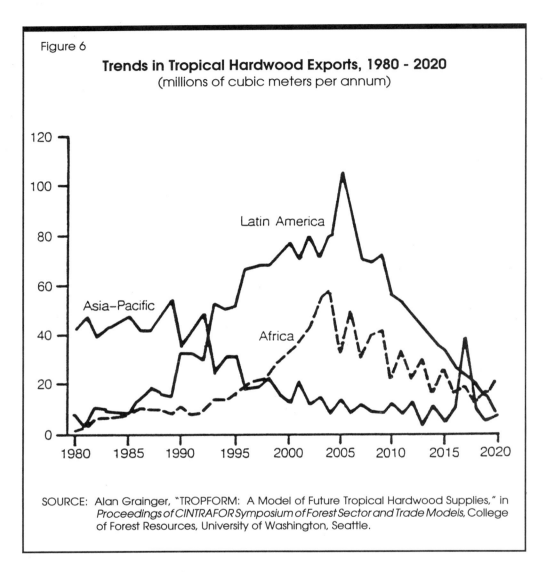

Figure 6

Trends in Tropical Hardwood Exports, 1980 - 2020
(millions of cubic meters per annum)

SOURCE: Alan Grainger, "TROPFORM: A Model of Future Tropical Hardwood Supplies," in *Proceedings of CINTRAFOR Symposium of Forest Sector and Trade Models*, College of Forest Resources, University of Washington, Seattle.

Shoddy logging practices exacerbate the deforestation trend. Ecosystem damage often accompanies logging, such as uprooting seedlings and residual trees that otherwise would form regrown forest. In many instances, harvesting only 5 to 20 percent of the standing trees results in damage to 20 to 50 percent or more of the remaining trees.[10] Undamaged standing trees become more vulnerable to windthrow from severe storms. Poor road alignment, construction and clearing, and logging on steeply sloped land lead to soil erosion and diminution of water quality. Logging roads also attract migrant farmers who move in and burn the remaining forest to plant crops.

Dry matter left behind after logging operations and the drying effect of opening the forest canopy enhances the forest's susceptibility to fire. Severe drought conditions in combination with logging on the island of Borneo (in tropical forests owned by Malaysia and Indonesia) caused one of the largest natural fires in history in 1982-83. More than 8.5 million acres—an area larger than Taiwan—burned. The market value of trees lost in East Kalimantan alone exceeded $5 billion.

As a result, deforestation itself has become an important factor in the contraction of the tropical timber trade. In regional terms, about half of the virgin productive closed forests in tropical Asia have been logged or burned, as have 25 percent of Africa's forests and 10 percent of those in Latin America. And for the reasons stated above, demand for tropical timber in developed countries has rarely driven this decline. In 1989, for example, only 34 percent of the industrial roundwood harvested in developing countries (excluding China) entered international trade—and many of these exports were to other developing countries.[11] Yet because of the continuing decline in tropical forest cover, only 10 of the world's 33 net tropical timber exporting countries are still expected to be able to export timber by the year 2000.[12]

The Asian Timber Market

Southeast Asia's rain forests have been the dominant source for the tropical hardwood market for nearly 30 years. The explosive growth of commercial logging has taken a heavy environmental toll, and reforestation programs are only now beginning. Japan, the world's largest importer of tropical timber, gets most of its wood from the Southeast Asian countries of Indonesia, Malaysia and Papua New Guinea. South Korea and Taiwan are the region's second and third largest importers, although their combined consumption amounts to only about 40 percent of Japan's.

The Philippines was the first country in Asia to develop a tropical export industry—and one of the first in the region to severely deplete its forest resource. Indonesia and Malaysia are the largest timber exporters in Asia today. The situation in each of these countries is summarized below.

The Philippines

As the first Southeast Asian nation to promote timber exports, the Philippines was the first exporter in the region to lose a startling amount of its forest cover. Commercial logging grew at phenomenal rates after World War II. The amount of land licensed for harvest in 1971 was double the amount licensed in 1960—more than 24 million acres.

As logging expanded, serious environmental problems surfaced. The loss of forests contributed to soil erosion, flooding, water shortages, dust storms and advancing sand dunes. Hardest hit were upland people who depend upon the forest for fruits, crops and wildlife to survive.

Growing pains and political realities greatly influenced the development of the logging industry in the Philippines. "Concession after concession was awarded to multinational corporations and to local rich minority and political powers who became entrepreneurs," says Eufresina Boado, formerly with the Philippine Forestry Bureau.[13] Among the American companies awarded logging concessions in the 1960s were **Boise Cascade, Georgia-Pacific, International Paper** and **Weyerhaeuser**, all of which operated on the island of Mindanao. Traditional landed elites and those who came to power as friends of President Ferdinand Marcos also were awarded logging concessions (a pattern repeated in Malaysia and Indonesia). Meanwhile, the Philippine Forestry Bureau was chronically understaffed with poorly educated workers. Morale was low, and corruption was rampant.

Selective logging (the process of taking only mature trees) has been rarely practiced in the Philippines. "Tree markers, who determine the trees to be cut and those to be left, are often inexperienced and easily fall prey to bribes," Boado says. As a result, many areas are overcut, and 30 to 70 percent of the trees remaining in harvest areas are heavily damaged.

Second-growth forest areas have not been properly managed, either. Consequently, they support more noncommercial trees species and weeds than commercial trees. The Filipino government failed to collect a substantial fee from loggers to protect the long-term value of the resource until 1970. But production was already dropping by 1975, and by 1984 it had plummeted to the 1955 level. The government subsequently banned logging in 64 of its 78 provinces, where forests are fast disappearing. By 1987, the nation's total forest cover dropped below 40,000 square miles, compared with 140,000 square miles in 1945. Less than 3 percent of the remaining forest is mature natural forest.[14]

Malaysia

As the Philippine export market dried up, Malaysia and Indonesia followed with their own timber booms, which continue today. Malaysia became a timber export power in the late 1950s, followed by Indonesia in the late 1960s. When Indonesia reduced its log exports to encourage domestic processing of logs in the 1980s, Malaysia surged ahead to become the world's top exporter of tropical logs. During the 1980s, timber revenues represented about one-eighth of Malaysia's gross domestic product and provided more than $2.5 billion in export income annually.[15]

Malaysia is composed of three geographical regions: peninsular Malaysia, Sabah and Sarawak, each of which has considerable autonomy. These provinces have some of the most commercially attractive forests in the humid tropics. Valuable trees grow close together and are easy to remove. Much of peninsular Malaysia has already been cleared and converted to tree crops of rubber and palm oil. In Sabah and Sarawak, shifting cultivation has been the leading cause of deforestation, although farmers often gained access to deforested areas through road building by loggers. As of 1983, Sarawak and Sabah were producing nearly two-thirds of the world's hardwood log exports.[16] In Sarawak, nearly two-thirds of the area has been licensed for logging.[17]

In Sabah, which boasts probably the richest, most dense tropical forests, **British Borneo Timber** had a monopoly on logging until 1952. Logging expanded quickly thereafter, with the entry of large foreign firms that received

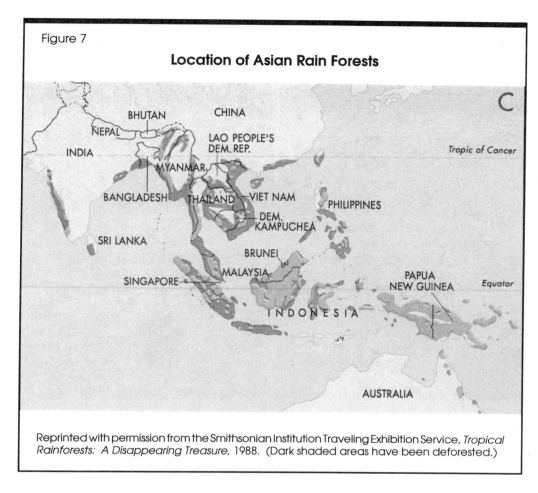

Figure 7

Location of Asian Rain Forests

Reprinted with permission from the Smithsonian Institution Traveling Exhibition Service, *Tropical Rainforests: A Disappearing Treasure*, 1988. (Dark shaded areas have been deforested.)

concessions of 21 to 25 years. **Weyerhaeuser** logged in Sabah from 1967 to 1988, for example. Other active companies such as **North Borneo Timber** and **Sabah Timber** were owned by British interests. Sabah subsequently reduced the concession period to only 10 years, and few large foreign firms were interested in working under such a short-term arrangement.

Logging in Sarawak has received international attention in recent years because of civil disobedience by the Penan forest people, who live in areas being decimated by the cut. The government of Sarawak says it wants to bring the Penan into the mainstream of society. While most of the Penan have been forced to settle in communities, about 500 remain nomadic.

In 1989, the International Tropical Timber Organization (ITTO), a coordinating body for tropical timber producers, sent a team of observers to Sarawak to evaluate the situation there. They concluded that the forest in Sarawak would be wiped out in 11 years if the rate of cutting were not reduced, eliminating the homelands of the Penan people. ITTO recommended a 30 percent reduction in the logging rate.[18]

In 1990, the Malaysian government promised to reduce logging in Sarawak to the levels sought by the ITTO observers. But it said the phase-down would occur over a 10- to 15-year period and did not say when the reduction would begin. The environmental group Greenpeace alleged that logging companies greatly intensified their rate of cutting in anticipation of the restrictions, and it urged a boycott of timber exports from Sarawak. According to Greenpeace's account, loggers worked around the clock and amassed a backlog of felled timber that clogged rivers for months. Logging in Sarawak rose from 14 million cubic meters in 1989 to 18 million cubic meters in 1990.[19]

Finally, in January 1992, the Malaysian government announced that logging in Sarawak would be reduced by 1.5 million cubic meters in 1992 and 1993, with total output dropping to 14.5 million cubic meters by the end of 1993. The government continues to deny that large-scale deforestation is taking place in Sarawak, however. It says only two to four trees per acre are harvested, with the rest of the forest allowed to regenerate and to continue to perform its normal ecological functions.

Lim Keng Yaik, Malaysian Minister of Primary Industries, contends that Malaysia is in fact ahead of developed countries in practicing sustainable forestry. "We are making headway toward ensuring our permanent forest estates are managed on a sustainable basis," Yaik maintains, "although the very criteria and definition of sustainability are still not resolved. Indeed, hardly any forests in the temperate countries can measure up to the current norms of sustainability without taking into account the fact that temperate forests are largely grown on a plantation basis depleted of biological diversity."[20]

Nevertheless, many observers remain leery of Malaysia's logging practices. Paul Senior, president of **Pat Brown Lumber**, says his company used to be a top American importer of wood from Sarawak. But Senior decided to drop all imports from Sarawak in late 1990 partly because "we were disappointed on their intransigence on reaching sustainability and partly for business reasons."[21] He concedes that there is a limited amount of pressure that U.S. importers can exert, however, because Japan, China and other Asian countries are much bigger customers in Malaysia.

Some believe the greatest leverage would come from the International Hardwood Products Association (IHPA), a trade group that represents importers of tropical timber. Ivan Ussach of the Rainforest Alliance, an environmental group based in New York, says a simple test of IHPA's influence would be for it to condemn the stepped-up logging operations in Sarawak that threaten the Penan forest people. "Here is a chance to take a stand on the most extreme example of unsustainable logging," Ussach believes. "If there ever was a case for a selective ban, this is it."[22] Meg Ruby, coordinator of Greenpeace's forest campaign, takes a similar stand. "If the IHPA is serious about pushing the industry toward sustainability," IHPA members "should immediately stop buying lumber from...Sarawak."[23]

Russell Stadelman, whose company is another top U.S. importer of Malaysian timber, for the most part agrees with Ussach and Ruby. "This would be a good chance for IHPA to say to Malaysia, 'You've got to move on this. You can't continue to cut timber at the rate you're cutting.'"[24] But while Stadelman has expressed his concerns to the Malaysian government, he continues to buy Malaysian wood. Sarawak imposes no quota or export tax on plywood sold abroad, he points out, while Indonesia has both a quota and an 8 percent export tax.

Meanwhile, IHPA Director Wendy Baer says her group has considered taking a position on the logging situation in Sarawak but has not reached a consensus on whether it would be appropriate to take a stand. The IHPA reports that logging was suspended in Sarawak during December 1992 in an effort to reduce harvest volumes by 30 percent—the level recommended previously by the ITTO mission.[25]

Indonesia

Indonesia is second only to Brazil in terms of rain forest acreage. More than two-fifths of the sprawling archipelago is classified as rain forest, especially Kalimantan, Sumatra and Irian Jaya. Taken together, Indonesia's islands are home to nearly 60 percent of all the tropical forests in Asia and perhaps 90 percent of the region's remaining virgin stands.

Indonesia has set aside 10 percent of its land area—48 million acres—as conservation areas. Yet it is losing an estimated 2.5 million acres of forest a year to shifting cultivation, commercial logging, fire and related causes. The country remains committed to logging on 158 million acres of tropical forest. More than 500 commercial logging concessions are in effect, with an average size of 250,000 acres.[26]

The export of tropical hardwoods is the second most important source of foreign exchange in Indonesia, after oil. In 1989, Indonesia produced more than 10 million cubic meters of sawnwood and 8 million cubic meters of plywood worth $4 billion, or 16 percent of the country's foreign exchange earnings.

After the Indonesian economy was opened to foreign investment in 1967, major exports of logs began from previously untouched tropical rain forests such as Kalimantan (the Indonesian portion of the island of Borneo). Commercial logging was responsible for the initial deforestation of Kalimantan and led to shifting cultivation and transmigration schemes in later years.

Like Malaysia, Indonesia offered 20-year concessions to foreign timber firms. Multinational companies like **Georgia-Pacific**, **Weyerhaeuser** and the subsidiaries of the Japanese conglomerates **Mitsui, Mitsubishi, Sumitomo** and **C. Itoh** were among those holding concessions. Indonesia's timber export earnings jumped during the 1970s from $110 million in 1970 to $2.1 billion in 1979.[27] The foreign timber boom lasted until 1980, when Indonesia curtailed log exports to encourage its domestic processing industries.

Indonesia's booming export market in the 1970s helped spawn large wood processing centers in neighboring countries such as Taiwan, Singapore and South Korea. These countries imported inexpensive tropical timber from Indonesia as well as Malaysia and processed it into a variety of products like plywood, furniture and veneer for sale on world markets. Indonesia then decided it, too, could benefit from domestic processing of logs. In 1980, it began to restrict the export of unprocessed logs in a policy shift to be phased in over five years.

Many of the wood processing plants in neighboring countries were forced to close or find new sources of timber. Meanwhile, Indonesia's processing capabilities expanded to the point where it was providing 70 percent of the world's hardwood plywood exports by 1984. But while the shift in policy provided more jobs for Indonesians, inefficiencies in domestic processing plants raised export prices and reduced stumpage values in the domestic market. The World Bank found that Indonesia managed to process only 43 percent of its industrial roundwood volume into salable products, for example, while comparable developing countries processed an average of 55 percent.[28]

Partly as a result of the change in government forest policy, the overall loss rate in Indonesia grew from an average of 741,000 acres a year in the 1970s to 2.2 million acres a year in the late 1980s. By the end of the period, government tree harvests and transmigration programs removed about 700,000 acres of forest a year, and commercial logging felled another 200,000 acres annually.[29] Most of the remainder of the forest loss was mainly from shifting cultivation and fires.

Human encroachment is a major problem in some of the Indonesian timber concessions. One logging road cleared through the timber concession of the **Kalimanis Group** (a large conglomerate that once was **Georgia-Pacific's** Indonesian partner) provides easy access for farmers migrating into the rain forest. An estimated 10 percent of the concession area already has been cleared for agriculture.[30]

As the rate of deforestation accelerates in Indonesia, the government has taken belated steps to curb the losses. In 1980, it imposed a reforestation tax of $4 on each cubic meter of logs harvested by timber concessionaires in Kalimantan and Sumatra. Companies engaged in their own reforestation efforts were exempt from the tax. Many loggers ignored the tax at first, and the government failed to channel the tax proceeds into reforestation projects.[31] The country achieved only 4.5 percent of its reforestation target from 1985 to 1990.

In 1989, however, the government raised the reforestation tax to $7 per cubic meter, and it raised the tax again to $10 per cubic meter in 1990. The law was also changed to require all companies to pay the fee and carry out reforestation programs directly. A campaign to collect delinquent back taxes netted $347 million through 1989. Much of this money is being used to finance the creation of new timber plantations through joint ventures with private companies.[32] Indonesia now seeks to reforest a total of 50 million acres of "particularly devastated land" at a cost of about $300 million a year. By 1994, it hopes to collect $1.5 billion a year in export taxes and reforestation fees.

The reforestation plan still faces a number of hurdles, however. One major problem is that little monitoring is done of timber concessionaires, so the government is almost entirely dependent on their reports to determine how much land is being cut annually (which in turn determines the volume of timber extracted and royalties paid). The World Bank has found that concessionaires often understate the volume and quality of timber they are cutting, and poor logging practices and breaches of regulations often still go undetected and uncorrected. While Indonesian forestry officials are aware of the problem and want to correct it, the World Bank says it is unlikely that the situation would improve even if the government increased its monitoring staff or took direct control of the concessions. "Instead, attention must be focused on incentives for better forest management by timber concessionaires and on changing development policies which contribute to deforestation," a bank report urges.[33]

Throughout Southeast Asia, government officials now sense there is an end to their "endless" forests. The World Resources Institute estimates that more than 133 million acres of denuded forest in the region may be suitable candidates for rehabilitation.[34] In Thailand, logging has reduced forest cover from 66 percent in 1950 to about 25 percent today; only 43 percent of its humid tropical forests remain. In 1988, devastating floods and landslides killed hundreds of people in deforested areas of Thailand, prompting a ban on commercial logging in early 1989. But illegal logging continues. In one six-month period following the ban, the Thai forestry department reported the arrest of 4,700 loggers and the destruction of an additional 94,000 acres of forest. Loggers in Thailand provide wood for furniture making and carving that is the main source of income for many rural people.[35]

Meanwhile, the ban on logging in Thailand has driven logging companies into the neighboring forests of Burma and Cambodia. Logging in Burma has increased to about 1.2 million acres a year, a rate five times higher than that of a decade ago. The military rulers of Burma have abandoned conservation plans for easy money received from the loggers of Thailand and other loggers from Singapore, Hong Kong, China and Taiwan.[36] Burma harvested more than 900,000 tons of teak in 1990, yielding more than $200 million in export earnings, mainly from the United States, Japan, Denmark and Italy. Burmese dissidents claim the military government has used these earnings to buy arms and fight rebel armies there. Partly for that reason, environmental groups are seeking to ban the importation of teak and teak products from Burma into the United States.

Producers of tropical timber often find ways to evade these bans, however. In Indonesia and the Philippines, producers get around a ban on raw log exports by smuggling logs to Sabah in Malaysia, which has no such ban. Once in Sabah, the logs are reshipped to Japanese and European markets. Indonesian producers skirt an export ban on sawnwood by minimally processing logs into oversize boards, with a slight molding on one side. Some timber exports simply aren't declared. Import records in Japan, for example, have consistently shown far more hardwood volume coming from the Philippines than export records in that country indicate. In some years, the discrepancies have exceeded 120 percent.[37]

Timber Imports from Southeast Asia

United States

While Southeast Asia dominates tropical timber imports into the United States, no major U.S. timber companies continue to have direct, company-owned operations in the region. **Georgia-Pacific** operated in Indonesia from 1960 to 1984 and in the Philippines from 1958 to 1982. **Weyerhaeuser** operated in the Philippines from 1966 to 1982, Malaysia from 1966 to 1988 and Indonesia from 1971 to 1981. **Boise Cascade, Bowater** and **Unilever**, a British-owned company, also held timber concessions in Southeast Asia. The only recent foray

Box 3A

Weyerhaeuser: An Indonesian Case Study

Weyerhaeuser, the world's largest private timber owner, obtained a 250,000-acre concession on the island of Kalimantan in Indonesia in 1971. The experience of **International Timber**—Weyerhaeuser's Indonesian division—highlights problems that multinational companies sometimes face when working in developing countries. Weyerhaeuser was seeking to increase its supply of tropical hardwoods in the early 1970s. (It also held concessions in Malaysia and the Philippines at the time.) Norman Johnson, Weyerhaeuser's vice president for research and former head of its Indonesian division, says the company went to Indonesia because of low stumpage prices, favorable tax incentives and that country's policy of not barring the expatriation of profits.[1a]

Before Weyerhaeuser arrived in Indonesia, loggers in the concession area had cut trees with handsaws and rolled them down hillsides into rivers. Then International Timber mechanized the operation, built roads and used heavy machinery to extract the commercially valuable dipterocarp species. (Dipterocarps are a family of tall tropical trees in Southeast Asia that are a valuable source of timber, aromatic oils and resins.) While mechanized logging caused more environmental damage than hand logging, Johnson believes it was the only way to harvest wood rapidly enough to keep up with the demand and remain profitable.

International Timber eventually logged about half the trees in its concession, taking trees larger than 10 inches in diameter. In 1977, the company exported 1.4 million cubic meters of wood from the area, worth $88 million. Then the harvest volume began to plummet—from 804,000 cubic meters in 1979 to only 300,000 cubic meters in 1980.

As time went by, International Timber also ran afoul of its Indonesian partner, **PT Tri Usaha Bhakti**, a company operated by retired military officers. The officers were not business people, nor did they know much about forestry, according to Robert Lowery, director of Weyerhaeuser's International Reforestation Project. Yet they sought to take over the project as soon as they learned how the timber operation worked. Lowery says the Indonesians also kept demanding cash infusions and a larger share of the project's profits. "That's the way things were there. They'd say, 'We need $100,000 here and another $100,000 there,' and we began to have ethical concerns about that."[2a]

Weyerhaeuser's Johnson recalls that International Timber wanted to reforest part

into the region by a U.S. timber company was **Scott Paper's** planned pulp mill and plantation in Irian Jaya in 1988. Scott withdrew from that project in 1989 before it got off the ground. (See Chapter 2 for details.)

Despite a lack of direct overseas investment, scores of U.S. timber companies continue to import tropical timber from Southeast Asia into the United States. By varying accounts, **Georgia-Pacific** probably is the first or second largest importer of tropical timber from the region, although definitive data are hard to obtain.

A compilation of 1990 data obtained by Greenpeace from the reporting service of the *Journal of Commerce* concluded that **Georgia-Pacific** probably was the largest importer of tropical timber from Indonesia, followed by **Russell Stadelman, Chesapeake Hardwood Products, Liberty Woods International,** of the concession but met resistance from its Indonesian partners, who apparently were more interested in maximizing short-term profits than in replanting. Making matters worse, no effort was made to prevent villagers from burning trees that remained in the concession area after the first harvest. Typically, the villagers would plant hill crops such as rice for a year. Then they would plant cassava or bananas in the second year. But by the third year the land usually was abandoned and had reverted to brush. The logged area typically was cut and burned again after about 15 years.

Another of Weyerhaeuser's frustrations was the 20-year concession limit for International Timber. The company had little incentive to replant the forest because it could not be certain it would hold the right to harvest new trees after they matured in 35 years. In addition, few dipterocarps replaced the felled trees naturally because so many of the species had been taken in the first cut. Consequently, International Timber decided to plant fast-growing trees that would mature before the end of its concession period.

In 1977, International Timber started a nursery and planted 833 acres of fast-growing eucalyptus, gmelina, acacia and albena in a demonstration plot. "We believed we could grow seven to 10 times more usable wood on the land than the yield we got from dipterocarps," Johnson recalls. But relations with the company's Indonesian partners continued to sour and "we were not sure we wanted to invest tens of millions of dollars into the operation." Weyerhaeuser eventually sold out to its Indonesian partners in 1981 for less than half of the project's estimated $50 million value.

International Timber offered about $1 million to continue reforestation experiments after it pulled out of the project. The research was to be conducted jointly by Indonesia's Agricultural Institute at Bogor and several American universities. But the Indonesians reportedly continued to show little interest in replanting and rejected the offer. Only about 2,200 acres of land was reforested at the time Weyerhaeuser left Indonesia, and no reforestation occurred over the next three years.[3a]

As recently as 1987, "local joint venture partners including governments-as-owners of timber stands have been unwilling to reinvest profits in this type of experiment since the financial rewards are, at best, in the distant future," observes Duke University's Malcolm Gillis.[4a] But with the strengthening of Indonesia's reforestation law in 1989, the local partners in International Timber's former concession area now are replanting about 400 to 800 acres of a year, Johnson reports.

Penrod, Mitsui USA, Pat Brown Lumber and C. Itoh Building Products.[38] The same data identified major importers of tropical woods from Malaysia as **Liberty Woods International, Russell Stadelman, Overseas Hardwoods, Pat Brown Lumber** and **Ihlo Sales & Imports. Stadelman** also imports tropical timber from Papua New Guinea. (More details on these firms are available in the company summary section at the end of this chapter.)

Weyerhaeuser once had a major direct stake in Southeast Asia, with operations in the Philippines, Malaysia and Indonesia. But in the 1970s it began to separate itself from its international subsidiaries through a series of planned divestments. Some environmental groups maintain that Weyerhaeuser effectively has established "front" corporations that make it harder to track its imports of tropical timber. As an example, the Task Force on Multinational

Corporations, based in Seattle, Wash., alleges that despite the company's sale of its Indonesian operations to **Chesapeake Hardwoods** in 1981, "Weyerhaeuser managers remain at the helm, and Weyerhaeuser remains a major customer and distributor for the new company." (Chesapeake itself was sold to a newly formed affiliate of the Indonesian **Kalimanis Group** in 1989.)[39]

Weyerhaeuser continues to purchase $10-15 million of tropical wood from Southeast Asia each year, including $500,000 of tropical luaun from Chesapeake Hardwoods. The Task Force on Multinational Corporations reported in 1992 that other companies in Southeast Asia with direct links to Weyerhaeuser include **Capricorn** in the Philippines; **Pacific Hardwood, Kennedy Bay Timber** and **Silam Forest Products** in Malaysia; and **Weyerhaeuser Far East**, based in Hong Kong. Weyerhaeuser confirms the investment in Capricorn but says that company is inactive. The other companies are no longer Weyerhaeuser holdings, according to Lowell Moholt, Weyerhaeuser's director of investor relations.[40]

Japan

Japan is the world's largest importer of tropical timber, logs, plywood, sawnwood and woodchips. It has many companies with direct investment in rain forest areas of the Philippines, Malaysia, Indonesia, Papua New Guinea and other countries. A 1989 study by World Wildlife Fund International, based in Gland, Switzerland, finds: "The main features of Japanese investment in forestry products have changed little during the last three decades. The desire for control—with no strings attached—of a given resource base, combined with the search for maximum profit yield in the short term, have acted and continue to act as the main thrust behind any investment."[41]

Trading houses associated with Japan's main "keiretsu," or corporate groupings, have the greatest involvement in commercial logging in tropical countries. **Mitsui** began logging in Kalimantan, Indonesia, in 1963. It later sold its concessions to **Sumitomo Forestry** and **Mitsubishi**. Sumitomo Forestry probably has been the Japanese company most heavily involved in logging through the years. Sumitomo Forestry had interests in more than 20 timber-related firms in Indonesia during the mid-1970s.[42]

The keiretsu structure, marked by cooperative ties between companies within a business group, encourages companies to sell their products to others within the group, regulate prices and sometimes exclude other companies. The crossholding of shares within a business group can make it difficult for outside firms to penetrate the group. The six major keiretsu in Japan are **Dai-Ichi Kangyo, Fuyo** (Fuji), **Mitsubishi, Mitsui, Sanwa** and **Sumitomo**. All have member companies that import significant amounts of tropical timber into Japan, according to the Japan Tropical Forest Action Network (Jatan), an environmental group based in Tokyo.

Within these keiretsu, trading companies heavily involved in the import of tropical timber include **C. Itoh, Marubeni, Nissho Iwai, Sumitomo Forestry** and other trading companies for **Mitsubishi** and **Mitsui**. Large pulp, paper and timber companies involved in tropical timber importing include **Honshu Paper**, a member of the Dai-Ichi Kangyo group; **Sanyo Kokusaku Pulp**, associated with

Table 4

Japanese Imports of Tropical Timber
from Southeast Asia, 1989

Business Group	Sarawak (cubic meters)	Total Imports of Tropical Timber (cubic meters)
Dai-Ichi Kangyo	774,000	1,768,000
Fuyo (Fuji)	791,000	1,642,000
Sanwa	759,000	1,388,000
Sumitomo	618,000	1,316,000
Mitsui	396,000	504,000
Mitsubishi	298,000	454,000

Dai-Ichi Kangyo Group: C. Itoh, Nissho Iwai*, Kawatetsu Shoji, Kanematsu-Gosho, Honshu Mokuzai.
Sanwa Group: Nissho Iwai*, Nichimen, Teijin Shoji.
Sumitomo Group: Sumitomo Forestry, Sumisho Lumber, Sumitomo Corp.
Fuyo (Fuji) Group: Marubeni, Marubeni Lumber, Okura Shoji, Sanyo Kokusaku Pulp.
Mitsubishi Group: Mitsubishi Corp., Meiwa Trading.
Mitsui Group: Mitsui & Co., Oji Mokuzai.

* Nissho Iwai belongs to two groups. The company's import statistics have been divided in two, with half being used for Dai-Ichi and half for Sanwa. Nissho Iwai is more closely associated with the Sanwa Group than Dai-Ichi Kangyo.

SOURCE: Japan Tropical Forest Action Network, based on data from the Japan Tropical Importers Association, February 1991.

the Fuyo group; and **Oji Paper**, a member of the Mitsui group. A further discussion of Japanese timber companies appears in the company summary section at the end of this chapter.

Japanese trading companies handle all aspects of the timber trade, from logging to transportation and importation. What is more, they often forge close ties with companies in developing nations and receive substantial funding from sources inside Japan. Such financing takes the form of grants, concessional yen credits, nonconcessional Export-Import Bank loans and private sector loans, explains Robert Orr, a professor of political science at Temple University Japan. Some trading companies have come to depend quite heavily on Japanese foreign aid. **C. Itoh**, Japan's largest trading company, receives $350 million to $400 million annually in all kinds of Japanese foreign assistance, according to Orr.[43]

The power these trading companies wield in some tropical countries is considerable. In Papua New Guinea, for instance, Japanese companies comprise 90 percent of the timber industry. Many of these companies have been found to bribe government officials, export more logs than their contracts permit, cheat landowners of royalties and benefits, and defraud the government of timber royalties, export duties and tax revenues.

One prominent inquiry convened by the government of Papua New Guinea in 1987 and headed by Judge Thomas Barnett concluded: "It would be fair to say of some of the companies that they are now roaming the countryside with the self-assurance of robber barons: bribing politicians and leaders, creating social disharmony and ignoring laws in order to gain access to, rip out and export the last remnants of the province's valuable timber."[44] Nineteen of the 20 companies examined in the Barnett inquiry were found to engage in fraud and illegal pricing practices on a regular basis. (An attempt was later made on Barnett's life and court documents perished in a mysterious fire.) The Barnett inquiry led to the resignation of Deputy Prime Minister Ted Diro, who was found guilty of 86 counts of corruption and other misconduct. Papua New Guinea subsequently placed a two-year ban on new logging permits in July 1990, although the government has since granted many exceptions to the moratorium, minimizing its effect.

Environmental groups increasingly are taking Japan's timber trading companies to task. Japanese environmentalists have criticized **Marubeni**, Japan's largest tropical importer, for logging mangroves in Irian Jaya, Indonesia, where mangroves are converted to wood chips and end up in pulp and paper products. The Indonesian government temporarily suspended Marubeni's logging license in 1990 for illegal cutting of mangroves in a conservation area and fined the company the equivalent of $590,000—the maximum fine allowable under Indonesian law.[45] Although the actual operator of the concession is an Indonesian logging company, **P.T. Bintuni Utama Murni Wood Industries**, "behind this company and the related operations is a complex network of joint venture capital outlays and materials processing and transportation activities controlled by the Marubeni Corp," says Jatan, the Japanese environmental group.[46]

In the United States, environmentalists led by Rainforest Action Network, Greenpeace and Earth First! have called for a boycott of products made by **Mitsubishi**. Through its **Daiya Malaysia** subsidiary, Mitsubishi is one of the top five Japanese importers of tropical hardwoods from Sarawak, Malaysia. And since Mitsubishi sells many consumer products through affiliated companies under the Mitsubishi brand name, activists consider it a prime target for a boycott. Mitsubishi owns 33 percent of **Mitsubishi Motors Cars**, for example. At the San Francisco auto show in November 1992, a 40-foot-tall inflatable Godzilla greeted visitors to the show with a banner that read: "Mitsubishi Destroys Rainforests: The word is getting around." Four protesters managed to get inside the hall and unfurl a similar banner.[47]

Some Japanese companies, including Mitsubishi, have beefed up their public relations staffs to counter attacks from the environmental community. Others have created new environmental divisions to address concerns about rain forest destruction. But for the most part, Japanese industry and government officials still deny playing a major role in tropical deforestation. The Japanese Foreign Ministry maintains that 49 percent of deforestation in tropical Asia is a result of slash-and-burn agriculture and that Japan is responsible for only 1.2 percent of tropical deforestation in the region.

Box 3B

Mitsubishi Man to the Rescue!

Some Japanese timber interests have taken "super-human" steps to counter mounting international criticism of their involvement in tropical deforestation. **Mitsubishi**, for one, has funded the publication of a 216-page comic book that features the exploits of "Hino, the Mitsubishi Man." The comic book was published by the Science and Technology Educational Association of Japan and distributed to Japanese high school students who were thinking of working for Mitsubishi and wanted to know more about the company and its activities.

In the comic-book story, Hino, the Mitsubishi Man, investigates charges that the company is destroying tropical rain forests, and not surprisingly, he finds the company innocent of any wrongdoing. The accusations against Mitsubishi concerning tropical deforestation "consist of misunderstanding and obvious distortions by the mass media," Hino concludes. The major cause of rain forest destruction, he says, is "shifting cultivation by local people."

Many objected to the comic book's publication. Japanese environmentalists brought four women from Sarawak, Malaysia (where Mitsubishi gets most of its tropical timber), to Japan to refute Hino's "investigation." One of the women, Lucy Uloi, told a newspaper that "traditional shifting cultivation carried out by Sarawak's natives for their very survival is small-scale and takes into consideration regeneration of the forest.... Logging carried out by Japanese companies using bulldozers destroys many times more forest than does shifting cultivation," she claimed.[1b]

Peter Hadfield, a newspaper columnist, also has criticized the comic-book story for being one-sided. "There is no hint anywhere in the story that the critics might be right and the company might be wrong. The symptoms of paranoia are obvious," Hadfield wrote in the *Daily Yomiuri*. "The story also betrays an appalling lack of methodology by anyone who is trying to determine the truth. Not once does Hino talk to people whose views differ from the company's creed," Hadfield observes.[2b] The Japanese Ministry of Education banned the cartoon book from school distribution in March 1992. It said the book constituted "propaganda."

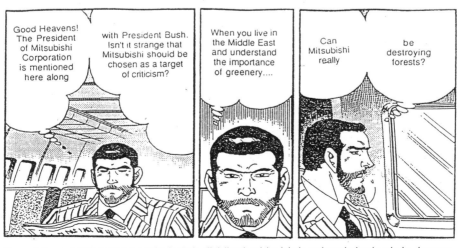

Panel from Mitsubishi comic book distributed to high school students in Japan.

Table 5

Japan's Role in Deforestation of Tropical Forests
(tentative government calculation)

	Average annual deforestation (thousands of acres)	Percentage of deforestation due to slash-and-burn farming	Japan's contribution to deforestation
Tropical Africa	9,080 (33%)	70%	(30 x 0.0007 =) 0.02%
Tropical America	13,859 (50%)	35%	(65 x 0.0001 =) 0.007%
Tropical Asia	4,979 (18%)	49%	(51 x 0.024 =) 1.2%
Worldwide	27,918 (100%)	49%	(51 x 0.0125 =) 0.6%

SOURCE: Japanese Foreign Ministry, citing *FAO Yearbook of Forest Products,* 1987; *FAO Tropical Forest Resources,* 1982.

"Although it is clear that Japan is the world's biggest importer of timber from tropical forests, it is quite misleading to say that Japan's imports are thus the primary cause of tropical forest devastation," insists Tomoo Aoyagi, a senior official on trade issues for the Japanese Forestry Agency.[48] Nevertheless, Japanese timber importers have moved voluntarily to restrict the import of tropical hardwoods in recent years, and the Japan Plywood Manufacturers Association has agreed to buy more temperate veneers, reports the U.S. Commerce Department.[49]

The African Timber Market

Africa's tropical forests have been severely depleted by a combination of commercial logging and shifting cultivation. The region briefly led the world in tropical timber exports after World War II. Since 1950, however, the Asian market has eclipsed the African market. Most of Africa's timber exports end up in Western European nations with ties to former African colonies.[50] No major U.S. timber companies are known to have direct investments in Africa, although many U.S. importers deal in African hardwoods.

Only shreds of rain forest remain in the West African countries of Liberia, Côte d'Ivoire, Ghana and Nigeria. These nations, with the exception of Nigeria, were the region's largest timber exporters during the mid-1980s.[51] Since then, logging in Cameroon and Gabon has accelerated as new roads make their forests

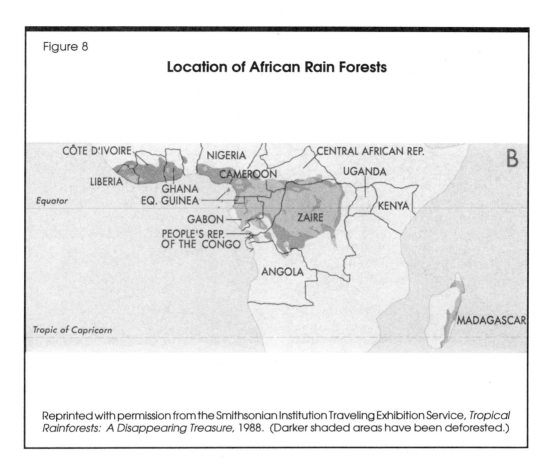

Figure 8

Location of African Rain Forests

Reprinted with permission from the Smithsonian Institution Traveling Exhibition Service, *Tropical Rainforests: A Disappearing Treasure*, 1988. (Darker shaded areas have been deforested.)

more accessible. By comparison, only one-quarter of Zaire's massive yet remote tropical rain forest area has been worked by loggers. Equatorial Guinea, Benin, The Congo and the Central African Republic also have large untouched remnants of rain forest. Yet 90 percent of Zaire's forest (the third largest tropical forest after Brazil's and Indonesia's) and 90 percent of the Central African Republic's rain forest have been parceled out to timber interests. Timber extraction has increased as European companies and European aid agencies provided funding for new roads in these countries.[52]

Africa's forests are home to about 150,000 so-called "Pygmy" people, including the Baka of Cameroon, the Aka of the Central African Republic and the Mbuti and Twa of Zaire. These hunting and gathering Pygmy groups trade forest products, such as meat and honey, with hundreds of thousands of Bantu farming villagers, who live along the fringes of the forest.

As in Southeast Asia, logging's destructive potential has been exacerbated by huge numbers of poor people who have followed in the wake of loggers and engaged in shifting agriculture. Yet in some areas, such as Côte d'Ivoire, logging itself has been a dominant force in tropical deforestation. Côte d'Ivoire once had the dubious distinction of the highest deforestation rate anywhere in the world—

estimated at more than 15 percent annually. A long-term drought and encroachment of the Sahara desert into the Sahel hastened the depletion of that country's
forests. The drought also brought 1.4 million refugees from neighboring
countries into Côte d'Ivoire by 1985.[53]

Today, the African countries with the fastest-growing timber markets are
Zaire, Cameroon and Gabon. The situation in each of these countries is analyzed
below.

Zaire

Zaire contains some of the most isolated rain forest on the African continent.
It is home to 11,000 plant species, one-third of which are unique to the region.
The remote location of Zaire's forest, combined with a lack of industrial
infrastructure, has kept the nation's rain forest largely intact. But the situation
is changing rapidly. Timber concessions have been granted on 90 percent of the
nation's 230 million acres of forest—mostly to political and military allies of
President Mobutu. One Canadian forester working in Zaire, Jacques Pierre,
estimates that the country's annual rate of logging will increase twentyfold by
the year 2000. That amount of production—10 million cubic meters of roundwood equivalent a year—would be the sustainable limit for Zaire, Pierre figures.[54]

Approximately 55 companies are logging in Zaire. These include the Italian
company **La Forestiere**, the German company **Stabach** and a host of other
Belgian, Italian and German firms. The largest timber concessions belong to the
German company **Karl Danzer**, which is working in a joint venture with the
Zairean government, known as the **Societe Industrielle et Forestiere Zairo-
Allemande** (Siforzal). President Mobutu has a large financial interest in Siforzal.
Danzer's 10 concessions amount to more than 22 million acres, or nearly 10
percent of Zaire's forests. Danzer's largest operation, totaling more than 2 million
acres, stretches for 175 miles along the banks of the Zaire River at Lokoko in the
northern part of the country.[55]

Danzer, one of Germany's largest timber firms, began its operation in Lokoko
in 1985. According to Virginia Luling, a British anthropologist, and Damien
Lewis, a British freelance journalist, Danzer is harvesting four hardwood species
in Lokoko—each with a value of about $5,000 to $10,000 per tree. While only 60
trees are felled daily, Danzer's operations affect a large area. The occurrence of
the valuable species is quite low—only one tree for every eight acres—so nearly
500 acres is affected by its daily operations. Huge "skidders," or tractors, drag
the trees through the forest to loading areas, where logging trucks wait to
transport the trees to the Zaire River. From there, the trees are loaded on to
barges to begin a 1,400 mile journey to the sea.[56]

Under Zairean law, Danzer must wait 25 years before it can re-cut harvested
areas. Some of the valuable hardwoods take more than 100 years to mature,
however. Danzer also pays the government a reforestation tax of $1 per acre.
Robert Grantham of the African Environment Network calculates that Danzer
pays about $10,000 annually in taxes to Zaire in return for exports valued at $16
million. Danzer has built schools and medical centers in the Lokoko region and
created 200 local jobs.[57]

Cameroon

Cameroon is a rain forest-rich country that has pushed timber exports aggressively to help out its sagging economy. Declining prices for oil, coffee and cocoa—its main export commodities—combined with $4 billion in foreign debt have led to greatly increased commercial logging activities. (Timber exports in 1989 totaled 525,000 metric tons.) A recent report by the Environmental Defense Fund claims that government controls on logging operations have been weak or nonexistent.[58] The government also has been criticized for its support of the "trans-Cameroon highway," which would extend across more than 400 miles of southern Cameroon and provide access to nearly 35 million acres of pristine rain forest, where Baka Pygmies live. (The World Bank has refused to fund the project, and it was put on hold in 1990.)

French, German, Dutch and Italian timber companies have operations in Cameroon. These include the German companies **Hinrich Feldmayer** and **Karl Danzer**; Dutch companies **Bekel** and **Wijma**; and the Italian firm **Alpi** as well as many French companies.[59] Feldmayer buys about 70,000 cubic meters of logs annually, mostly from Lebanese entrepreneurs "whose logging practices are based on the sole principle of cutting as many trees as quickly as possible," according to Korinna Horta of the Environmental Defense Fund.[60] Bilateral lending institutions also have financed timber operations. The German **Kreditanstalt fur Wiederaufbau**, for one, has financed road building projects in the south and western parts of Cameroon. In 1992, Cameroon President Paul Biya reportedly contacted Japan's Foreign Affairs Ministry to seek funding for completion of the trans-Cameroon highway.[61]

Brookside Veneers, a privately held New Jersey veneer company, imports obeche and koto from Cameroon through the Italian-based **Alpi**. David Thomsson, president of Brookside Veneers, says he works only with suppliers of "well-managed" logging operations whose goal is sustainable yield. Thomsson estimates that 90 percent of his timber is coming from "well-managed forest programs," with an average of about one tree removed per acre. Thomsson says that Alpi's forest management practices are better than those of many other companies operating in Cameroon, because the company has invested heavily in processing in the country—building a veneer and plywood mill—and is dedicated to carrying out its own forest management plan.[62]

Gabon

With 49 million acres of rain forest—much of it undisturbed—Gabon has become a major log exporter in recent years with substantial investments by foreign (mostly French) multinationals. France is the main market for Gabon's two primary export species, okoume and azibo. Areas previously not accessible soon will be open to logging as the trans-Gabon railway project is completed in the southeastern portion of the country.

A subsidiary of **St. Gobain**, one of France's 12 largest companies, is logging in Gabon.[63] The subsidiary, **Rougier-Ocean-Landex**, holds many timber concessions in Africa and is the second largest plywood manufacturer in France.

(ROL's timber production in 1985 was 200,000 cubic meters from all sources of wood. As of 1988, **Banque National de Paris** held an 11 percent interest in the company.) Other foreign-owned firms in Gabon include the French family-owned firms **CCAF** of the **Corbbet-Marti** group and **Gabexfo** of the Bernardini family. In addition, the Spanish holding company **Alena SA** owns a Gabonese logging company, **Societe l'Oukome de la N'Goume**, which exports timber for plywood production at its factory in Tarragone, Spain. The German firm **Hinrich Feldmayer** also holds a 6 percent stake in a Gabonese logging firm.

Joint ventures between development banks and Gabonese companies have also promoted timber investments in the country. **Compagnie Forestiere du Gabon** is a large joint venture between two state agencies, the French **Caisse Centrale de Corporation Economique** and the **Dutch Development Bank**, and several timber companies, the French **Empain**, the Dutch **Bruynnzell** and the German **Hinrich Feldmayer**. Germany's **Karl Danzer** also has operations in Cameroon.[64]

The Latin American Timber Market

Latin America's tropical forests are the last of the great rain forest areas to be developed for commercial logging. Latin America possesses 55 percent of the world's closed tropical hardwood trees, yet it has not been a major exporting force in the postwar period. The region's timber exports account for less than one-tenth of world timber production. The United States imports more than 60 percent of Latin America's tropical timber exports (although this amounted to only 500,000 cubic meters in 1980).

Large timber companies originally passed over Latin America because its forests are more homogeneous than those in Asia or Africa, with fewer desirable trees per acre, and they are situated farther from end-use markets. As Asia and, to a lesser extent, Africa deplete their virgin timber supplies, however, attention of both industry and environmental groups is shifting to Latin America. Some multinational companies are investing in the region in the hope that Latin American forests can serve as a new supply source as these other forests are depleted. Environmentalists want development to proceed with much more planning for resource conservation and sustainable timber management to prevent a repetition of the unrestrained boom eras in Asia and Africa.

While only 10 percent of the exploitable area in Latin America has been logged, the majority of forests in several Central American and Caribbean countries have been severely deforested. Haiti's forests are gone, 90 percent of the Dominican Republic's forests have been logged, Guatemala's and Mexico's rain forests have shrunk by half, and Costa Rica is expected to be a net importer of tropical hardwood before the end of the decade.

By contrast, the Amazon forest of South America is still relatively intact. As the world's largest contiguous rain forest, the Amazon extends into nine South American countries, all of which share (to one degree or another) the triple threat of population booms, soaring poverty and large external debt. In recent years, the Brazilian Amazon rain forest has dominated popular concern about rain forest destruction. Brazil's portion of the Amazon (60 percent of the total) stretches over 1.9 million square miles —a land mass equal to the United States east of the Mississippi River. Yet a forest area twice the size of the state of Delaware went up in smoke in Brazil in 1991 alone. Rio de Janeiro, the site of the 1992 Earth Summit, sits in the middle of an Atlantic coastal forest that has shrunk to only 3 percent of its original size.

The situation in Brazil has caught the world's attention because it ranks first in terms of biological diversity yet also ranks high in habitat destruction. Costa Rica faces a similar situation, albeit on a much smaller scale. The commercial logging activities of each of these countries are analyzed below.

Brazil

Logging has been a tradition in Brazil for generations. The country, in fact, was named after a tree harvested by Portuguese colonists. Brazil's Atlantic rain forest

Figure 9

Location of Latin American Rain Forests

Reprinted with permission from the Smithsonian Institution Traveling Exhibition Service, *Tropical Rainforests: A Disappearing Treasure,* 1988. (Darker shaded areas have been deforested.)

was cut down in the 19th century to make way for the expansive cities of Rio de Janeiro and Sao Paulo. To the north, the tropical and subtropical rain forests of Minas Gerais soon gave way to fields of grain, soybeans, coffee and cacao and, later, cattle pasture.

On the whole, cattle ranching and shifting cultivation have played a far greater role in deforestation in Brazil than commercial logging. But timber extraction is a burgeoning part of the Brazilian economy and, by some accounts, has become a leading industrial sector.[65] While Brazil supplies only 5 percent of the world's tropical wood products today, its share is expected to increase steadily.

Four of the Amazon region's six states and territories depend on wood products for more than 25 percent of their industrial output. In the states of

Rondonia and Roraima, wood products account for more than 60 percent of industrial output. The increase in wood production is evidenced by the steep increase in government licensed sawmills—from 194 in 1965 to 1,639 in 1981 and 2,892 in 1987. Encroachment on the Amazon rain forest is evident as well. In 1976, only 14 percent of Brazilian sawnwood was derived from rain forest areas; recently the figure was 44 percent.[66]

U.S. imports of Brazilian wood: Only Indonesia supplies more tropical wood to the United States than Brazil. As such, the United States is Brazil's single largest foreign market for solid wood products. Tropical hardwood and wood product imports from Brazil were valued at $182 million in 1987, representing 3 percent of the $5.7 billion U.S. wood import trade that year. Timber imports from Brazil have dropped precipitously since then: the value of imports (mainly tropical lumber) fell to $39 million in 1989 before rebounding to nearly $54 million in 1991.[67]

Most commercial logging in Brazil is done by domestic companies. American wood products companies generally buy Brazilian timber on the open market or through contractual arrangements with established domestic firms. Several private, medium-sized U.S. companies have processing plants or export offices in Brazil, including **Castell Exports, Russell Stadelman, Robinson Lumber** and **Pat Brown Lumber**.

Two major U.S. paper companies, **Champion International** and **Westvaco**, have pulp plantations in southeastern Brazil. Champion's operation is on or adjacent to land that once was part of Brazil's Atlantic rain forest. **Georgia-Pacific** operated a small veneer and plywood mill in Brazil from 1965 to 1990, but it sold the mill to the plant's manager, Bruce Larson, in 1990. Japanese companies in Brazil include **Eidai**, which is 50 percent owned by **Mitsubishi**, and **C. Itoh**. Eidai operates inside the Amazon rain forest. C. Itoh's plantations and pulp mills are south of the Amazon and not on rain forest land.

Brazilian logging practices: Commercial logging in Brazil traditionally has been done in an unsustainable manner on land with uncertain title. A series of government decrees have tried to end such logging practices. Brazil's first forestry laws encouraged clearcutting of virgin forests and the establishment of forestry plantations. These laws were intended for the south of the country and did not apply well to the Amazon, where only a few commercially valuable species grow per acre.[68] The law also required that one new tree be planted for every tree cut, and it allowed loggers to contract with third parties to plant trees on areas already deforested to offset their own logging. The practice was widely abused and susceptible to corruption and has since been discontinued.

The Brazilian government's new forestry laws require commercial loggers to have secure title to their land and submit a forestry management plan for approval by the national environmental agency, Ibama. The main requirements of the plan are that logging of mature trees not interfere with the natural growth of the forest and that trees be cut at a rate to ensure a steady future supply. Replanting usually is not required in the Amazon because selective cutting opens up the canopy and fosters new growth in the areas exposed to direct sunlight.

Several timber companies operating in the vicinity of the northern port of Belem, which is a center for the Amazonian timber industry, say they have started reforestation programs and implemented selective cutting practices. **The Majinco Group,** a large Brazilian timber company that supplies several U.S. companies, reports that about 50 percent of its land (98,000 acres) is selectively cut. Corridors are opened to harvest commercially valuable mature trees while road building and disruption of the forest floor reportedly are kept to a minimum. Maginco President Danilo Remor cautions, however, that "enormous" tracts of land will be needed to sustain this type of cutting. He estimates that the costs of selective harvesting are about $30 per cubic meter more than traditional harvesting methods.[69]

Several U.S. timber brokers concede that Brazil's forestry laws are easily circumvented and that a lot of lumber remains on the market from questionable sources. In a few highly publicized cases, Ibama has slapped fines on companies that have not complied with the government's forestry laws. But Brazil's environmental agency does not have the manpower or the financial resources to police all of the extractive activities going on in the Amazon.

In coastal areas, Brazil lifted a ban on all commercial uses of its dwindling Atlantic forests in early 1993. (The ban, which went into effect in 1990, had been widely flouted.) The new forestry plan places 24,000 square miles under the protection of state and local governments, which will share oversight responsibility with federal agencies. New roads can be built into the protected areas as long as there is a plan to minimize overall environmental damage from the incursion.[70]

Bruce Larson of **Larson Wood Products** believes that previous government policies were largely responsible for the loss of rain forest in Brazil and that selective forest extraction is preferable to an outright ban on logging. "There are about 50,000 people in and near Portel, where our plant is located (west of Belem). If you take jobs away from these people, the forest will no longer have value and most of them will have no choice but to burn forests and raise crops to survive, just as the Indians did before," Larson says.[71]

Costa Rica

Much has been written about Costa Rica's dazzling rain forests, its commitment to conservation and its unique system of national parks and forest preserves. Yet the combination of a politically stable government and a high foreign debt has led to more foreign investment than in neighboring countries. As a result, more of its forests have been cut for commercial timber or agricultural purposes than in other parts of Central America.

A 1990 study by the World Resources Institute found that Costa Rica registered the highest annual rate of forest loss—7.6 percent (or 247,000 acres annually)—of nine crucial tropical rain forest countries it surveyed.[72] Like most deforestation data, this figure reflects many uncertainties. Previous estimates had put the rate of forest loss in Costa Rica at 148,000 acres annually. The administration of President Oscar Arias claimed that the rate of deforestation had been cut in half in 1989, to only 74,000 acres. Other estimates place the share of deforestation resulting from logging activities alone at between 81,000 acres and 123,000 acres per year.[73] In addition, two World Bank economists who

(continued on p. 64)

Box 3C

National Forest Policies...

Flawed economics, misguided policies, land tenure disputes and corruption all contribute to government's role in tropical deforestation. Governments often sell off publicly owned timber too cheaply—undervaluing nontimber assets of standing forests while promoting wasteful, resource-depleting logging practices. Harvest fees typically are set well below the actual cost of managing forest resources, which encourages rapid, wasteful logging practices, including logging in critical watersheds. Moreover, royalties charged without regard to species, size or grade of wood lead to "highgrading," taking only the most valuable species, which in turn expands the forest area disturbed during a harvest.[1c]

Log-export restrictions in many tropical forested nations also reduce the stumpage value of timber and hence the value of forests relative to alternative land uses. Artificially low prices for roundwood stimulate rapid conversion of forests and diminish investment returns on long-term sustainable management practices. Some land tenure policies encourage deforestation as well. Forests often are treated as if timber and the agricultural land thought to lie beneath it are the only resources of value. Accordingly, many tropical forested nations consider land clearing an improvement of the land and, indeed, the only way to claim property rights. Even in Hawaii, government tax policies encourage cutting rain forests for cattle ranches yet provide no incentives for tree planting or conservation.

Import trade barriers also skew forest management decisions. As more developing countries ban log exports to stimulate domestic processing of wood, importing countries have raised tariffs to protect their own wood product industries. International forums such as the General Agreement on Tariffs and Trade (GATT) have succeeded to some extent in reducing tariff escalation and in removing nontariff barriers to processed wood imports from tropical countries. Today, tariffs on processed wood imports in developed countries are comparable or lower than on many other products, and they are generally lower than corresponding import tariffs in developing countries.[2c]

One way to promote more sustainable forest management practices would be to award logging concessions for longer periods. Robert Repetto, an economist with the World Resources Institute, and Malcolm Gillis, a professor at Duke University, recommend that logging concessions last at least 70 years.[3c] Such a duration would put the onus of conservation on loggers, who now claim they have little incentive to replant. This action by itself might not be enough to stop unsustainable logging, however. Repetto and Gillis point out that 99-year leases in Ghana have not resulted in better forest management there. "The oft-repeated claims that longer concession durations are more conducive to good forest management practices mean little," Repetto and Gillis maintain, "without complementary measures to curtail forest depletion," such as required silvicultural treatment and enforcement of logging violations.[4c]

Many observers point to corruption as another major stumbling block in the creation of sound forest management practices. Awarding concessions to political allies and outright bribes of forestry officials are accepted ways of doing business in many tropical forested nations. In Papua New Guinea, 19 out of 20 timber companies examined by a government commission were found to engage regularly in fraud and illegal pricing practices. Deputy Prime Minister Ted Diro was found guilty of 86

...and Tropical Deforestation

charges, most of which related to influence peddling in the timber industry, and he was forced to resign in 1991.

Transfer pricing—the intentional undervaluing or overvaluing of timber—is another widespread practice. Logging companies may declare a sales price for timber that is far below its actual market value and then deposit the difference in an offshore tax haven. Such price rigging greatly reduces the amount of royalties and export duties paid and can reduce a company's declared profits to the point where it pays no income tax to the host government. As part of the inquiry that led to the downfall of Deputy Prime Minister Diro, it was determined that transfer pricing on log sales in 1986 and 1987 alone deprived the Papua New Guinea government of $27.5 million in foreign currency earnings and $4.3 million in tax revenues on "hidden" profits. **Stettin Bay Lumber**, owned by the large Japanese firm **Nissho Iwai**, made hidden profits of $3 million in 1986 and 1987, the inquiry found, while **Mitsubishi** concealed $1.5 million in profits through undervalued purchases from **United Timbers**, an "independent" company created with loans from Mitsubishi. No logging company operating in Papua New Guinea showed a profit before 1986, in fact, despite a timber boom that was well underway.

The Papua New Guinea inquiry revealed other abuses as well. **Bunnings**, an Australian company operating in Vanimo, was found to have engaged in "reckless felling" and "mass destruction" of forests—breaking all of the environmental clauses in its contract with the government. **Jant**, a subsidiary of **Honshu Paper**, was also cited for logging too close to streams and lagging behind in its reforestation efforts. Some environmental groups maintain that if companies like Mitsubishi and Honshu are engaged in transfer pricing and flouting environmental codes in Papua New Guinea, the integrity of their operations in other tropical timber countries is brought into question as well.

Even some within the forest products industry question the integrity of tropical timber operators. "Anyone who tells you sincerely that they are faithfully following government reforestation guidelines has to be full of crap," says Paul Senior, president of **Pat Brown Lumber**. "The larger the exporter the less likelihood there is that they are following the law, because of their greater ability to bribe and influence officials."[5c]

Mark Baker, another American who ran a Brazilian timber import business in Massachusetts for six years, says that tropical timber exported from Brazil to the United States is often falsely documented or underpriced. Making matters worse, Baker believes that Brazil is not benefitting from its timber extraction because most timber profits are leaving the country. Baker's own payments were not made to the Brazilian companies from which he bought wood, for instance. Instead, he was directed to deposit the money in a bank in the Grand Cayman Islands, and the money eventually ended up in **Deutsche Bank**. "All the timber brokers in Manaus hid their money somewhere outside of Brazil," Baker says, to avoid paying Brazilian taxes and to guard against inflation.[6c]

The Indonesian government is trying to clean up corruption in its own timber industry by contracting with a Swiss detective agency, **Societe General de Surveillance**. The Swiss company already has been successful in reducing payoffs to customs officers at Indonesian ports. Now it has a four year contract to monitor logging practices in three Indonesian provinces.[7c]

have reviewed the available data conclude that, at present, "most of the deforestation [in Costa Rica] is taking place by logging and other commercial interests."[74]

Two major U.S. timber companies, **Stone Container** and **Scott Paper**, have modest plantation projects in Costa Rica. In nearby Honduras, Stone Container sought to develop a huge, 3 million acre area of native pine (not tropical) forest, but the Honduran government backed out of the deal in early 1992. In Guatemala, **Simpson Paper**, a Seattle company, is planting gmelina trees for pulp in a deforested area.

"The fate of the forests of Costa Rica is one of the saddest cases of natural resources mismanagement in Central America," says Henry Tschinkel, a forester for the U.S. Agency for International Development. "In many cases only remnants of the original natural forest reserves remain as islands in vast expanses of degraded secondary forests and agricultural lands."[75]

Up to 26 percent of Costa Rica's land is protected in some way, however, and 12 percent consists of national parks that cannot be developed at all. Yet sizable areas of the forest preserves have been invaded by squatters; many are political refugees from neighboring Nicaragua who have cleared large rain forest tracts. Nearly all of the land outside of these "protected" areas has been deforested.

In the 1960s and 1970s, deforestation rates in Costa Rica ran as high as 250,000 acres a year, as vast areas were cleared for cattle ranching. Large agricultural operations that grow export crops such as bananas and coffee have also taken an enormous toll on Costa Rica's virgin forest cover. As the nation runs out of unprotected forest areas later this decade, conservationists fear that loggers will begin to invade the park areas. "The chainsaws are already running at the edges of the parks," says Raul Solorzano, president of the Tropical Science Center, a Costa Rican research group. "It's a very imminent danger."[76]

Costa Rica's timber industry has already been affected by the dwindling forest base. The number of sawmills in the country decreased from 220 in 1984 to 160 in 1990. Multinational timber companies, such as Taiwan's **Equipe Enterprises**, now are eyeing the relatively untouched forests of Nicaragua as a more attractive place to obtain wood in Central America. Costa Rica even sent a delegation to Chile in 1989 to investigate the possibility of importing logs.

The Costa Rican government has announced a massive reforestation project to replant as much of the country's tropical forests as possible. Even in this relatively well-off developing country, however, achieving this ambitious goal will be difficult. Plans called initially for more than 60,000 acres of land to be reforested over a four year period. In 1989, however, only 37,000 acres were replanted because of a lack of available funds.[77]

Beyond its reforestation plans, Costa Rica has strict laws prohibiting logging without a permit or within 50 yards of a stream. Illegal logging recently was made a felony. As in Brazil, however, convictions do not come easily. Those who witness illegal logging often lack the resources to win a case and risk being sued if they lose. In addition, illegal logging frequently occurs at night or on weekends and holidays, when forestry inspectors do not work.[78] Costa Rica is fortunate to have nearly $50 million in funds from recent debt-for-nature swaps, some of which is being spent to guard against illegal logging adjacent to its national parks.

'Sustainable' Forest Management Practices

Sustainability is the buzzword of all parties now taking part in the debate over how to save tropical forests. Yet defining precisely what sustainability is has been difficult for environmental, forestry and industry officials. Foresters traditionally have referred to sustainability in terms of the continuous yield of marketable timber; the size of the cut is based on the annual growth rates of trees. Ecologists argue that such a definition ignores the effects of a timber harvest on the entire forest ecosystem, which is damaged in the logging process. Therefore, they believe a better definition of sustainability is using forests for human purposes in a manner that maintains environmental services (such as watershed protection and erosion control) and biological quality (such as diversity of plants and animals) in a substantially unimpaired condition.

The tropical timber importing industry appears to be moving closer to the ecologists' definition. "You should be able to leave it as you find it," says Keister Evans, a former consultant to the International Hardwood Products Association (IHPA), which represents U.S. importers of tropical timber. "Trees should have the opportunity to recover and all ecological impact—soil, water, animals— should also be allowed to renew themselves."[79] Still, officials of IHPA recognize that the practices of its wood suppliers are far from ideal. The association acknowledges, for example, that "current exploitation of tropical forests, ranging from highly selective removal of a few choice trees (without taking the necessary steps to ensure regeneration of the stand), to deforestation, burning, cultivation, and pasturing, is not forestry, in that it degrades remaining forests and the soil as a source of future benefits and products."[80]

The International Tropical Timber Organization (ITTO), an influential group that promotes both trade and conservation of tropical timber, has weighed in with its own definition of sustainable forest management that recognizes the importance of nontimber resources. It defines the process as "managing permanent forest land to achieve one or more clearly specified objectives of management with regard to a continuous flow of desired forest products and services without undue reduction in its inherent values and future productivity and without undue undesirable effects on the physical and social environment."[81]

With such a definition, ITTO surveyed the implementation of sustainable forestry practices around the globe as of 1989. The ITTO survey found very little sustainable forestry being practiced in tropical areas, even in developed nations like Australia. Out of 2 billion acres of land under production in ITTO member countries, only 185,000 acres—on the Caribbean islands of Trinidad and Tobago—were considered sustainably managed. Of that total, only 39,000 acres had been fully regenerated after logging. The survey cited commendable forestry management practices in selected forests of Australia and Malaysia, but those forests could not be judged as fully sustainably managed. Therefore, tropical forest areas under sustainable management apparently represented only two-tenths of 1 percent of worldwide tropical timber production as of 1989.

Robert Goodland, an ecologist at the World Bank, believes that sustained yield tropical forestry can be achieved (at least in theory) by using highly selective extraction of a small number of trees per acre and then leaving harvested areas alone for decades to allow for regeneration—exercising tight control over the interim.[82] But even if all these steps are followed, cautions Duncan Poore, a forester who conducted the ITTO survey, sustainability in any silvicultural system can be proven only after at least three harvests. The first cut of a forest does not establish a baseline against which others can be gauged, Poore maintains, because the forest may have taken up to a thousand years to evolve.[83] Even after three full rotations, which could take 90 to 180 years, adds Goodland, "we can only say that the system tried is more likely to be sustainable than other alternatives."[84]

Given these complexities, some question whether "sustainability" itself is a realistic goal. Bruce Cabarle, a forestry expert with the World Resources Institute, believes absolute sustainability is generally unattainable under the strictest criteria, because any intrusion into the forest may cause some irreversible degradation. "Instead," Cabarle says, "we may have to talk about the need to strive for best practices or the most benign or appropriate technology available."[85]

Government Bans of Tropical Hardwoods

A variety of legislative measures have been taken to nudge tropical timber producing countries in the direction of sustainability. Europe has been more active than the United States in setting tropical timber trade restraints, partly because it is a higher priority with many environmental groups there. Some 200 city councils in Germany, half of the municipalities in the Netherlands and several hamlets in Belgium have banned purchases of tropical timber altogether.[86] The minister for buildings in Germany announced in 1989 that the federal government of Germany had also stopped purchasing tropical timber. The Dutch government also plans to ban "nonsustainable" tropical imports after 1994. The European Parliament of the European Community also passed a resolution for all 12 member countries to ban imports from the Malaysian state of Sarawak, where the deforestation rate is especially high, but the European Commission later rejected the proposal. Meanwhile, some environmental groups have urged a consumer boycott of all products made from tropical timbers.

In the United States, Arizona, California, New York and the city of Minneapolis are among the jurisdictions that have banned or considered banning tropical timbers in public construction projects, except from certified sources. A proposal by the U.S. Conference of Mayors to ban tropical hardwoods in all municipal projects was defeated in June 1991 after last-minute lobbying by the timber importers' lobby.[87] A labeling bill introduced in Congress in 1991 by then-Sen. Albert Gore Jr. (D-Tenn.) also died in committee. The bill would have required labels on all tropical woods and wood products imported into the United States, indicating the species and country of origin. Tropical timber importers objected to the bill partly because the labeling requirement would not help consumers determine whether the imported timber had been grown and harvested in a sustainable manner. The International Hardwoods Products Association said the bill could "unfairly punish producers who are making an effort to carefully manage concessions, if others in that country are not exhibiting good forest management concessions."

Recently, another approach has been taken to stem the trade of especially endangered tropical hardwood species. In March 1992, signatories to the Convention on International Trade in Endangered Species of Wild Fauna and Flora prohibited further trade in Brazilian rosewood because it is so depleted, and trade in three other endangered tropical timber species, including Central American species of true mahogany, afrormosia and lignum vitae, also was restricted. These three species now must have permits that document traded volumes and paperwork confirming the species' conservation status. Some countries have objected to listed tropical timber species under the CITES convention, arguing that such matters should be left to the International Tropical Timber Organization.[88]

International Tropical Timber Organization

Many are looking to the International Tropical Timber Organization as the forum to bring about a worldwide effort to change forestry management practices. ITTO is the only international forum that assembles major tropical producer nations and consumer nations to discuss tropical forestry issues. The organization was created in 1983 under the International Tropical Timbers Agreement (negotiated through the United Nations Conference on Trade and Development), but it was not formally organized until 1987. The accord that established the 49 nation group expires in March 1994. Negotiations on a new pact are bogged down by a dispute about whether all timber producers—not just those in the tropics—should abide by its conservation standards.

Since its inception, ITTO has been plagued by political and protocol issues, and it is not clear whether it can—or should—be the group to implement swift reform of timber harvesting practices. ITTO can pass resolutions, but it has no authority to force its members to implement them. Consequently, its potential may be more as a vehicle to persuade tropical timber exporting nations to develop sustainable management practices and to persuade importing nations to help pay for this effort.

In 1990, ITTO guidelines set the year 2000 as the time when all tropical timber exports should be derived from sustainable sources. The target date has yet to be endorsed by its governing council, however. Even moderate environmental groups like the World Wildlife Fund accuse ITTO of foot-dragging in implementing the mandate of its charter for forest conservation. As Robert Buschbacher, the fund's tropical forestry program director in the United States, remarked in 1991, "Since ITTO was created, nearly 85 million hectares of tropical forests—roughly the size of Venezuela—have disappeared. Unfortunately, after five years of work, ITTO has failed to lift its written policy off paper and into action."[89] ITTO's most recent semiannual council meeting adjourned in May 1993 with the group still divided on setting conservation standards for timber exporting countries. Many of these nations dispute allegations that they are depleting a vital natural resource and insist that a new pact should cover all timber producers, not just those in the tropics.[90]

(continued on p. 70)

Box 3D

Natural Forest Management Practices

Natural forest management practices restrict timber harvests to protect ecological functions that sustain the forest and its inhabitants. When practiced properly, such silvicultural methods can raise the value and total output of products from the forest, albeit at the expense of maximizing timber production (as in plantation forestry). Under natural forest management, nontimber forest products such as fruits, nuts and resins can be harvested alongside a limited supply of timber. The livelihood of forest dwellers is sustained by this process, provided that sufficient markets exist for their products. Commercial as well as community-based natural forest management experiments are being tried throughout the world. Three such projects in Latin America are described below.

Portico: Portico, a large private Costa Rican company with U.S. financial backing, is trying to demonstrate how natural forest regeneration can be practiced successfully when commercial timber operators have sufficient capital and operating expertise to implement selective harvesting practices. Portico owns 49,000 acres of prime swamp forest in the northeastern part of the country and holds options on another 43,000 acres of forest. It harvests a wood related to mahogany—caobilla—for hand-carved doors.

Portico's plan is to remove only one or two trees from each acre of its holdings on a 15 year cycle, leaving the forest largely intact. The company employs directional felling to minimize damage to other trees and takes only trees that are more than two feet in diameter. The number of seed-bearing species left in the forest should allow natural regeneration to occur without the need for additional plantings, reports company president Mario Barrenechea.[1d] Portico also clears some noncommercial species to promote the growth of mahogany. It is monitoring the impact of its operations on the biodiversity of the forests to determine if such thinning practices attract exotic plants or animals.

Some foresters object to Portico's logging activities within the Barra del Colorado Wildlife Refuge, however. (Costa Rican law does not prevent logging in a refuge if the management plan is approved by the government.) Some critics also claim that Portico is practicing a form of "high-grading"—harvesting only the most commercially valuable trees in the forest—needlessly destroying other trees in the process. A site visit by the author in November 1990 found some thinning of the forest area, but overall it appeared thick, lush and vital. It was in far better condition than a clear-cut operation on adjacent land that had left that area stripped of ground cover, void of animals and vulnerable to erosion. Portico has purchased a 98 acre tract of such deforested land and is growing a secondary forest with a mixture of natural and artificial regeneration techniques. That forest should be ready for its first selective harvest in 12 years.

Portico's Barrenechea estimates that the costs of natural forest regeneration are double those of a traditional logging operation. Barrenechea was able to attract investors by emphasizing that his company aims to preserve the long-term viability of the species, which assures continued operations. **Norwest Banks** of Minneapolis owns 30 percent of Portico's stock through a debt-for-equity swap with the Costa Rican government. The Overseas Private Investment Corp. insured Norwest's investment.

World Wildlife Fund ecologist Gary Hartshorn says he is impressed with Portico's operation and calls it "one of the least destructive operations I have seen in the American tropics."[2d] But Portico's experiment may not be repeated in Costa Rica because of the scarcity of remaining undisturbed forest.

Yanesha Forestry Cooperative: In 1986, five communities in the Palcazu Valley of central Peru formed the Yanesha Forestry Cooperative. It is believed to be the first native forestry cooperative in the Amazon, with about 150 members and 27 employees. The cooperative is employing a "strip shelterbelt" system to preserve a diverse selection of regional species. Narrow strips of forest, usually 30 to 50 yards wide and 200 to 500 yards long, are clear-cut to create gaps in the forest canopy that simulate what occurs naturally when a mature tree falls down. The gaps allow sunlight to penetrate the canopy and stimulate the growth of fast-growing native species, which mature in 30 to 40 years.

Initial results of the project are promising. To date, the narrow gaps do not threaten large areas of animal habitat or contribute to erosion. A 1988 inventory of cuts made two and three years earlier showed that 209 species were growing in one strip and 285 species in a second strip—more than twice the number of species identified before the original cut. The project plan calls for cutting several new strips a year, each located at least 100 yards from others recently cut. The forestry cooperative produces lumber in its own sawmill and also treats lumber for use as posts and railroad ties.[3d]

Carton de Colombia: Carton de Colombia, operated by **Smurfit/Latin America**, a Colombian subsidiary of **Container Corp.**, has pioneered the use of tropical hardwoods for pulp and paper production in a rain forest area. Colombia was completely dependent on paper imports (and paper from waste paper, rice straw and sugarcane bagasse) when Carton de Colombia started its operation in 1947. Since imported wood fibers were very expensive, the company developed a process to pulp mixed tropical hardwoods. By 1988, nearly all of Colombia's paper demands, except for newsprint, were met by domestic production.

Carton de Colombia takes special care to promote regeneration and minimize disturbance of the forest. It practices selective harvesting on a 148,000 acre concession of tropical rain forest that has one of the highest rates of rainfall in the world and tremendous biodiversity. An aerial cable system is used to minimize disturbance to the forest. Logs are piled by hand and lifted straight up and out of the forest, eliminating the need for loaders and skids. Roads are constructed of an expensive geotextile fabric to make them stable and prevent erosion.

Carton de Colombia has done extensive research on its site and found that sustainable pulp production can be achieved through natural regeneration. However, the company is also considering a move to exotic species like eucalyptus and gmelina, which some studies show provide a higher yield of pulpwood at a lower cost than natural forest management. The company now is researching the potential of eucalyptus and pine plantations in the Andes and expects to complete a move toward plantations by the time its concession near the Pacific coast of Colombia ends in 2004.[4d]

(More information on these and other innovative forestry projects is provided in Chapter 8.)

International Hardwood Products Association

Tropical wood importers and exporters may look more favorably on proposals brought forward by industry groups such as the International Hardwood Products Association. Members of IHPA account for 85 percent of U.S. tropical timber import purchases, and they are generally opposed to governmental constraints on trade, arguing that such measures would depress the value of the forests and lead people to burn or otherwise exploit them more freely. A consensus statement issued by IHPA in 1990 did recognize, however, that "selective constraints could be beneficial in some areas where logging exposes rare species, national parks, indigenous lands, or open frontier regions to intensive over-exploitation."[91]

In 1989, IHPA adopted a program called Conservation, Utilization, Reforestation and Education (CURE) as its first step toward dealing with rapid deforestation. The program encourages tropical timber importers to fund research on sustained yield practices and reforestation programs and to promote policies of free trade for wood products on the world market. (Increased trade would help provide more revenue for sustained yield management, the group maintains.) In 1990, in collaboration with the Smithsonian Institution, IHPA issued a more focused and committed consensus statement that includes the following recommendations:[92]

- Encourage suppliers and their governments to minimize timber losses through more efficient logging operations, improved recovery techniques and wood preservation;
- Encourage suppliers and their governments to involve local people in forest management, establish long-term and secure tenure over forest resources, and promote development of verifiable guidelines and criteria for defining sustainable management of timber; and
- Improve effectiveness of current policies to buy timber only from legal sources.

How many of IHPA's 140 members have endorsed this position statement is not known; IHPA is a voluntary association and cannot force members to adopt its policies. IHPA Executive Director Wendy Baer believes, however, that 90 percent of its members have taken some action to carry out the recommendations.[93] Donald Schramm, general manager for international operations at **Georgia-Pacific**, one of the largest importers of tropical timber, reports that his company has notified its suppliers that tropical wood must be derived from sustainable sources. About 85 percent of Georgia-Pacific's imports come from Indonesia, and Schramm believes that country already is committed to sustainable forestry. He bases his assessment on statements by the Indonesian Director of Forestry that 100 percent of the nation's logging will be "selective" by 1996. "I think that virtually everything we're importing is sustainable or on track to be sustainable. If we don't move in that direction we're out of business. It's in our interest to make sure it happens."[94]

Other timber importers agree. "We understand the need for sustainable yield timber policies because without it we will be out of business," echoes Howard Steinberg, president of **Ply-Gem Manufacturing**, a publicly traded company based in New York that imports tropical timber from Malaysia and Indonesia. Steinberg is convinced that some countries, including Indonesia, are being responsive to public opinion. "Indonesia is very serious about this issue. They know where every cubic meter of wood comes from."[95]

Former timber importer Mark Baker is skeptical that IHPA will use its influence to promote sustainable forestry, however. He maintains that the IHPA initiative is tantamount to a "big lie—a giant smokescreen. I used to sit in their offices and hear them justify how they tried to get around forestry laws." Baker says "what will drive the industry, as always, is price and demand. It is not in their interest to put money into forest management systems. The member companies are already competing with each other."[96]

Nels Johnson and Bruce Cabarle of the World Resources Institute concur that sustainable management practices are more expensive, at least over the short term, and that timber producers may be discouraged from adopting them. Extra planning, training and monitoring of the forest resource as well as meeting secondary ecological objectives raise both up-front costs and lost revenue, they say. But they also believe that sustainable management practices may be competitive if measured over the length of the harvest cycle—some 20 to 40 years.[97]

In any event, IHPA has taken some concrete steps to promote sustainable forestry. In 1990, it founded the Tropical Forest Foundation, a nonprofit group aimed at providing information to policymakers and the public about the benefits of sustainable forest management. Keister Evans, formerly a consultant to IHPA, is the foundation's executive director. Evans reports that the foundation is involved in efforts to bring timber importers and environmental groups together to see if they can agree on voluntary standards to determine which imports are coming from sustainable sources—as an alternative to mandatory labeling requirements. Major industries on the board of directors include **Caterpillar, Georgia-Pacific, Herman Miller** and **Mitsubishi**. The World Wildlife Fund is the only environmental group represented in the foundation.

World Wildlife Fund ecologist Gary Hartshorn says the foundation is working toward the creation of a voluntary monitoring program in 1993. Members of the foundation, like many others, are suspicious of claims made by some tropical wood exporters that their wood is being grown in a sustainable fashion. "We're concerned because the volume of wood being sold as sustainable is sometimes five times the amount we think the forest can handle," Hartshorn explains. The IHPA program would identify the source of the wood sold by logging companies that make such claims and follow it through the production and delivery process. The goal is to ensure that wood is harvested under the guidelines developed by the foundation and that a chain-of-custody monitoring process prevents the delivery of unsustainably grown wood. Hartshorn estimates that several dozen companies are involved in this private effort.[98]

Voluntary Wood Certification Efforts

Three U.S. organizations are working to certify the sources of tropical timber to assist consumers and major wood customers (such as furniture manufacturers) in their purchasing decisions. Smart Wood is a project of the Rain Forest Alliance, a nonprofit group based in New York City dedicated to rainforest preservation. Green Cross Certification is a not-for-profit division of **Scientific Certification Systems** of Oakland, Calif. Pacific Certified Ecological Forest Products is a project of the Institute for Sustainable Forestry, also based in California, which aims to bring ecological and economic stability to forest communities.

Smart Wood

The Smart Wood project certifies U.S. timber importers, wholesalers and retailers who purchase all of their tropical timber from sources that do not contribute to the destruction of tropical forest ecosystems. The Rainforest Alliance uses broad principles to evaluate sources of tropical timber, such as maintenance of environmental functions, sustained yield production and positive impact on local communities. Trees harvested or slated for harvest in the next cutting cycle must be physically marked before they are logged, and a post-logging inventory must be completed within six months of the harvest to evaluate the environmental impact on the site. All tropical timber sources are eligible for Smart Wood certification, including natural forests and plantations, large commercial concessions and small community forestry projects. Retailers who sell products from Smart Wood sources only are designated as "Smart Wood Companies." Retailers who sell Smart Wood products, among others, are listed as participants in the certification effort.

Smart Wood's criteria for evaluating sustained yield are quite explicit. They were developed in cooperation with foresters, ecologists and social scientists in accord with guidelines issued by ITTO and the International Union for the Conservation of Nature. The guidelines address such issues as security of long-term tenure of operations, harvesting rate, residual damage (not to exceed 25 percent of remaining trees), buffer strips and socio-economic impacts. Qualified personnel, including professional foresters, ecologists and social scientists, conduct field audits on a yearly basis. Operations found to be in strict adherence with the principles by the Smart Wood program's review board are certified as "sustainable" sources of tropical timber. Those demonstrating a strong opera-tional commitment to the principles are classified "well managed." Two sources that Smart Wood has certified as "well managed" are state forestry plantations in Indonesia that grow teak, pine, mahogany and rosewood, and several forestry cooperatives approved by the Broadleaf Development Project in Honduras.

Green Cross

The Green Cross certification process does not try to label certain wood harvesting techniques as "sustainable" because of the difficulty in defining the term. Instead, Green Cross employs a variety of experts who conduct a life-cycle assessment of timber resources. Life-cycle assessment looks not only at traditional factors like cutting cycles but also at natural regeneration potential, energy usage and wood waste minimization. Potential air and water pollution problems, socio-economic impacts and ecosystem biodiversity are evaluated as well. A chain-of-custody process ensures that certified wood is the same wood that ends up with the retailer.

Green Cross has analyzed timber resources in Cameroon, the Caribbean, Honduras and Mexico. A team of field inspectors considers five main technical criteria: logging and milling operations, silvicultural techniques, soil conservation, species preservation and wood utilization. Their work is then reviewed by experts in eight fields: botany, mammalogy, entomology, anthropology, ornithology, herpetology, silviculture and ecology. Inspectors return every six months to evaluate the forest resource and grade it in a fashion similar to a report card.

The Knoll Group, a major designer and manufacturer of office furniture and a subsidiary of **Westinghouse Electric**, paid start-up costs for the Green Cross certification program. Knoll wants to find alternatives to mahogany that it imports from Brazil for its office furniture.[99]

Pacific Certified Ecological Forest Products

Like the Rainforest Alliance's Smart Wood project, the Institute for Sustainable Forestry has explicit guidelines for technical forest management. To receive the institute's certification as an ecological forest product, a producer must meet 10 criteria for maintaining or restoring natural forest processes. Synthetic fertilizers and pesticides cannot be applied. Forest practioners also must address the need for local employment and community stability and abide by the institute's call for a moratorium on logging in ancient forests. Presently, the institute employs exclusive licensing agreements with domestic sawmills that process logs only from certified sources. All lumber from these mills is stamped with the Pacific Certified Ecological Forest Products label at the mill site.

Other Players

The Woodworkers Alliance for Rainforest Protection (WARP), an association of North American woodworkers and related industry representatives, was founded in 1989. The group's main objectives are to make more efficient use and reduce overall consumption of tropical hardwoods as well as promote sustainable development in tropical countries. WARP director Scott Landis reports that the group also is recommending the use of lesser known species to take the pressure off heavily logged tropical species. WARP is developing an in-shop testing program for such new marketable species and operates a phone line to provide information on tropical species to woodworkers and architects.

Forest Stewardship Council: At its founding meeting, WARP proposed the creation of a Forest Stewardship Council to bring together representatives of certification groups, tropical timber producers and retailers and environmental organizations. The council, which formed in 1991, is re-evaluating the criteria

(continued on p. 76)

Table 6

Underutilized Sources of

Species	Description/Working Properties
Almendro *Caryocar glabrum*	Attains height of 170 ft. with straight-bole diameters of 5 ft. to 7 ft.; free of branches for 60 ft. to 70 ft. Interlocked grain with a ribbon figure. Heartwood is honey color; sapwood is white. Resistant to rot and marine borers. Moderately abundant. Moderately difficult to saw; fair results from planing; sands smoothly and turns well. Used in boatbuilding, furniture, floor-ing and applications requiring wear resistance.
Cachimbo *Cariniana sp.*	Attains height of 150 ft. with trunk up to 30 in. in diameter; free of branches to 70 ft. Grain is roey with a fine texture. Heartwood and sapwood are indistinguishable when dry and can be yellowish-, pinkish-, or reddish-brown with purple tinge and dark streaks. It is easy to saw, plane, turn and bore; it sands well and takes a smooth, glossy finish. Some species have a high silica content and will dull tools. Used for construction, furniture, ship-building, flooring, veneering and turnery.
Chontaquiro Amarillo *Diplotropis martiusii*	Attains height of 120 ft. with straight trunk of 30 in. or more in diameter; may be free of branches to 70 ft. Texture is coarse with yellowish sapwood and light- to dark-brown heartwood, which is very resistant to rot. Trees are relatively abundant. Works well with saws and edge tools, and sands to a fine finish; only fair turning results are reported. Used in construction, furniture, parquetry, cabinetry and interior finish.
Marupá *Simarouba amara*	Attains height of 140 ft. with a straight trunk up to 36 in. in dia-meter; may be free of branches to 90 ft. Wood is straight grained and has uniform texture. Sapwood and heartwood are indistinguishable and become yellowish-white when exposed. Somewhat susceptible to some rots and stains. Trees are fast growing and abundant. Wood is reported to saw easily. Planing results are excellent; it turns fairly well and sands well. Wood stains and finishes easily and glues well. Uses include interior construction, boxes, furniture, veneering, pat-ternmaking, millwork and particleboard. Reported to be excellent for carving.
Quinilla Colorada *Manilkara bidentata*	Reaches height of 100 ft. to 150 ft. and trunk diameters of 2 ft. to 4 ft. Boles are clear and straight to 60 ft. Wood is hard and heavy; grain is usually straight with occasional waviness; texture is fine. Heartwood is light- to dark-reddish-brown, but often not

SOURCE: Woodworkers Alliance for Rainforest Protection, *Fine Woodworking*, May/June 1990.

Tropical Hardwoods

Species	Description/Working Properties
	distinct from whitish or pale-brown sapwood. Trees are widely distributed and highly frequent. Reported to be moderately difficult to saw and sand, but all other sharp-edge tool working properties are rated excellent. Gluing requires special care. Steam-bending properties are rated excellent. Uses include construction, turnery, boat frames, bent work, violin bows and billiard cues.
Requia *Guarea sp.*	Suggested as a mahogany substitute. Reaches height of 150 ft. with diameters to 4 ft.; free of branches to one-third its height. Its straight, interlocked grain produces a ribbon figure with a medium texture. Sapwood is yellowish and heartwood is pinkish-, brownish- to reddish-mahogany, which is resistant to rot, fungus and insects. Its frequency is reported to be medium and it's widely distributed. Easily worked with all tools. It has a tendency to tear when bored. Uses include furniture, cabinetry, turned pieces, musical instruments, boat planking, veneering and millwork.
Tornillo *Cedrelinga catenaeformis*	Attains height of 150 ft. with straight, well-formed trunk over 4 ft. in diameter; free of branches for 80 ft. Wood is straight grained to roey with occasional wavy grain. Sapwood is off-white and heartwood is pink to golden brown. Texture is medium to coarse. It is fairly durable. Behind eucalyptus, it's the second most frequently sawn wood and accounts for more than 14% of woods produced by Peruvian sawmills. Easy to saw, but leaves woolly surfaces. Planing requires sharp edges to produce smooth surfaces in interlocking or cross-grain pieces. Turns and bores easily. Uses include interior carpentry, furniture, turnery, carvings and drawer sides.
Turupay *Clarisia racemosa*	Attains height of 130 ft. with well-formed trunks to 40 in. in diameter; free of branches to 60 ft. Grain is usually interlocked, producing a ribbon figure on the radial surface. It has a medium texture. Heartwood is pale to bright yellow and remains golden on exposure. Sapwood is white. Trees are widely distributed in scattered clumps. Easily worked. Rated fair to good in all machining operations. Requires sharp tools to produce a smooth surface. Sawing often produces woolly surfaces. Uses in construction, flooring, furniture and millwork.

used to rate tropical timber—given the difficulty in defining "sustainably grown" wood. Alternative descriptions are being sought for sound forest management practices, in particular, for wood grown outside of plantations. One of the key goals for the council is to maintain forests in a natural state to the maximum extent possible, ensuring that the rate of harvesting of forest products does not exceed the regeneration rate of these same forest species.

The Forest Stewardship Council may represent one of the brightest hopes for the fledgling "green wood" marketing effort. Large home improvement chains, such as **B&Q** in the United Kingdom and **Home Depot** in the United States, have expressed interest in purchasing tropical timber exclusively from sustainably grown sources by as early as 1995. While the current market for "green wood" represents perhaps only 2 to 3 percent of all tropical hardwood imported into North America and Europe, the market could boom if consumers thought retailers' "green" claims were credible.[100]

The Forest Stewardship Council may facilitate this process by establishing a set of sustainable forestry guidelines that is agreeable to all parties—and then working to ensure that policies, laws and regulations in timber importing and exporting countries are consistent with those guidelines. A larger challenge will be to convince consumers that it is worth paying more for sustainably grown wood than for other sources of timber and to convince local producers of sustainably grown wood that their extra efforts will be rewarded.

"The ultimate challenge, however, remains creating the public awareness and political will needed to amend the macroeconomic and land-use policies that ultimately dictate the forest's fate," write Nels Johnson and Bruce Cabarle of the World Resources Institute in their 1993 report, *Surviving the Cut: Natural Forest Management in the Humid Tropics*.[101] In the interim, Johnson and Cabarle recommend that sustainable forestry guidelines and standards be extended to nontimber forest products. Such certification programs in combination with "green" consumers may catalyze larger reforms—and serve as a pro-active alternative to bans and boycotts—yet still slow the deforestation trend.

Chapter Three Appendix

Timber Companies with Tropical Forest Operations or Policies

The four industry chapters of this book include appendices that summarize the activities of major corporations in tropical forest areas. Virtually all of the companies listed were contacted by IRRC in 1990, 1991 and 1992 and were given the opportunity to discuss their tropical forest operations and measures they are taking to minimize ecological damage. Additional information has been obtained from government agencies and from human rights and environmental organizations that monitor corporate activities in the tropics. Some of the companies listed have no tropical forest operations but have instituted policies with regard to purchases of products from tropical forest regions.

Within the forest products industry, few U.S. companies own facilities in the tropics (although several did more than a decade ago). At least 150 companies import tropical timber into the United States, however. Summaries of the operations and import arrangements of major forest products companies, tropical timber wholesalers and leading furniture makers are provided below.

United States

ARMSTRONG WORLD INDUSTRIES INC.: Armstrong World Industries, based in Lancaster, Pa., owns **Thomasville Furniture Industries**, a leading furniture maker. Thomasville's "sole rain forest raw material is mahogany with wood coming from selected, individual trees and not from any cutting that eliminates vast acreage of rain forest," according to Armstrong's 1990 annual report. When IRRC contacted the company to confirm this information, Armstrong said its annual report was in error and that the company does not import mahogany from tropical rain forests. Sonny Koontz, vice president for Thomasville's wood operations, reports that **Impar Co.**, its Brazilian supplier, has assured Thomasville that the wood comes from an area in the southern part of the state of Para, near the Araguaia River, that is 600 miles from rain forest. A map of rain forest areas by the World Conservation Monitoring Center pinpoints the location of Impar's operation as being adjacent to or in former rain forest area, however. Impar has told Thomasville that the area where it is logging is "partly rolling hills and partly pasture land with some areas of jungle and many rivers." (The word "jungle" typically is a euphemism for rain forest.)

Koontz told IRRC, "Our supplier has convinced us that [its wood] is being grown in a sustainable manner." Reportedly, only one or two mahogany trees are cut per acre each year, and 40 trees are planted for every one cut. Thomasville sells an estimated $22 million worth of products a year containing tropical hardwoods, representing about 4.5 percent of its wood product sales, Koontz reports.[102]

PAT BROWN LUMBER CO.: Pat Brown Lumber of Lexington, N.C., was one of the top 10 importers of tropical timber from Southeast Asia and Brazil until 1990. Company President Paul Senior says he stopped buying from Sarawak, Malaysia, in late 1990 partly because he was disappointed with the Sarawak government's lack of progress in adopting sustainable forestry practices. Most of Pat Brown's tropical timber now comes from Brazil in the form of mahogany, andiroba and virola. Andiroba can be used as a substitute for mahogany, and virola is suitable for general millwork applications. Both are harvested from flooded forests called varzea and from swampy land near the islands at the mouth of the Amazon River.

Pat Brown's affiliate in Brazil, **Tradelink**, purchases mahogany that has been certified under the Brazilian forestry laws as coming from "well-managed" forests. Senior acknowledges that it is difficult for importers to monitor whether the required reforestation is taking place, however. He believes that varzea logging (in flooded forests) does less damage to rain forests because it is cut by loggers from canoes and then floated out to mills. This method of harvest does not damage soil or require access to roads. Varzea trees regenerate quickly and can be harvested again in about 15 to 20 years. Enough andiroba has been logged, however, that conservationists are concerned about its survival. Andiroba has been proposed for inclusion in the Convention on International Trade in Endangered Species.[103]

CHAMPION INTERNATIONAL CORP.: Champion International, based in Stamford, Conn., owns **Champion Papel e Celulose Ltda**., one of Brazil's largest producers of eucalyptus short-fiber bleached chemical pulp and printing and writing papers. The company grows eucalyptus on 100,000 acres about 80 miles north of Sao Paulo. The terrain is a mixture of grasslands, plains and light forest. A company publication, "Champion-Brazil and the Environment," notes that the plantation is "approximately 2,600 kilometers from the tropical rain forest," apparently referring to the Amazon. "In recent years, pulp and paper producers and other industries have been criticized by ecologists and environmentalists for endangering the Amazon tropical rain forest by overcutting and generally wasting the resources of the land. We have never been involved in these activities," the publication says.

Champion's Brazilian plantation is adjacent to, if not part of, what used to be the Atlantic rain forest, which has only 3 percent of its original forest cover remaining. Champion spokesman Ed Clem told IRRC that the area had been cleared for sugar cane plantations or other agricultural purposes when Champion purchased the land. He acknowledged that possibly as much as 500 acres of the plantation previously was rain forest. He said Champion is working with the government to plant native trees in areas not suitable for plantation crops.[104]

GEORGIA-PACIFIC CORP.: Georgia-Pacific (G-P), based in Atlanta, Ga., has no direct foreign investments in tropical rain forest areas. It sold its last such holding, a Brazilian veneer and plywood plant, in 1990. It once held large concessions in the Philippines and Indonesia but sold those operations in the early 1980s. G-P continues to be one of the top—if not the top—importers of tropical hardwoods into the United States, however, with major purchases from Indonesia, Malaysia and its former Brazilian facility, now owned by its former manager, Bruce Larson (see **Larson Wood Products**).

Brazil: Until 1990, G-P exported logs from Portel, Brazil, near the port of Belem at the mouth of the Amazon River. The company returned an estimated 1.85 million acres of land to the Brazilian government at the time of the 1990 sale because of a long-simmering dispute over land titles and taxes. Land titles in the Amazon often are disputed because of the remote location of Amazon land and conflicting ownership claims. G-P objected to paying taxes on lands where it was not sure it held actual title. The government threatened to seize areas it believed had belonged to G-P, but where taxes had not been paid for years. The company decided to give the land back to the government when it sold the plant to settle the dispute, according to Bruce Larson, the former plant manager, who now owns the mill facility.[105]

Larson reports that there was occasional logging on the land before it was returned to the government—but not on an ongoing basis. "Independent loggers who cut for G-P felled timber on G-P land or on land adjacent to the company's holdings," Larson says. (Such a statement may be at odds with G-P's own pledge that it "has never harvested or logged any timber" from its Brazilian lands.) Larson thinks public concern over disappearing rain forests was partly responsible for G-P's decision to sell its Brazilian plant, although G-P says pressure from environmentalists was not a factor in its decision.[106]

Indonesia: From 1960 until 1983, G-P operated three sawmills and logged and manufactured plywood in East Kalimantan in a joint venture with Mohammad "Bob" Hassan, who is now a major player in the Indonesian timber market. According to one account, in 1977 G-P exported 118,075 cubic meters of roundwood valued at $6.4 million.[107] "It was very bureaucratic and difficult to operate," according to G-P's Michael Vidan. "Being politically wired is critical to success in the Third World," he maintains, adding that G-P's capital and technological expertise was needed only until its Indonesian partners gained more experience and stature.[108] The company finally sold out to Hassan in a leveraged buyout when G-P Chairman Marshall Hahn decided to divest operations that were not part of the company's core business.

While G-P no longer has direct investments in Indonesia, a number of U.S. expatriates—several of whom used to be G-P employees—are still working in both the processing and forest management sides of Hassan's operation, according to a forestry consultant who visited the former G-P concession in 1990. "They emphasized the need to keep a low profile within the company," the consultant's report said, "because of government pressure on the private sector to employ Indonesian expertise."[109]

G-P continues to import substantial amounts of tropical hardwoods, with more than 70 percent coming from Indonesia. Records suggest that G-P imported 144,500 tons of finished tropical hardwoods in 1989, for example.[110] A company position paper on tropical forests states that G-P is not the principal U.S. importer of tropical hardwoods, however. A 1990 compilation of Commerce Department import data, assembled by Greenpeace, ranked G-P as the second largest importer of tropical wood from Indonesia.[111] Rainforest Action Network claims that G-P is the top U.S. importer of tropical hardwoods.

Donald Schramm, G-P's general manager for international operations, told IRRC that the company's "intentions are to purchase products only from companies that practice sustained yield forest management."[112] G-P asked suppliers to inform the company in as much detail as possible how their forests are being managed. The company's timber suppliers in Indonesia and Thailand each wrote half-page letters that did not clearly answer the question. The only company to respond in detail was **Portico Co.**, a Costa Rican company discussed earlier in this chapter.

HERMAN MILLER CO.: Herman Miller of Zeeland, Mich., is one of the largest business furniture manufacturers in the United States. Spokesman Robert Johnston told IRRC that the company's policy is to purchase tropical hardwoods only from sources believed to be sustainably managed. Since that policy went into effect in early 1990, the company no longer imports Brazilian rosewood used in its well-known Eames chairs and sofas. The company has also dropped imports of Honduran mahogany and is trying to influence its suppliers to move towards sustainable forestry management practices, says Johnston.[113]

KNOLL INTERNATIONAL INC.: The Knoll Group of East Greenville, Pa., is a subsidiary of **Westinghouse Electric Corp.** and another leading manufacturer of office furniture. George Wilmot, Knoll's vice president for advanced research, reports that the company is looking for alternatives to the Brazilian mahogany that it has traditionally imported for use in its furniture. Knoll uses almost 9 million square feet of veneer annually and is seeking ways to take pressure off of expensive veneers such as mahogany by replacing it with lesser-known species like obeche. The majority of Knoll's veneers now come from obeche, a fast-growing, plentiful wood from Cameroon that can be reconstituted to resemble more expensive hardwoods. Obeche wood is peeled to obtain large runs of clear blond veneer that are glued together to achieve common grain configurations. The finished veneers can resemble mahogany, maple or cherry. Wilmot says the manufacturing process makes efficient use of the wood, utilizing 90 to 95 percent of the felled obeche versus an average 35 percent utilization rate for natural veneer.[114]

Knoll hopes to prove that a ban on tropical timber imports is unnecessary by demonstrating that sustainable sources are available. Yet the company is wary of certifications of sustainability that accompany some imported wood. Knoll has funded Green Cross certification efforts, which are intended to identify timber from sustainable forest operations. (A discussion of Green Cross appears earlier in this chapter.) Green Cross has certified mahogany from a forestry cooperative in a tropical rain forest in the state of Quintana Roo, Mexico, as "well managed." Knoll hopes to use the cooperative as a source of alternatives to mahogany as well. Knoll also is experimenting with ramon, a very common species in Mexico that has no commercial value at present. Ramon may serve as a substitute for European beech from the former Yugoslavia, where civil strife has virtually eliminated timber exports.

LARSON WOOD PRODUCTS INC.: Larson Wood Products, incorporated in Delaware, operates **Georgia-Pacific's** former veneer and plywood production facility in the Brazilian Amazon. Georgia-Pacific ran the facility from 1965 until 1990 and then sold it to the plant's manager, Bruce Larson. The new private company derives its timber from 120,000 acres of land near Portel, 120 miles west of the city of Belem. The plant processes about 80,000 cubic meters of tropical hardwoods a year and exports about 25,000 cubic meters of plywood for the U.S. market. The mill employs about 600 workers. Another 600 workers are involved in timber extraction. Larson says that sales amount to $4 million to $6 million a year and that G-P remains a major customer.[115] Larson also operates a small pine plantation in Brazil, encompassing about 500 acres, that is used for pulp for the Jari operation.

Larson Wood Products' most commonly harvested species are kapok (sumauma), bajeira (esponga) and breu (sucuruba), which are transported by river to its mill in Portel. Some cutting occurs in the varzea portion of the tropical forest, which is flooded by the Amazon River during the rainy season.

New forestry laws in Brazil are supposed to phase out independent logging and allow logging only on land with secure title and managed forests. For a company to export logs, it must own the land and manage it or purchase logs from managed sources. About half of Larson's timber is derived from forests managed by other companies. It is about to start logging its own 120,000 acres under a forestry management plan.

LIBERTY WOODS INTERNATIONAL INC.: Liberty Woods International of Orange, Calif., is one of the five top importers of tropical timber from Indonesia, according to U.S. Commerce Department data analyzed by Greenpeace.[116] It also imports tropical timber from Sarawak, Malaysia. "Our company supports the sustained yield program in Indonesia," says Liberty Woods Vice President John Chaffin, but he acknowledges the company has no way to confirm that the program is working. "We don't have the technical expertise to do it properly," he told IRRC. Chaffin says his company "came close" to telling its contacts in Sarawak that it could not continue to purchase timber from them unless they enacted a sustained yield program, but elected not to.[117]

PLY-GEM MANUFACTURING CO.: Ply-Gem Manufacturing of New York, N.Y., is a publicly traded company that imports meranti plywood from Malaysia and Indonesia. Company President Howard Steinberg estimates that less than $20 million of its annual sales of $500 million involve tropical timber. Company officials make site visits every other year to see whether the mills are adhering to national reforestation standards.[118]

PLYWOOD PANELS INC.: Plywood Panels of New Orleans, La., is one of the largest U.S. importers of tropical plywood from Indonesia and Malaysia. The company's estimated annual sales are $160 million. Donald MacMaster, Plywood Panel's vice president, has served as president of the International Hardwood Products Association. MacMaster told IRRC that he has talked to suppliers about the need to develop sustainable sources of tropical timber. He reports that Indonesian suppliers are responding "quite well" and appear to be committing the necessary resources to reforestation. Malaysia is farther behind in its consciousness regarding the importance of conservation, however; MacMaster says it is where Indonesia was six years ago. The U.S. federal government temporarily became majority owner of Plywood Panels after the Federal Deposit Insurance Corp. took over a troubled bank that was Plywood Panels' majority stockholder.[119]

PLYWOOD TROPICS USA INC.: Plywood Tropics USA, a private company based in Portland, Ore., is one of the largest importers of tropical timber into the United States. The company is co-owned by Richard Newman, a former director of international forestry operations for **Georgia-Pacific**, and Indonesian business-man Mohammed "Bob" Hassan, who dominates that country's plywood timber trade. Newman says he believes that Indonesia has faced up to its forest depletion problems and heralds the nation's tropical forestry action plan as an "absolutely dynamite document." He predicts that pressure to use forests for fuelwood will be relieved as the number of Indonesian forest plantations increases.[120]

ROBINSON LUMBER CO.: Robinson Lumber, based in New Orleans, La., is one of the largest U.S. timber exporters from Brazil. It also exports tropical timber from Bolivia and Honduras and once had operations in Nicaragua. Samuel Robinson Jr., vice president for procurement, reported in 1990 that Robinson Lumber exports 10 million board feet a year from Bolivia and 8.9 million board feet a year from Brazil.[121] The Brazilian government has set quotas on mahogany and banak (virola), which have been depleted because of their popularity. The company can export only 100,000 cubic meters of mahogany and 85,000 cubic meters of virola each year.

Bolivia: Robinson purchases lumber from domestic companies operating near Santa Cruz and exports the wood through the port of Curitiba to the United Kingdom. Exported species include mahogany and Spanish cedar. Logging is conducted in the Chimanes forest in the Beni Biosphere Reserve, the result of a controversial debt-for-nature swap. Indian groups say that domestic logging companies have encroached on their lands. Conservation International, a group that was supposed to assist the government in supervising the timber cutting, withdrew from the area after loggers declined to follow sustainable forestry practices, according to James Nations, Conservation International's vice president for Latin America.[122] Robinson maintains that the biggest threat to the forests is the Peruvian government's own Agriculture Ministry, which allows colonists to burn forests for pasture. Mine closures in the Andes have caused a migration to eastern forests. A lucrative cocaine market also exists in the region, and many farmers burn forests to grow coca.

Brazil: Robinson Lumber has operated a small factory and kiln in Breves for more than 15 years, where it makes moldings. The company purchases most of its wood in Brazil from a domestic company, **Majinco**. Majinco reports that it has been reforesting logged areas since 1984. By 1988, Majinco had planted 2.5 million seedlings, 60 percent of which are mahogany. The mahogany timber is rough-sawn in Brazil, and then Robinson Lumber exports it to North Carolina, where it is made into house frames. Robinson also exports virola, a white wood used for picture frames; cedar, for house frames; and jatoba, used in beams and flooring.

Robinson Lumber has purchased 2,400 acres for selective cutting purposes to comply with Brazil's new forestry law. The company says it has been experimenting with ways to manage the land so that it will regenerate and remain profitable. The company's forester, Gil Amaral, is taking an inventory of commercially valuable species and may "enhance" the land by pruning noncommercial species to allow more sunlight to reach desired species. Robinson believes it is the only U.S. company in the area that is nearing completion of the experimental phase. Small areas already cut will be planted with a variety of species.

SCOTT PAPER CO.: Scott Paper, based in Philadelphia, Pa., has a small timber operation in Costa Rica, consisting of two 1,400 acre plantations—one planted with Caribbean pine and the other with gmelina, which is used for pulp. The Pabones plantation, located on former grazing land, consists of 1,000 acres of pine, 370 acres of gmelina, 243 acres of natural forest and 93 acres of crops. Natural forests remain along the rivers in both plantation areas and will not be cut, according to Theodore Clayton, Scott's director of Costa Rican operations. The plantation allows Scott to rely on local raw materials for pulp rather than importing it.

As the pine trees are cut, they will be replaced with fast-growing gmelina because it is easier to make pulp out of gmelina, Clayton reports. (Pine is generally not the best choice for paper production because of its high resin content.) As for the impact of the harvests on wildlife habitat, Clayton says, "As long as a bird doesn't mind moving its nest to a new tree, we are not destroying habitat."[123]

About 10 to 15 percent of the forest plantation area is cut at any one time. Pine is grown on a 10 to 15 year rotation; gmelina matures in just seven years. Scott has reforested 29,000 acres at other sites in Costa Rica and provides seeds at 50 percent of the international price to anyone who wants them. "We intend to be here for the next 50 to 100 years. We are thinking in terms of our long-term survival here," Clayton says.

Scott had proposed a major investment in an Indonesian rain forest in the late 1980s but withdrew from the project in 1989. (See Chapter 2 for details.)

SIMPSON INVESTMENT CO.: Simpson Investment, based in Seattle, Wash., owns **Simpson Timber** and **Simpson Paper**. Simpson is planting fast-growing gmelina trees on 24,000 acres of former rain forest in Guatemala for pulp export to the United States. John Walker, Simpson's vice president for land and timber, reports that the six year old project is using land that was logged more than 30 years ago and has been used since for cattle grazing. The gmelina will be harvested after only five years, by which time they should be 50 to 60 feet tall. About 3,400 acres will be harvested annually to produce the 250,000 cubic meters of chips necessary to make the operation cost-effective. As of 1991, 5,400 acres had been planted; the harvest date is set for 1995. A wood chip facility is being built near the plantation, and a barge port will ship the chips north. Walker estimates that the project has the potential to provide employment for 500 people. Simpson has invested more than $10 million in the project and plans to operate it indefinitely. The company does not plan to harvest any wood from natural rain forest areas, Walker says.[124]

RUSSELL STADELMAN & CO.: Russell Stadelman of Germantown, Tenn., is a major importer of tropical timber from Southeast Asia and Brazil, with annual sales of approximately $40 million. Russell Stadelman II told IRRC that his company is concerned about overcutting in Sarawak, Malaysia, and has asked his suppliers to address the issue. "They are studying the problem but I don't think that's good enough," he said. Stadelman would like the International Hardwood Products Association to take a stronger stand on the issue.[125]

STONE CONTAINER CO.: Stone Container, based in Chicago, Ill., has operations in Costa Rica and announced plans in October 1991 to harvest up to 2.5 million acres of pine forests on the "Mosquito Coast" of Honduras for pulp export to the United States. An agreement between Stone and the government of Honduras was suspended in February 1992, however, after protests from environmental groups. Environmentalists complained that there was no environmental assessment or reforestation plan in the contract with the Honduran government. They also were concerned that while no rain forests were slated to be cut, they might have been damaged anyway by operations in nearby pine forests. The Honduran Congress has turned down the project, and it now appears dead.

Honduras: The pine plantation that Stone Container had planned in Honduras would have created up to 3,000 jobs and generated $20 million a year for the Honduran economy. The massive project was not in tropical rain forest but in pine belts similar to those in Florida and South Carolina, according to Paul Howell, Stone's general manager for the project. (Scientists from the College of Forest Professionals in Honduras maintain, however, that some of the cutting would have been in tropical forest.) Howell says the reforestation plan would have resulted in 12 million cubic meters of new growth each year, compared with harvests of "just 3 or 4 million cubic meters. We will leave more than we take."[126] Stone maintains that it was committed to replanting the forest in conjunction with the government under a long-term management program, including silvicultural practices to increase the size and vitality of the forest.

Costa Rica: Stone Container has begun what it claims is the largest plantation reforestation project yet undertaken in Costa Rica. The company plans to plant 27 million gmelina trees on 59,000 acres between 1989 and 1994. **Ston Forestal**, Stone Container's Costa Rican subsidiary, expects to plant 9,000 acres of gmelina annually, which will grow to an average circumference of 10 inches and be ready for harvest in six years. The harvested wood will be shipped to the United States for use as pulp and paper.

The Costa Rican project is on abandoned agricultural and pasture lands leased by the company in the southwest part of the country, near the Osa Peninsula. No natural forest is included in the project area. The plantation is near the Corcovado National Park, however, which has been nominated to become a United Nations World Heritage Site and Biosphere Reserve. Some environmentalists are concerned that the project may affect animal and bird behavior, disrupt the local fishing industry and degrade the quality of life for members of local communities.[127]

The departure of a banana company in 1985 left the Osa Peninsula region with a high unemployment rate. Stone estimates that between 600 and 900 people will be employed during the planting process and another 1,000 temporary workers will be used during harvest seasons. (Four hundred people were on the payroll when IRRC visited the project in late 1990.) Workers are paid a minimum wage equal to about $1.15 per hour.

Ston Forestal reported in 1990 that it had fallen behind its goal of planting 10,000 acres a year. It planted only 750 acres in 1989 and 6,700 acres in 1990 because of drainage problems. About 2.5 million seedlings are growing in the company's nurseries, but a longer dry season than anticipated stunted early growth of the seedlings. The first harvest is expected in 1996.

WEYERHAEUSER CO.: Weyerhaeuser of Tacoma, Wash., is the world's largest private owner of timberland. It no longer has direct investments in tropical forests—although it did for 30 years. The company sold its last rain forest operation, a sawmill in Sabah, Malaysia, in 1988. Previously, it had sizable operations in the Philippines and Indonesia. (See the box on pp. 48-49 for a discussion of Weyerhaeuser's former operation in Indonesia.) Tropical timber operations formerly owned by Weyerhaeuser or run by former Weyerhaeuser employees remain in Guatemala, Indonesia, Malaysia, the Philippines and Venezuela.

In 1989, Weyerhaeuser sold its wall paneling business (the largest in the United States) to **Chesapeake Hardwood Products Inc.**, an affiliate of the **Kalimanis Group**, one of Indonesia's largest lumber and plywood manufacturers. The operation is owned by Mohammed "Bob" Hassan, **Georgia-Pacific's** former Indonesian partner. Weyerhaeuser continues to sell an estimated $10 million to $15 million of tropical timber annually in the form of plywood panels from about three dozen wholesale distribution centers. But Weyerhaeuser purchases the wood from other U.S. tropical timber importers rather than directly from overseas producers, reports Lowell Moholt, Weyerhaeuser's director of investor relations.[128] Accordingly, the company's response to public inquiries is that "Weyerhaeuser does not import tropical woods." But it does sell tropical timber that other companies have imported.

Weyerhaeuser says it wants to teach tropical timber operators better reforestation practices. Robert Lowery, director of the company's International Reforestation division, says it is working with Indonesia on a memorandum of understanding to consult on natural forest management.[129]

Germany

KARL DANZER: Karl Danzer is one of Germany's largest timber firms. It holds the largest timber concessions in Zaire in a joint venture with the Zairean government, known as the **Societe Industrielle et Forestiere Zairo-Allemande** (Siforzal). President Mobutu has a large financial interest in Siforzal. Danzer's 10 concessions amount to more than 22 million acres, or nearly 10 percent of Zaire's forests. Danzer's largest operation, totaling more than 2 million acres, stretches for 175 miles along the banks of the Zaire River at Lokoko in the northern part of the country. Danzer began its operation in Lokoko in 1985. Danzer also has timber operations in Cameroon and Gabon.[130]

HINRICH FELDMAYER: Hinrich Feldmayer, another large German timber firm, has operations in Cameroon and Gabon. In Cameroon, Feldmayer buys about 70,000 cubic meters of logs annually. An Environmental Defense Fund study says that most of its purchases are from Lebanese entrepreneurs "whose logging practices are based on the sole principle of cutting as many trees as quickly as possible."[131]

Japan

HONSHU PAPER CO.: Honshu Paper is Japan's fifth largest paper manufacturer. Its subsidiary in Papua New Guinea, **Jant Pty. Ltd.**, has been cutting tropical rain forest timber in the Gogol-Naru Valley since 1974 and converting it to woodchips for pulp and paper products. The company says it harvests trees in strict accordance with government regulations, although it did not say how many acres of trees it has cut. Keiichi Ohashi, Honshu's general manager for international business development, told IRRC that the Jant operation is utilizing "unused second-growth forest in Gogol and Naru to develop the land for plantation, agriculture and other business after being logged."[132] The company started experimental reforestation in 1976 and by the end of 1990 it had replanted 12,400 acres. Ohashi estimates that 40 percent of the total annual harvest of 170,000 cubic meters of wood is now derived from reforested trees. A new project will begin in 1998 that involves planting 2,700 acres of trees a year and eventually harvesting them.

Rainforest Action Newtwork claims that Jant has clearcut more than 120,000 acres of forest in Papua New Guinea. Some of the group's members who have visited the area assert that the cutting has caused severe erosion and topsoil disturbance. They also allege that river sedimentation and turbidity has damaged fishing grounds and that standing water in the clearcut has led to a sharp increase in the mosquito population, causing health officials to spray the area with DDT for fear of malaria. The environmental group says valley residents have shut down Jant operations three times in protest. In October 1990, they presented the government with a petition signed by 2,500 residents calling for renegotiation of Jant's contracts and $15 million in compensation for environmental damage and failure to deliver promised services. Jant plans to expand its operations into another 145,000 acres of rain forest, according to Colleen Murphy-Dunning of Rainforest Action Network.[133]

Jant maintains that "any serious land erosion or disturbance has not been reported after logging." The company says it has built 100 miles of roads and bridges in the area, invests $1 million annually in infrastructure and pays $1.4 million a year in taxes. Rainforest Action Network says the company avoids paying more taxes because of transfer pricing.

C. ITOH & CO. LTD.: C. Itoh is part of the "Big Three" Japanese general trading firms, along with Mitsubishi and Mitsui. Its well-known brand names include **Asahi Optics** (Pentax lenses), **Fuji Electric**, **Fujitsu** and **Isuzu**. C. Itoh imports logs and plywood from Sarawak, Malaysia, and owns part of a Brazilian pulp and paper company operating in an area that was formerly Atlantic coastal rain forest. While the company reports that it owns no operations in Malaysia, the Japan Tropical Forest Action Network says that C. Itoh owns 39 percent of **Mados-C. Itoh-Daiken-Sdn. Bhd.**, a plywood and veneer manufacturing company in Johor in peninsular Malaysia. The **Dai-Ichi Kangyo** business group, of which C. Itoh is a member, was Japan's largest importer of tropical logs in 1989, importing 1.7 million cubic meters of wood, according to statistics compiled by Jatan. C. Itoh alone imported 922,000 cubic meters of tropical roundwood into Japan in 1989.

In the United States, **C. Itoh Building Products** imported 14.2 million kilograms of tropical timber from Indonesia in 1990, according to U.S. Commerce Department records compiled by Greenpeace. In 1990, C. Itoh established an environment department to conduct environmental assessments of its overseas projects and help restore tropical rain forests. Industry observers have told the *Japan Times*, however, that the department does not have enough authority to stop the company from carrying out development projects even if they are found to be environmentally destructive.[134]

MARUBENI CORP.: Marubeni is another of Japan's leading general trading firms. Its familiar brand names include **Canon** office machines and cameras and **Nissan**. Marubeni sold in excess of $8 billion of forest products in 1990. The company did not respond to IRRC's inquiries about its activities in tropical forest regions. It did say that it buys timber from "those suppliers who implement sustainable forest management under government forestry regulations in the producing country."[135] A 1989 study by World Wildlife Fund International reported that Marubeni controls **Great Pacific Timber and Development Corp.** in the Philippines, which produces logs and sawnwood, and that it holds a 25 percent interest in **Capital Veneers Sdn. Bhd.** in Sabah, Malaysia.[136]

Marubeni was Japan's single largest importer of tropical timber in 1989, importing more than 1 million cubic meters, according to statistics compiled by Jatan from the Japan Lumber Importers Association. Jatan gave its "Rainforest Destruction Award" to Marubeni in 1989 for its alleged continued involvement in rain forest destruction. Jatan alleges that Marubeni is involved in large-scale mangrove cutting and woodchipping on 338,000 acres of pristine mangrove wetlands at Bintuni Bay, Irian Jaya, in Indonesia. "The Bintuni Bay area is the final refuge for a significant number of wildlife species of natural mangroves and a wetland of great international importance," says Jatan researcher Joseph Rinkevich.[137] The Indonesian government fined **P.T. Bintuni Utama Murni**, a Marubeni subsidiary, $590,000 in 1990 for illegally logging tropical mangroves in a conservation area. Indonesian law prohibits cutting mangroves within 200 meters of seashore.

A new Marubeni subsidiary, **Malaysian Fibreboard Sdn. Bhd.**, manufactures fiberboard from old rubber trees previously burned as waste. Marubeni also is trying to replace some tropical timber with conifers in some applications because conifer forest management "has already been well established to realize sustainable development," says Fukashi Furukawa, general manager of the company's environmental protection department, which was created in 1990.[138]

MITSUBISHI CORP.: Mitsubishi is Japan's largest general trading firm. It owns 60 percent of **J/V Logging Co.** in Malaysia, also known as **Daiya Malaysia**. Mitsubishi is Japan's largest importer of tropical plywood from Indonesia. It also owns 50 percent of **Eidai do Brasil**, which exports approximately 30,000 cubic meters of virola annually. The company has purchased 40,000 acres of land in Brazil on which it plans to practice a mixture of reforestation and natural forest management or selective cutting. Mitsubishi operating companies also are involved in logging in Bolivia and Colombia and mining in Ecuador.

Mitsubishi imported 454,000 cubic meters of tropical timber into Japan in 1989, according to the Japan Tropical Forestry Action Network (based on data from the Japan Lumber Importers Association). In 1990, its American subsidiary, **Mitsubishi International**, imported 8.6 million kilograms of tropical timber from Indonesia into the United States and 6.4 million kilograms of timber from Brazil, according to U.S. Commerce Department data reviewed by Greenpeace.

Mitsubishi is the target of a U.S. boycott by Rainforest Action Network and a European boycott being led by European environmental groups. Dick Shinohara, vice president and general manager of the Forest Products Division of Mitsubishi International, told IRRC that the company is carrying out "selective cutting" on the basis of local regulations and that Mitsubishi's operations have not resulted in deforestation anywhere in the world.[139] Mitsubishi employs a narrow definition of deforestation that is used by the UN Food and Agricultural Organization. That definition does not recognize an area as deforested unless 90 percent of the trees have been removed. Mitsubishi says that more than 10 percent of the forests remain in areas where it is operating.

Mitsubishi established an Environmental Affairs Department in 1990 to begin to work on solutions to environmental problems such as deforestation. One of its first projects is a rain forest reforestation study in Malaysia to be conducted by a professor from Yokohama National University. The study will provide guidance for future reforestation projects.

MITSUI & CO. LTD.: Mitsui is Japan's second largest general trading company. **The Mitsui Business Group** imported 504,000 cubic meters of tropical timber in 1989, according to the Japan Tropical Forestry Action Network (based on data from the Japan Lumber Importers Association). Mitsui Co. alone imported 319,000 cubic meters. A spokesman for **Mitsui USA**, based in New York City, reports that Mitsui imports plywood from Taiwan and Indonesia to the United States as well as Japan. Mitsui USA imported 16.3 million kilograms of tropical timber from Indonesia into the United States in 1990, according to U.S. Commerce Department data reviewed by Greenpeace. World Wildlife Fund International reports that Mitsui controls 10 percent of **United Industrial Paper Products Manufacturing Co.** of Malaysia and 45 percent of **P.T. Katingan Timber Co.** in Indonesia.

The Netherlands

ROYAL DUTCH SHELL: Shell has a vision of becoming the largest forest products company in the world. It has established fast-growing tree plantations with plans for operations in The Congo, Brazil and Thailand. The company reports that none of its operations has had any impacts on rain forests. Shell is in a joint venture with a Congolese company to develop 61,000 acres of eucalyptus to produce pulp logs for export to Europe. Philip Maxwell of Shell's forestry management team says the Congo plantation is in savannah, not rain forest. Floryl, a Brazilian pine and eucalyptus plantation in the state of Bahia, also is in savannah. A third plantation would be established on degraded agricultural land in Chantaburi province in southeast Thailand. Shell is awaiting approval from the Thai government. Shell has denied published reports that the project involves cutting rain forest areas and forcing local people to sell land against their will.[140]

Taiwan

EQUIPE ENTERPRISES: Equipe Enterprises, which has major logging operations in Malaysia, was close to signing a contract with the Nicaraguan government for a 20 year concession to log more than 1 million acres of tropical forest. But the Nicaraguan government backed out of the deal in 1992 after an environmental panel rejected the company's reforestation plans as inadequate. Another possible motive for suspension of the project was apparent pressure from the U.S. State Department, which was concerned that high-ranking Sandinista Army officers would benefit personally from the sale. The State Department allegedly held up a $25 million foreign aid payment and suggested that its release was conditional upon a satisfactory resolution of the environmental dispute, according to Guillermo Castilleja, Latin American program officer for the World Wildlife Fund.[141]

The $100 million investment contract would have allowed the harvest of more than 2 million trees a year and generated an estimated $70 million in timber exports. Environmental and human rights groups criticized the plan because of the ecological damage they say it would have caused to the largest rain forest north of the Amazon, and because it could have displaced thousands of Sumo and Miskito Indians who live in the area.

Bianca Jagger, who spearheaded opposition to the plan in the United States, claims the Nicaraguan government had struck a deal to promote Taiwanese investment in Nicaragua after Taiwan pledged to lend the struggling government $30 million to cover part of the arrears payments on its foreign debt. Under the agreement, about 666,000 acres would have been cut over 20 years to supply a plywood and a lumber mill, and an additional 490,000 acres would have been cut to supply a pulp mill—both to have been built by Equipe. The government estimated that about 42,000 acres would have been harvested each year, and the company eventually would have been required to reforest 494,000 acres on the Atlantic coast.

At one point, the transaction appeared to be proceeding over the objections of Jaime Incer, head of the Nicaraguan environmental agency, Irena. Incer had visited Equipe's logging operation in Malaysia and concluded that it had no experience in sustainable utilization and reforestation of tropical rain forests—nor were the expected returns on the Nicaraguan contract adequate to finance such management. Officially, however, Incer defended the project, maintaining that Equipe would use sustainable logging techniques that would not destroy the rain forest.

United Kingdom

BAT INDUSTRIES: British-American Tobacco (profiled in Chapter 6 for its tobacco operation) owns a portion of the Aracruz plantation in Brazil, which is not in the tropical rain forest but is a successful plantation operation.

B&Q: B&Q, the largest do-it-yourself home improvement chain in the United Kingdom, has committed to sell only sustainably grown timber—temperate or tropical—by the end of 1995. After that, B&Q "will not buy timber whose harvesting has caused the destruction of or severe damage to a natural forest," the company's new policy states. Timber that is clear-cut, even to establish plantations, will not be stocked by B&Q. The retailer notified its suppliers of its new policy in late 1992 and has asked them to complete a questionnaire about the origins of their timber.

B&Q is phasing out the use of labels on its timber, which could be confusing or misleading to consumers. Alan Knight, B&Q's environmental coordinator, says that a credible system of timber certification and labeling must be established for the company to implement its new policy. B&Q has worked closely with and provided funding for organizations involved in the Forest Stewardship Council, an international body that has been formed to encourage good stewardship of forests worldwide. B&Q also is funding field research to support a small-scale community-based forestry project in Papua New Guinea. Its long-term plan is to stock timber from such sustainable projects.[142]

UNILEVER: Unilever, best known for its soap and detergent products, owns a 40 percent share of **UAC of Nigeria Ltd.** UAC, a diversified business, is part of **African Timber and Plywood** (ATP), based in Sapele, Nigeria. ATP is logging in tropical rain forests. In 1990, it felled 122,000 cubic meters to supply domestic markets in Nigeria. A Unilever spokesman says the operation is "well managed, allowing for natural regeneration within the concession." A plantation of fast-growing gmelina was planted in 1983, and commercial harvest began in 1991. The plantation is expected to supply all of the firm's particle board needs in 1993. The company is considering planting an additional 60 square miles of forest area with indigenous trees to be managed sustainably.[143]

Chapter 4
Oil Production in the Tropics

T he oil industry accounts for the largest share of U.S. multinational investment in humid tropical forests. A ceaseless search for hydrocarbons has no fewer than 15 U.S. oil companies involved in exploration and production activities, constituting a multibillion dollar investment around the globe. Several environmental groups have launched campaigns to show how considerable pollution and degradation can occur in rain forest areas because of oil-related activities. Some oil companies have responded with their own campaigns to show how oil extraction can take place with only minimal harm to the environment. While recent oil development plans demonstrate far more respect for the rain forest environment and indigenous cultures than in the past, questions remain about implementation and monitoring of these plans and the legacy of oil development that has already occurred.

Oil production in rain forests has caused some dissension in the oil industry and within the environmental community. In Ecuador and Peru, for example, **Conoco** and **Texas Crude** agreed to pull out of protected rain forest areas in 1991, even as other companies like **Maxus Energy** and **Atlantic Richfield** have gone forward with efforts to produce oil there. Pressure from U.S. environmental and human rights groups—and their increasingly sophisticated Latin American counterparts—appears to have been a factor in some oil companies' decisions to scale back their activities in rain forest areas. But the environmental community is itself divided over whether to cooperate with oil companies that continue to operate in such sensitive regions.

Most oil companies and some conservationists defend multinational activities in rain forest areas. They contend that state-owned oil companies in tropical countries often have few or no environmental rules and that some of their remedial measures make matters worse. Companies unfamiliar with oil spill response techniques, for instance, often try to burn the spilled oil by felling nearby trees and setting them ablaze. This process leaves a significant amount of oil on the ground, however, so a bulldozer usually is brought in to cover the remaining spill with soil. Eventually, the oil returns to the surface.

"What is sad is that it's not necessary to make that kind of mess," says Paul Driver, director of the conservation services division of the International Union for Conservation of Nature, based near Geneva. "If they had left it alone there would have been less damage. But now you have burned trees and bulldozed soil and you still haven't cleaned up the mess."[1] Consequently, multinational oil companies sometimes find themselves teaching state-owned companies basic ways to minimize damage and respond to oil spills in rain forest areas.

But even the big multinational companies do not always use the kind of environmental protection procedures that would be required in the United States. "I've seen some environmental impact statements by other companies that wouldn't come close to being approved in the United States," says Charles Goodwin, environmental manager for international operations of **Occidental Petroleum**.[2] Occidental, for one, says it is committed to abiding by the functional equivalent of U.S. rules at all of its foreign facilities. Yet monitoring compliance in remote rain forest areas can be extremely difficult. Companies for the most part have to work on an honor system.

The financial arrangements under which a company operates also can influence how much attention is paid to the environment. In Peru, foreign investment is so badly needed that responsibly minded oil companies have good leverage with the government to insist on protective measures—if they want them. In Ecuador, on the other hand, multinational companies have contracted with the state-owned oil company, **Petroecuador**. Petroecuador reimburses U.S. companies for their services, but it is sometimes reticent to pay for expensive environmental protection programs.

This chapter reviews the standard procedures for oil exploration and production and the particular challenges of operating in a rain forest environment. Three case studies of oil development in Ecuador, Peru and Papua New Guinea illustrate the difficulties that companies often face when environmentalists and indigenous groups oppose their efforts—and highlight the potential to resolve at least some of these difficulties through collaborative efforts and state-of-the-art oil development practices. The rain forest activities of more than two dozen companies are summarized in an appendix to this chapter.

Environmental Impacts of Oil Production

Oil and gas production in the rain forest can cause tremendous disruption when comprehensive environmental plans are lacking or are neglected in the field. Construction of roads usually constitutes the biggest threat to the forest and its dwellers. Roads open up remote areas for colonization and can turn minor, short-term damage into widespread deforestation and social calamity over time. Other stages of the exploration and production process may degrade the forest and its inhabitants as well—and spills can have a catastrophic effect. Improper disposal of production wastes can pose a health threat long after drilling has ceased.[3]

Seismic Testing

Exploratory oil drilling commonly begins with seismic exploration to assess an area's geophysics. Cables are laid in straight lines on the ground, and explosive charges are detonated in holes usually 60 feet deep to generate sound waves deep into the earth. The energy is converted into electrical impulses recorded on tape to render a cross-section of the subsurface. Accordingly, areas must be cleared to allow passage of equipment and personnel. Clearing width usually ranges from about three to nine feet and can be achieved in various ways. The use of machetes to clear a path just wide enough for a person to pass and cable to be laid is the least intrusive clearing method. By contrast, use of bulldozers knocks down many trees and leaves topsoil exposed.

The most environmentally benign seismic testing method is a portable dynamite survey. Seismic traverses are cleared by hand, and hand-held drills are used to place the charges. Helicopters can be used to avoid cutting paths or roads into the forest (although small landing pads still must be cleared). This testing method is not used very often, however, because it tends to be more expensive and labor-intensive than the others.

Exploratory Drilling

Once seismic data are recorded, exploratory drilling begins. The drill site usually involves clearing anywhere from one to 10 acres, depending on the size of the reserve pits used to store drilling muds. Drilling muds are routinely used to help maintain pressure balance, prevent blowouts and cool the hole in exploration wells. Reserve pits store surplus mud and drill cuttings. Ideally, exploratory drilling plans include a means for safe permanent disposal of mud and mud wastes. High technology mud cleaners can be used for efficient recycling of mud on site and between wells. If an exploratory well is unsuccessful, the most efficient means of disposal is simply to dump the mud back down the borehole. (The best practice in the United States is to ship muds and drilling wastes to offsite treatment facilities.)

Muds generally fall into two categories: water-based muds, which can be made with fresh or saline water and are used for most types of drilling, and oil-based muds, which are used when water is not appropriate. Sometimes additives are used to control the chemical, physical and biological properties of muds. Occasionally, chemicals and oil wastes are improperly deposited in these pits. Unlined pits in rain forests may leak their contents into underground aquifers or be swept over the top of the pit during rain storms. Partly for this reason, drilling sites and reserve pits are ideally situated far away from bodies of water—but water is omnipresent in the rain forest.

Wellhead blowouts can occur when the weight of mud in the borehole cannot contain the pressure from the oil formations below. Blow-out prevention technology, well-planned emergency procedures and on-site storage of equipment for control and cleanup can minimize the environmental effects of such blowouts. Other impacts on the rain forest can come from exhaust and noise generated by diesel- and gasoline-powered drilling equipment. Exploratory drilling often lasts for six months or longer.

Production Drilling

Production drilling is similar to exploratory drilling in many respects, but its environmental impact is longer-lasting. A developer's goal is to drill the fewest wells in order to drain an oil reservoir. Cluster development—a recently developed procedure where several wells are drilled at an angle from a single pad—can minimize the area of land affected by drilling.

Water removed from the earth during the drilling process is called formation water (or produced water). While the contents of this water vary, most is strongly saline. It also contains varying quantities of petroleum hydrocarbons and naturally occurring metals and additives from the production process. These additives include coagulants, corrosion inhibitors, cleaners, dispersants, emulsion breakers, paraffin control agents, reverse emulsion breakers and scale inhibitors.

The American Petroleum Institute says the primary environmental concern from formation water is contamination of soil, vegetation and sources of potable water. In the United States, API recommends three disposal options: underground injection into subsurface reservoirs usually located deep below aquifers, discharge to a water source if treated according to Clean Water Act regulations, or discharge to land through percolation and evaporation where fresh water is not present or located such that contamination from formation water cannot occur.[4]

In tropical forest areas, however, formation water often is stored in open, unlined pits and is a major source of blight and pollution. As with mud pits, formation water and any chemical additives kept in these pits can leak into drinking-water aquifers or be swept into rivers during storms. In addition, birds and other animals may become trapped if they land on an open waste pit or pond. Reinjection of formation water into a deep well or into a special horizontally drilled hole is one solution in remote areas, which typically have no treatment facilities.

—Photo courtesy of Maxus Energy Corp.

Oil drilling platform in the Ecuadoran rain forest. The drill site normally requires clearing up to 10 acres of forest.

Pipeline Construction

The other major threat to rain forests in the oil production phase is the impact of pipeline construction. Pipelines usually require the clearing of a path at least 100 feet wide during construction. Moreover, areas for construction camps, pump stations, helipads and housing facilities for workers must be erected. As with the seismic phase, pipeline construction can introduce large numbers of workers into a region and provide a potential migration route for colonists. The route of a pipeline also is important. Routes that follow rivers are easier to construct but generally mean more contact with indigenous peoples who tend to live near rivers and more potential to contaminate those rivers in the event of spills.

Oil Industry Guidelines for Rain Forests

The Oil Industry Exploration and Production Forum, an international association of 36 oil companies and 13 industry organizations operating in 52 countries, has published a set of guidelines for oil companies operating in rain forest areas. The guidelines, issued in April 1991, are not a set of binding regulations, however; they are suggestions on how to minimize forest impact. They are prefaced with the caveat that "economics as well as environmental protection will be considered" in negotiations with host countries and that not all measures will be appropriate in all geographical areas.[5]

The guidelines recommend, for example, that "the circumstances under which bulldozers are used should be strictly controlled" and, "where practical, construction of roads should be avoided." In hilly terrain, restoration is recommended to prevent erosion and flooding. "For a sloping site, consideration should be given to restoration of something like the original contours. At a minimum, the site should be left with terrain of comparable contours which will not erode or act as a focus for instability." The guidelines say no oily wastes should be allowed in mud pits and that the pits should be constructed from impermeable membrane (often synthetic liners) and soil materials and surrounded by a raised bank to prevent run-off into adjacent areas. The guidelines say steel tanks should be used for storage if oil-based muds are used.

Several major oil companies, including **Arco, Conoco, Exxon, Maxus, Shell Oil** and **Texaco** say they are committed to following the guidelines in all future rain forest exploration and production activities.

Oil Boom in Ecuador

The United States imports about 4 percent of its crude oil from seven South American countries; most of it comes from Colombia, Ecuador and Trinidad and Tobago. In the last several years, however, international attention has focused on Ecuador, a tropical-forested country where many oil companies are active. Located on the Pacific coast of South America, Ecuador contains 32 million acres of tropical rain forest, mostly in the Oriente region in the eastern half of the nation, which slopes down the Andes Mountains into the Amazon basin, forming the headwaters of the Amazon River. Ecuador (along with neighboring Peru) plans to double its oil production in the next five years.

Ecuador's rain forests are regarded as among the most biologically rich on earth. They are home to perhaps 10 percent of the world's plant and animal species, including 120 species of mammals, 500 species of fish, 600 species of birds, and at least 12,000 plant species. Ecuador's rain forests also are home to 250,000 indigenous peoples, including the Achuar, Cofan, Huaorani, Quichua Secoya and Siona. The World Resources Institute estimates that Ecuador has the highest rate of deforestation in South America, losing more than 100,000 acres, or 2 percent, of its forests annually. Much of this deforestation is attributed to opening up the oil frontier in the Oriente region.[6]

Ecuador's oil boom began in 1967 when a **Texaco/Gulf** consortium discovered oil near Lago Agrio, followed by giant finds at Sacha and Shushufindi. Multinational firms such as **Amoco, Chevron** and **W.R. Grace** were awarded concessions and started exploratory drilling. When the Ecuadoran government realized the money to be made from oil, it reclaimed many concessions and raised taxes and royalties on the foreign companies. A national oil company, **Petroecuador**, was created in 1971 and has held a monopoly on oil production in Ecuador ever since. Other companies have continued to provide support services for Petroecuador.

In 1972, **Texaco** completed a pipeline traversing the Andes to transport oil from the Oriente to the Pacific port of Esmeraldas. **Gulf** pulled out of Ecuador in 1976 as the Government of Ecuador demanded a majority financial share in the Texaco/Gulf consortium—but Texaco remained. In the early 1980s, the Ecuadoran government encouraged more foreign investment, resulting in new exploration contracts with **Arco, British Petroleum, Conoco, Exxon, Occidental, Tenneco** and **Unocal**. The oil boom during the 1980s boosted Ecuador's economy with more than $7 billion in oil revenue but also led to unrestrained borrowing practices that created more than $12 billion in foreign debt.

Today, the Ecuadoran economy runs largely on oil; the government even proclaimed 1992 as "the year of oil development." Half of Ecuador's export earnings and 40 percent of the state budget are generated from petroleum revenues. However, about half of the country's known oil reserves have been pumped and the other half may be depleted by 2010. Part of the pressure to develop oil rapidly comes from the need to service the country's enormous foreign debt. Oil exports finance three-quarters of the interest payments on that debt.

Ecuador elected a new government in July 1992, and Sixton Duran Ballen became president. Ballen wants to stimulate oil production further by withdrawing Ecuador from the Organization of Petroleum Exporting Countries and doubling its oil production targets from the 273,000-barrel-a-day limit set by OPEC to 576,000 barrels a day by 1996. In October 1992, Ecuador's minister of energy and mines opened a new round of bidding for oil development rights and declared that **Petroecuador** would end its monopoly on oil production in the country. The government's new energy plan does not include provisions to protect the rights of indigenous peoples who live in the Oriente region, however.

As Ecuadoran oil production soared in the 1970s and 1980s, scant attention

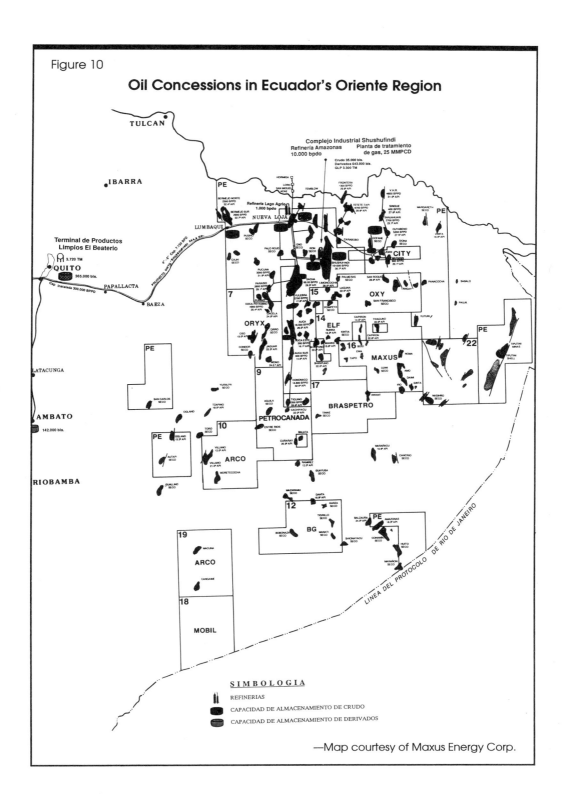

Figure 10

Oil Concessions in Ecuador's Oriente Region

—Map courtesy of Maxus Energy Corp.

was paid to spills and other environmental and social impacts of the boom. Judith Kimerling, an attorney and formerly a Latin American representative with the Natural Resources Defense Council, spent 18 months in Ecuador researching the impact of oil development in the Oriente, resulting in NRDC's publication of *Amazon Crude* in 1991. The book offers a detailed account of the impacts of oil drilling in tropical rain forests. Kimerling regards the Oriente an "environmental free-fire zone" that has operated with virtually no environmental or public health controls. She estimates that oil production spans 2.5 million acres, with 400 wells and 29 production stations pumping 283,000 barrels per day. Another 7.4 million acres—more than 30 percent of the Oriente—is under exploration. While **Texaco** has had the longest and greatest ties to the region, several other companies— including **Atlantic Richfield, Maxus, Occidental Petroleum, Oryx** and **Elf-Aquitaine**—recently completed oil exploration and now are building production facilities. (Occidental and Oryx already are producing oil from their tracts.)

Texaco's Involvement with Petroecuador

Texaco's operations in Ecuador's rain forests date back to the mid-1960s, when the Texaco/Gulf consortium discovered oil near Lago Agrio, Sacha and Shushufindi. Texaco subsequently acquired a 37.5 percent non-operating interest in **Petroecuador**. At the time of peak production, Texaco and Petroecuador produced 220,000 barrels of oil a day from 230 wells in 15 oil fields. (The largest field, at Sacha, still produces 60,000 barrels of oil per day from 94 wells.) Texaco's 1972 contract agreement required it to surrender its operations to Petroecuador in 20 years. Texaco did so in June 1992.

A 1990 study by J.F. Sandoval Moreano, an Ecuadoran engineer, found that the rate of new settlements accelerated greatly along roads built by Texaco and Gulf, beginning in 1965. The result was a significant increase in pioneer settlement and deforestation. Moreano also reviewed reports by the Ecuadoran environmental agency, Digema, and found that only 40 percent of the production oil well platforms operated by Petroecuador, Texaco and Gulf were considered to have a good level of maintenance. In addition, water used for cooling equipment at the Lago Agrio refinery and Shushufindi gas plant reportedly was contaminated by oil residues and released untreated into waterways.[7]

As the years passed, the environmental damage mounted. "Texaco's 1960s wells have never been cleared up," says World Wide Fund for Nature forest conservation officer Frances Sullivan. "Polluted water and oil are still leaking into rivers."[8]

Kimerling is especially critical of the way Texaco and other oil companies have disposed of production wastes in Ecuador. In the United States, "oil producers commonly reinject production wastes into the original formation or into nearby dry wells," she writes in *Amazon Crude*. "In Ecuador, these same companies simply dump their wastes into local creeks or 'production pits,' which are unlined and unstable holes dug in the ground or on the side of the earthen drill platform....Each pit has an overflow pipe to a nearby body of water. The toxic soups also percolate through soils into the groundwater or flood into lakes or streams when the pits collapse."[9]

"The only treatment occurs when the oil companies burn the pits to reduce their petroleum content," Kimerling adds, and that produces more problems. A campesina woman told her, "When they burn their pits, smoke falls in pieces from the sky, then we have black rains and the particles drop on our crops and animals and into the lake where we get our water. In October of 1989, ash rained on all of us from Texaco's central facility in Lago Agrio and the children got skin problems. But usually they don't bother to burn and they just let the petroleum flow into the creeks. Everything here stinks of the chemical that they put in the pits."[10]

In February 1992, the International Water Tribunal, a private review panel that hears citizens' grievances about transboundary water disputes, found "sufficient evidence" that Texaco's and Petroecuador's operations in the Ecuadoran Amazon region resulted in "large quantities of hydrocarbons, salts and hazardous substances associated with oil exploration and production…in waste waters and surface waters discharged or spilled on soil and into surface waters." The tribunal, based in Amsterdam, also found safeguards lacking to prevent spills from reserve pits that store drilling mud and formation water.[11] (The International Water Tribunal has no judicial power, however. It was established in 1981 with funding from the Dutch government. Its judges are former government officials, water resource professionals, scientists and court judges.)

In its own defense, Texaco maintains that the reserve pits were lined with naturally occurring clay to prevent the movement of hydrocarbons, salts and hazardous substances into groundwater. Moreover, it says it is not aware of any instances in which discharges of substances from these pits resulted in water contamination. One company analysis of water samples near the Sacha field found these samples comparable to water samples adjacent to oil fields in the United States. While Texaco does acknowledge that ethyl benzene, xylene and toluene are among the contaminants associated with oil production in Ecuador, it says the presence of these naturally occurring components of crude oil is reduced "far below any level of concern" by separating the crude oil from formation water before the water's release into the environment.[12]

How much area has been affected by Texaco's and Petroecuador's operations in the Oriente also is a matter of dispute. While the concession area encompasses more than 1.2 million acres, Texaco says the consortium's operations have directly affected only about 12,000 acres. Texaco does not dispute that nearly 300,000 barrels of oil spilled from the Trans-Andean pipeline during the 17 years it operated the pipeline. But the company points out that 1.3 billion barrels of oil were transported safely through the pipeline over the period, so that the spills accounted for only 0.02 percent of all the oil transported. Moreover, Texaco attributes 18 of 27 major spills from the pipeline to force majeure events such as floods, landslides and earthquakes.[13] One 57,000 barrel spill occurred during a 1987 earthquake, spreading oil all the way to the Atlantic Ocean—passing through Ecuador, Peru and Brazil in the space of about two weeks. Kimerling says the pipeline's design allowed it to spill oil for days before the flow could be stopped.

Perhaps the greatest point of contention is the effect of oil development on those who live in the Oriente region of Ecuador. According to one account in *The*

New York Times, Texaco's operations with Petroecuador have dramatically transformed portions of the landscape in the Cuyabeno Wildlife Production Reserve and the lives of those who live nearby. "The forest, once thick, has been pockmarked by dirt roads, subsistence farms, oil pumping stations where yellow flames burn off gas 24 hours a day, and open, unlined pits for storing liquid drilling wastes." Roads built through the area gave 1,000 families access to half of the reserve area. Settlers reportedly suffered from skin rashes, allergies, abscesses and infections after drinking water from areas near the unlined oil waste pits. In addition, large numbers of rare pink dolphins apparently died from contact with contaminated water. "Without a doubt, the oil exploration actions in the Cuyabeno Reserve are an environmental disaster and have caused considerable degradation of the rain forest," maintains Gregory Miller, Ecuadoran project director for the Nature Conservancy.[14]

Cofan Indians also have been decimated by oil development in the Cuyabeno Reserve. Touribe, a young Cofan leader, told National Public Radio in September 1991 that seismic explosions scared away animals, settlers streamed in on roads built by the companies, oil and chemical spills killed fish and turned some rivers into dead bodies of water that gave his people rashes. "With the coming of the petroleum companies came the epidemics," he said. "We didn't know anything about the flu, the measles; almost all the region was hit. Many fled from here. Those that stayed were finished. So now we don't all live together like we used to. Some live downriver, others live upriver in Colombia....It was all contaminated. There were 70,000 of us. Now there are only about 3,000 of us."[15]

Health officials say a combination of diseases and a sense of hopelessness resulting from the introduction of prostitution and alcoholism contributed to the demise of the Cofan. Not far away, oil workers lived with modern comforts, such as air conditioned compounds, swimming pools, electricity, telephones and occasional hunting expeditions in a company helicopter.

In October 1990, the Natural Resources Defense Council publicly criticized Texaco and other oil companies for purportedly disregarding the environment in the Oriente. Their practices, NRDC alleged, have resulted in "shocking impacts of oil spills and waste discharges upon the rain forest, its native peoples and settlers." The environmental group asked Texaco to establish a $50 million fund to undertake emergency cleanups, conduct health and environmental studies, and establish environmental controls.

Texaco denies any wrongdoing in its 20 years of operations in the Oriente, however. "To allege that Texaco is responsible for the local population's use of roads for colonization and agricultural development is both dishonest and unrealistic," it says in a 15 page company document called *Setting the Record Straight*. "As a private company, Texaco would have no authority or right to restrict citizens of Ecuador from using these roads or to interfere in Ecuador's national programs and planning for colonization of the region."[16]

Michael Trevino, public affairs manager for Texaco Latin America/West Africa, adds that the company's operations "have always been conducted in strict accordance with the laws of the countries in which we were operating and the environmental practices of the time."[17] However, an environmental manager for **Occidental Petroleum** who has worked in Ecuador points out that the country had no real means of implementing or monitoring its environmental protection laws until 1990. The oil industry, in other words, was essentially self-regulated.

Texaco/Petroecuador audit: While Texaco withdrew from Ecuador in 1992, the impact of its past operations there is still being assessed. Texaco and its former partners in the oil consortium, Petroecuador and the Government of Ecuador, are conducting a joint environmental audit with assistance from **HBT Agra** of Calgary, Canada, a consulting firm that is knowledgeable about oil industry practices in the rain forest. The audit began in early 1993 and will take most of the year to complete. Texaco says the audit has two major tasks: to determine "acceptable international oil industry practices for rain forests and Ecuadoran environmental law and regulation" during the time the consortium operated (1964 through 1990), and to use these practices and laws, once they are determined, as audit criteria for evaluating the consortium's facilities and operations in Ecuador.

Environmental and indigenous groups are seeking to participate in the audit process, although it remains to be seen whether their requests will be granted. Rather than focusing exclusively on past environmental management practices in relation to Ecuadoran law, these groups would like to see the scope of the audit broadened. The indigenous groups would like to include social impacts in the evaluation, possibly leading to indemnification of communities and individuals that have been adversely affected by oil development. Environmental groups want the audit to identify measures to clean up and restore damaged areas and to modernize oil facilities that have passed hands from Texaco to Petroecuador.

"To date, indications are that the audit...will not be independent, comprehensive or transparent," maintains Judith Kimerling (who returned to Ecuador in July 1993 to study Ecuadoran environmental law under a grant from the MacArthur Foundation).[18] Texaco spokesman Michael Gallagher says he does not know whether Texaco will release the results of the audit to the public once it is completed, although he assumes the Ecuadoran government will do so. "Texaco is confident that the joint environmental audit will show the consortium's operations were at or above applicable oil industry standards for the period," Gallagher predicts.[19] But that is not to say that Texaco's management practices were as environmentally sound as they could have been. As another Texaco official for environmental and product safety, Ulysses Henderson, told *The New York Times* in 1991, "The operations are quite comparable to the way the oil patch was operated in the U.S. 20 years ago. If we were starting an activity...today, we would do things differently."[20]

Conoco's Bid To Do Better

As Texaco reviews its past management practices in Ecuador, other companies are moving ahead with plans to extract more oil from the rain forest. An oil consortium—led by **Conoco** initially and now by **Maxus**—has struck oil in the vicinity of Yasuni National Park, a tropical rain forest preserve. The amount of oil thought to reside in the area is 300 million barrels, or about one-fifth of Ecuador's known reserves. Conoco, which found oil in five of seven exploratory wells, pledged in 1990 to go beyond current operating practices and, in the words of Alex Chapman, manager of Conoco's environmental protection project, "establish a world-standard model rain forest operation that will demonstrate how environmental and indigenous people concerns can be economically integrated into an oil development" project.[21]

Oil development in the Yasuni region is controversial because portions of one exploration block (Block 22) are within the park's boundaries, which has been designated as a Biosphere Reserve by the United Nations and is home to nomadic Huaorani Indians, a group of about 1,200 hunters and gatherers. Another exploration block (Block 16) is on lands titled to Huaorani who have settled in a more densely populated protectorate, where Catholic missionaries have been present for the last 20 years. The Huaorani were given legal title to 1.5 million acres of ancestral lands in April 1990, but the land titles exempt subsurface rights, enabling companies to search for and extract oil.

Conoco outlined a detailed environmental protection program with an aim of convincing environmental and human rights groups that it could produce oil without damaging the rain forest or its inhabitants. A 90 mile access road would not be linked to any existing road, for example; instead it would start at the Napo River. Patrols by Conoco and the government would seek to prevent settlers from using the access road, and the roadbed itself would be constructed of a plastic geogrid material, reducing by 70 percent the number of trees normally harvested to provide a roadbed.

A connecting pipeline would be buried underground, reducing the width of the area to be cleared by more than half (to 82 feet). Wells would be drilled in clusters, with as many as 12 wells directionally drilled from a single platform. Conoco estimated total clearing for the road and production facilities at 1,000 acres. In addition, it designed several programs to minimize toxic waste and eliminate the release of oil into rain run-off areas. Water used in the production process was to be reinjected into wells rather than dumped into unlined pits. New drilling mud and chemical technology also was to be used in an attempt to eliminate all drilling pit wastes. Conoco also pledged to prevent oil spills through use of catchment systems and to prepare oil spill contingency plans that would be completed before operation.

Some critics claim, however, that Conoco's record did not quite match its rhetoric. While acknowledging Conoco's desire to be a "green" oil company, Kimerling reports that the Ecuadoran government cited Conoco for illegally discharging drilling wastes into the environment and contaminating a brook. She says Conoco also denied her requests for information about its activities in the field and the quantities and chemical composition of drilling muds and other wastes dumped into unlined pits during oil exploration. And since Conoco planned to patrol the road it built from the Napo River, she says, ecologists could have been barred from making their own on-site inspections.[22]

An even greater concern of many observers is the fate of the Huaorani. The population is spread among 17 communities, three of which are nomadic and four or five of which keep more than one home. (The rest of the population are settled into single village locations within the protectorate.) The Huaorani are an egalitarian people; organization and leadership have been foreign to them. The impending arrival of oil companies compelled the Huaorani to organize quickly.

Figure 11

Maxus Holdings in Ecuador

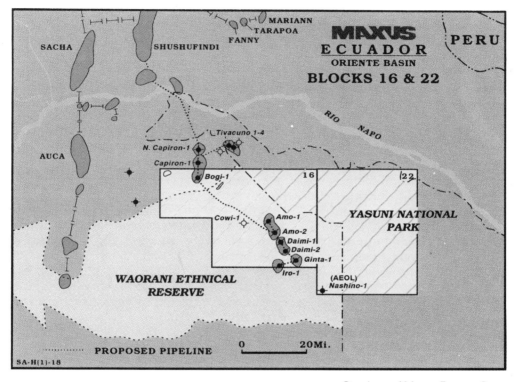

—Courtesy of Maxus Energy Corp.

Huaorani communities had been threatened once before, during the rubber boom of the early 20th century. Many Huaorani fought against Peruvian soldiers who encroached on their lands. Now, with the arrival of the oil companies, several oil workers and at least two missionaries hired by Conoco to induce the Huaorani to accept oil development have been killed.

The recent battle has been mainly a political one, however. After the first assembly and Congress of the Huaorani nation in 1990, the Organizacion de la Nacionalidad Huaorani de la Amazonia Ecuatoriana (Onhae) was founded. Onhae provided a common front for the Huaorani nation and sought to discourage oil companies or government representatives from negotiating directly with individual Huaorani communities. Onhae wrote to Conoco to express opposition to road construction in Huaorani territory and to reject oil development activity there as a source of pollution and human illnesses.[23]

Environmental and human rights groups also came to the defense of the Huaorani. The Confederacion de Nacionalidades Indigenas de la Amazonia Ecuatoriana (Confeniae), which represents Ecuadoran indigenous groups living in the Amazon, filed petitions jointly with Onhae to the Organization of American States. The petitions alleged that oil development activity in the Yasuni region would violate the "rights of Huaorani to life and to health and well-being, as well as human treatment, protection of family, freedom of movement and of religion, inviolability of the home and to property and privacy." The two groups also requested an on-site visit from human rights commissioners with the OAS and sought a 10 year moratorium on oil production to allow the Huaorani to develop the ability to interact knowledgeably with outsiders.[24]

Natural Resources Defense Council intervention: In October 1990, the Natural Resources Defense Council called for Conoco to withdraw from the Yasuni project. The company replied that other companies would remain even if Conoco pulled out, but it said it was willing to have independent oversight of its activities and to fund community development activities for the Huaorani. NRDC attorneys S. Jacob Scherr and Robert F. Kennedy Jr. subsequently met with Conoco and discussed the creation of such a foundation or fund.

When an account of the NRDC-Conoco meeting was circulated, environmental groups in Ecuador reacted angrily, charging that the environmental group was negotiating the fate of the Huaorani without consulting them. In the meeting, Scherr reportedly told Conoco that if NRDC went forward with the plan, "they would be sticking their necks out but they would do their best to bring people (in the environmental community) around."[25] NRDC maintains, however, that "it was clear to everyone at the meeting that these were not negotiations nor were they intended to be, since concerned parties were not represented and would in no way be bound by our discussions."[26] The group rejected allegations that it had undertaken "secret negotiations" with Conoco and said that Ecuadoran environmental groups had been fully and repeatedly briefed on the matter.

Some other U.S. environmental groups did not support NRDC's intervention, either. Barbara Bramble, director of international programs for the National Wildlife Federation, told *The Washington Post* that NRDC had erred in moving forward before a consensus emerged in the tenuous alliance of Ecuador's environmental and indigenous groups. "Whether they intended it or not, they were hiding things from people who were known to be naysayers or skeptical....You can't get around them. I don't quarrel that [they] may have been [seeking] the best solution, but they ruined it," she said.[27]

NRDC subsequently held discussions in Ecuador with Confeniae, the umbrella group of Ecuadoran Indian organizations that is part of the regional Amazonian Indian federation. But the controversy surrounding NRDC's role as well as internal disagreement within the Indian group led to an impasse, and the group decided it would negotiate directly with Conoco without further involvement of NRDC. These direct talks reportedly led nowhere.

Conoco Withdraws, Maxus Advances

With Onhae and Confeniae formally opposed to near-term oil development in the Yasuni National Park area, Conoco withdrew from the project in October 1991, claiming there were higher profits to be made elsewhere. However, other partners in the project, led by **Maxus Energy**, are pressing forward with development. Maxus, based in Dallas, Tex., has a 34 percent stake. The other partners are **Taiwanese Overseas Petroleum and Investment Corp.** (31 percent); **Canam Offshore Ltd.** and **Murphy Oil Co.**, both subsidiaries of **Murphy Oil Corp.** of El Dorado, Ark., (20 percent); and **Nomeco Ecuador Oil Co.**, a subsidiary of **CMS Energy Corp.**, based in Jackson, Mich. (14 percent). Ironically, environmental groups fear that Conoco's departure could make matters worse, since the remaining partners may not be as committed to protecting the rain forest.

Maxus and its partners have pledged, however, to follow the operating plans designed by Conoco for Block 16, a 700,000 acre tract of rain forest. The consortium has also kept intact almost all of the staff and infrastructure relied upon by Conoco in Ecuador. "We are fully aware of the highly sensitive nature of the Oriente area," says C.L. Blackburn, chairman and chief executive officer of Maxus. Operators of the project "pledge that they will responsibly carry out the consortium's plan to develop the oil properties," he maintains.[28]

Maxus began development drilling in its Block 16 concession in the spring of 1992. It expects oil production to begin in early 1994, reaching approximately 15,000 barrels a day later that year. The company expects production to reach 50,000 barrels a day in 1995, and average 40,000 to 50,000 barrels a day for five to seven years, before production starts to decline. The Maxus consortium also has been awarded Block 22, which is adjacent to Block 16, although no agreement has been reached with Petroecuador regarding the exploration of this block.

Altogether, the Ecuadoran government has authorized eight oil companies to operate on Huaorani lands. One of these companies, **Petro Canada**, has abandoned its block and withdrawn from the country. Two other companies, **Unocal** and Brazil's **Petrobras**, have suspended their activities pending further negotiations with the Ecuadoran government. **Arco, Elf-Aquitaine, Maxus, Mobil** and **Occidental Petroleum** remain active in the area.

Maxus has pledged to execute an environmental management plan to develop Block 16 "in an environmentally responsible manner" and to work with the Ecuadoran Museum of Natural Sciences and the Missouri Botanical Society to collect and study forest canopy flora and fauna. The Sierra Club Legal Defense Fund has recognized Maxus, along with **Arco**, for showing "a somewhat more 'open' attitude toward the public....Maxus in particular has made its study more easily available to the public than other companies." At the same time, however, the Sierra Club contends that "the operative plans of Arco and Maxus, despite exceeding the government's requirements for environmental and social control in oil development activities, are not safe, either for indigenous peoples or for the environment."[29]

Maxus says it plans to limit tree cutting in Block 16 to only 1,000 acres of rain forest, where it will drill 100 wells. It has also pledged to abide by guidelines to restore sites as nearly as possible to their original condition and to make roads and campsites inaccessible and to take down bridges when leaving an area. Maxus's 70 employees in Block 16 have been instructed to avoid interacting with the Huaorani. "Maxus employees aren't even allowed to talk to Indians," says

William Hutton, on-site general manager of Maxus Ecuador. "If they do, they're fired. We aren't getting into the Indians' culture."[30]

Yet some interaction with the Huaorani seems inevitable. In September 1992, a Maxus employee approached the president of Onhae and a few other Huaorani individuals to reach an agreement whereby Maxus would operate on the lands of certain Huaorani communities in the protectorate, and the Indians would receive electricity from a power plant and some other goods. (The Onhae president and the Huaonari Congress repudiated the agreement one month later, and 100 Huaorani men and women then traveled to Quito to demonstrate in front of the offices of Maxus Ecuador and several government agencies.)[31]

While some Huaorani in Onhae favor a moratorium on oil development in their communities, other Huaorani and their representatives (especially those from the protectorate) welcome the construction of a road that would provide easier access to markets and a faster way to get to the hospital. But it is unclear whether the Huaorani fully understand the implications of giving consent for oil production on their lands. The oil developers claim that local people have consented to exploration activities; anthropologists who have studied the Huaorani are not so sure.

What is known is that the Huaorani's traditional way of life is already changing. By some estimates, 90 percent of Huaorani adults have now worked at least once for a seismic test company, usually for short periods to cut seismic lines through the forest by hand.[32] The work has given Huaorani access to money and fostered a desire for products from the "outside world." Their diets also are changing as they relinquish hunting and garden farming. Illnesses are more frequent. Alcoholism and prostitution, previously unknown, are becoming common vices.

At the same time, colonization along the roads is difficult to control. While Maxus has pledged to prevent such colonization, some contend that the company has no detailed plan to prevent it, nor has it said what will happen to security along the road once oil production stops. The road Maxus is building may stretch more than 100 miles eventually, penetrating deep into the Yasuni National Park, which is home to Quichua Indians as well as the nomadic Huaorani. The road, which will take six years and cost more than $20 million to construct, will connect seven exploratory wells drilled by Conoco and facilitate the construction and maintenance of an oil pipeline linked with the Trans-Ecuadoran transportation system of the Northern Oriente.

Texas Crude in Peru

Another story involving a U.S. oil company, environmental groups and a rain forest played out in Peru in 1991. Peru, in desperate need of foreign investment, granted **Texas Crude Exploration** exploration rights to a 2.4 million acre tract in the northern Amazon jungle. About three-quarters of the tract is in the Pacaya-Samiria National Reserve, a largely unspoiled riverine forest habitat with more than 150 lakes and many rare animals such as pink river dolphins, black and speckled caiman, Amazon manatees and giant South American river turtles.

Biologists warn that an oil spill there would be disastrous, because the reserve is in a flood zone with slow moving waters.

About half of the fishing in the Peruvian Amazon is done in the Pacaya-Samiria National Reserve. More than 700 fresh water species of fish, nearly 200 species of birds and 80 kinds of mammals have been discovered. The value of the animals, wood, fish, fruit and other commodities harbored by the reserve is estimated by one Peruvian environmental group at more than $10 billion.[33] The areas bordering the reserve are highly valued for their nontimber forest products.

Environmental groups in Peru, aided by like-minded organizations in the United States, contested the oil concession granted Texas Crude. They said the agreement violated a law signed by President Alberto Fujimori in 1990 that outlawed exploration for nonrenewable resources in natural reserves. In their view, a proposed contract between the national oil company **PetroPeru** and Texas Crude was void.

But PetroPeru had already entered the reserve to explore for oil. The environmental groups further alleged that PetroPeru had damaged the reserve during its exploration efforts. "Residual petrochemicals of high salinity are being discarded in the lower lands of the Yanayacu Grande exploratory zone without treatment or control," claimed the Peruvian Society of Environmental Law (Spda), an environmental group. Just north of the reserve, a residue depository built by PetroPeru leaked into the Corrientes River, poisoning the water and causing the deaths of several children, the group alleged.[34]

As a compromise, the environmental groups suggested that the Peruvian government swap the exploration tract inside the reserve for one outside its boundaries. At first, Texas Crude vehemently opposed such a swap. In a letter to Spda, the company derided suggestions that indigenous peoples living in the reserve would be hostile to Texas Crude's oil development plan. "I would imagine that even the dimmest bulb could perceive the desirable economic benefits which would flow to Peru if Peru rejoined the select group of oil exporting countries," said Scott Baum Jr., a Texas Crude vice president. And to the suggestion that the Peruvian government had violated the law in negotiating with Texas Crude, Baum shot back, "Please identify the culprits and bring them before the proper judicial authorities for prosecution to the fullest extent of the law."[35]

When Spda suggested negotiations should be undertaken to provide Texas Crude with a block outside the reserve, the company responded, "Perhaps your organization will advance the funds, time and personnel to this project. Please do not confine your activities, in this regard, to Peru." Just three months later, Texas Crude withdrew its offer to invest $400 million for oil exploration in the Peruvian Amazon. Peruvian Energy Minister Fernando Sanchez Albavera reported that the company's decision was a result of the pressure from environmentalists.

As in the Oriente of Ecuador, however, the oil development story is far from over in the Peruvian Amazon. **Edward Callan Interests** and **Halliburton Geophysical Services**, both based in Houston, Tex., reportedly have begun prospecting for oil in the upper Maranon River basin in northwestern Peru.[36] **Mobil** has a major exploration effort underway in the Huallaga basin of northern

Peru. **Santa Fe Energy Resources** and **Great Western Resources** also are seeking contracts with PetroPeru to explore for oil. **Royal Dutch Shell** is exploring for oil in southern Peru and is considering a return to the Camisea rain forest, where it had invested $175 million in exploratory drilling for natural gas before contract negotiations broke down with PetroPeru in 1989. **Occidental**, meanwhile, has had operations in the Peruvian rain forest for 20 years.

Chevron in Papua New Guinea

Perhaps the most ambitious effort to develop oil in an environmentally sensitive rain forest area is underway in Papua New Guinea. A consortium led by **Chevron** has been granted a production license for recent oil discoveries in a pristine rain forest area near Lake Kutubu in the country's southern highlands. Other members of the Kutubu Petroleum Development Project are **Broken Hill Properties** of Australia, **British Petroleum** and the **Mitsubishi Group**. Chevron and its partners reportedly have invested $1.4 billion in the project.

"We've tried to make this a model effort for development that is environmentally sound and socially responsible," says William Fraizer, the Kutubu project's director of environment and safety.[37] Exploration work has been carried out by helicopter, although a limited road network is in place for the production phase. The project also features a 159 mile gravity-fed pipeline drilled under river beds to the Gulf of Papua and then 25 miles offshore to a floating loading and storage facility. The underground route reportedly added tens of millions of dollars in construction costs but avoids impacts on mangrove ecosystems or the Neiru Wildlife Management Area.

For the Kutubu project, Chevron developed a comprehensive environmental plan and submitted it for government approval. The plan forbids Chevron employees to hunt animals or disturb plants near the project area. Contractors must take measures to preserve topsoil and prevent landslides during construction. Contractors also are required to prepare oil spill response plans for their work areas and have secondary containment systems for fuel storage areas. Bruce Bunting, vice president of the Asia and Pacific program of the World Wildlife Fund-U.S., has visited the Chevron project and was impressed. "They have gone to incredible lengths to minimize damage," he says.[38] Chevron has donated $1 million to the World Wildlife Fund to promote rain forest protection efforts.

Oil production from the Kutubu project began in August 1992. Initial production was 120,000 barrels a day; the reserve itself is estimated to contain 220 million barrels of oil. Chevron estimates that about 3,200 acres of rain forest will be disturbed by the project, including oil production facilities, a pipeline corridor and support facilities. Only 1,500 acres will be permanently deforested, according to the company.[39]

As has been the case in the western Amazon, however, oil development has caused considerable upheaval among inhabitants of Kutubu's rain forests in Papua New Guinea. Chevron official Steven North says the company has made

Box 4A

Building Better Corporate-Environmental Relationships

Not all relations between oil companies and conservation groups in rain forest areas are acrimonious. The International Union for the Conservation of Nature, for one, operates a support service to help developing countries write environmental impact statements for oil projects. The IUCN and the World Wildlife Fund also have advised large companies like **Chevron** and **British Petroleum** on protective measures for rain forests. "There's no reason why you shouldn't be able to take oil out of rain forests without damaging them," argues Jeff Sayer, director of the IUCN's Forest Conservation Program. Most of the countries with tropical rain forests are still below the threshold of basic economic activity needed to support their people, he said. "I find it hard to tell them they can't mine in a forest in Guinea because there are endemic frogs in it that the people in the North are concerned about."[1a]

In Belize, two U.S. companies have acted responsibly while searching for oil in a nature preserve, according to a conservation organization that owns much of the land. **Valco International** of Houston and **Pentagon Petroleum** of Baton Rouge, La., have a four year license to explore in an area covering 260,000 acres—much of it tropical rain forest—and to drill at least one test well. The Program for Belize owns 152,000 acres of protected land within the tract, although Belizean law allows mineral explorations anywhere on private land. Arnold Brown, the U.S. executive director of the Program for Belize, says that while his group is not happy about oil exploration in the conservation area, the government of Belize has agreed to several conditions requested by the group to minimize forest damage. No roads may be cut without permission of the program, for example, nor may any archaeological sites be disturbed. Dumping drillhole tailings or chemicals into waterways is prohibited as well. **Halliburton Energy Co.**, the subcontractor doing seismic exploration, has agreed not to use heavy machinery or to allow employees to carry weapons or hunt. Some of the trails being cut for exploration may end up being useful for survey work being performed by the Program for Belize.[2a]

extensive efforts to identify landowners in the Iagifu-Hedinia region. But in such a tribal society, several tribes can hold title to the same land at different times of year; one group might have hunting rights and another grazing rights. Some tribes have repudiated agreements with Chevron because of intertribal animosities and claims that Chevron has not fulfilled its promises.

Chevron has pledged $45 million to build a highway, schools and clinics. The 66 mile crushed-limestone highway—requested by local landowners—was only half-finished when oil production began. Violence in the region has increased because of outsiders who have traveled along the highway. Now the landowners want Chevron to police the road. Highlands tribes also want public access to a track cleared above the underground pipeline, but Chevron is reluctant to open up the track because of safety and environmental concerns. Several logging companies reportedly are trying to buy timber along the pipeline track. There are also disputes over who should pay for teachers' salaries in schools built by Chevron, how much should be paid to local tribes as royalties for oil production and whether Chevron should fulfill promises made—and broken—by the government to build airstrips, health centers and post offices in the oil area.

"The landowners feel they will be cheated out of their royalties and there are fears they may violently attack the project as they did at the Bougainville mine" in Papua New Guinea, warns Colleen Murphy-Dunning, a campaign coordinator for Rainforest Action Network. Murphy-Dunning visited the Kutubu area in late 1991. She says Chevron could face an "environmental disaster" if the pipeline were sabotaged.[40] Chevron has not discussed the potential for sabotage or accidents with the villagers, according to press accounts.

Chevron officials have expressed concern for what will ultimately become of Papua New Guinea's tribal peoples, however. James Harrington, Chevron's manager of land and government relations in Papua New Guinea, told *The Wall Street Journal* in 1992, "You put in roads, you introduce amounts of money that have never been seen before....It all invites change, and often it's not change that really helps people."[41]

Tribal leader Hewabe Siri is a symbol of the change that Harrington refers to. "They promised us much, but look around you: What has changed?," Siri wondered aloud. As the *Journal* article described him: "He sits on the porch of a hut decorated with magazine pictures of warriors in traditional tribal dress— nose bones, war paint and feathered headdresses. Mr. Siri sometimes dons such garb himself, but today he sips a Pepsi and waves an arm toward the rooting pigs and mud-splattered children in the red dirt. 'When our oil is gone and Chevron goes home, what will we have to show for it?'"[42]

Chapter Four Appendix

Oil Companies with Tropical Forest Operations or Policies

United States

AMOCO CORP.: Amoco, based in Chicago, Ill., has produced oil from rain forest areas in the Congo and plans to explore for oil in Gabon, reports Harry Partlow, Amoco's General Manager for Environmental Affairs and Safety.[43] Amoco also is involved in discussions with Colombia, Mexico and Indonesia regarding oil exploration. Amoco searched for oil unsuccessfully in the Peruvian Amazon in the 1970s, according to Spda, a Peruvian environmental group. Amoco also owns 30 percent of the Ok Tedi copper mine in Papua New Guinea. (See company summary in Chapter Five for details.)

ATLANTIC RICHFIELD CO.: Arco, based in Los Angeles, Calif., is developing a 494,000 acre tract in Pastaza in the Oriente region of Ecuador. An exploratory drilling operation was completed recently. The company has made significant finds of oil near Villano and Moretecocha and is negotiating terms for extraction. The Pastaza tract is on lands inhabited by Quichua Indians who have been involved in disagreements with Arco and the government about the boundaries of their land. Arco reported in late 1991 that it had cleared 500 acres of land and was taking special precautions to minimize disturbance.[44]

Rainforest Action Network cites a report by an Ecuadoran government commission, however, that says Arco has cleared 2,500 acres of forest for its exploration activities, felled 400,000 trees, created 300 miles of roads, destroyed agricultural subsistence lands (known as "purinas") as well as sites of Indian deities that are considered sacred. The Ecuadoran government signed a treaty with the Indians that promised compensation for damage caused by Arco's exploration activities, but the Indian group says it has not received the proceeds.[45]

Government troops were sent to the Pastaza area in July 1990 after threats of violence emerged. Arco said it received permission from the village of Moretecocha to drill at the site. But once construction began, nearby Sarayacu Indians "decided to extend their ownership claims to include this land," according to Arco's Chamberlain. After Sarayacu threats of violence, he says, the government placed troops at the well site "for the protection of all concerned, people at the rig, the Moretecochas as well as the Sarayacus."[46]

The Sierra Club Legal Defense Fund reports that Arco is now moving some of its exploratory operations north to a tract near the Curaray River, where the largest number of Huaorani Indians live. Sources from Petroecuador have indicated that a road may be extended south across the Curaray River to facilitate the development of Arco's wells, among others. The road would cut through the middle of Huaorani territory.[47]

Arco has presented its guidelines for oil development in Ecuador to the Center for Environmental Design Research, an independent group based at the University of California at Berkeley. The group found many positive elements in Arco's guidelines, but it also had some criticisms. The guidelines were developed 18 months after exploratory drilling had already begun, and they did not offer a specific strategy for implementation and monitoring of the guidelines. The center also found that Arco made little effort to present documentation on the social, cultural and public health conditions of the area, or to foresee the impacts of oil exploration on indigenous communities. The guidelines do exceed the environmental control requirements established by the Ecuadoran government, however.[48]

CHEVRON CORP.: Chevron, based in San Francisco, Calif., is the operator of a giant oil development complex in Papua New Guinea. The company has operations in former rain forest areas of Nigeria, and it is engaged in exploratory drilling in the Congo. Chevron also is a joint venture partner in **Caltex Pacific Indonesia**, which operates with **Texaco** in Indonesia.

Papua New Guinea: Chevron's Papua New Guinea exploration and development effort is in the Iagifu-Hedinia region. A consortium led by Chevron is producing oil from a rain forest area near Lake Kutubu in the country's southern highlands. Other members of the Kutubu Petroleum Development Project are **Broken Hill Properties** of Australia, **British Petroleum** and the **Mitsubishi Group**. Chevron and its partners reportedly have invested $1.4 billion in the project. Political risk insurance has been provided by the Overseas Private Investment Corp. and the Australian export credit agency. Oil production in Kutubu began in mid-1992. Chevron estimates that 3,200 acres of rain forest will be disturbed by the project, including oil production facilities, a pipeline corridor and support facilities. Only 1,500 acres will be permanently deforested, according to the company. (More information on Chevron's operations in Papua New Guinea appears on pp. 110-112 of this chapter.)

Indonesia: **Caltex Pacific Indonesia** is a partnership of Chevron and **Texaco** in Indonesia, serving as a contractor for the state-owned **Pertamina Oil Co.** The partnership has been operating in Indonesia since 1934 and was involved in the discovery and development of the giant Duri oilfield in Sumatra in 1941. Since 1939, Caltex has drilled more than 330 exploratory wells, resulting in 120 oil discoveries. Today, Caltex is Indonesia's largest oil producer, pumping nearly 700,000 barrels per day, accounting for 50 percent of Indonesia's oil production. Caltex has sought to use enhanced oil recovery to improve recovery rates from declining oilfields. About $2 billion has been invested in a 15,000 acre steamflood project at Duri. (Steamflooding is an alternative method of oil extraction; steam is injected into the ground to heat the oil and make it flow easily into production wells.) Chevron did not provide IRRC with information on the portion of Duri that is in rain forest.

The Congo: Chevron is conducting exploratory drilling in the Congo. It may contract with the International Union for the Conservation of Nature to conduct an environmental assessment and to identify measures to minimize impacts of oil drilling in the rain forest.

E.I. DU PONT DE NEMOURS & CO.: DuPont, based in Wilmington, Del., does not have active oil production facilities in rain forest areas, but its subsidiary, **Conoco**, is exploring for oil in the Congo, Gabon, Indonesia and Papua New Guinea. Conoco's concessions around the world range in size from several thousand acres to hundreds of thousands of acres. Until October 1991, Conoco was the operator of a partnership to explore for oil in the Oriente region of Ecuador and held a concession to Block 16. (See pp. 103-106 for details on Conoco's involvement in Ecuador.)

EXXON CORP.: Exxon, based in Irving, Tex., is not engaged in "any activities of consequence" in rain forest areas but is conducting exploration in forested areas of Gabon, Indonesia and southern Trinidad, according to company spokesman C.R. Ball.[49] One account of Exxon's activities in tropical countries says that company subsidiaries also are exploring for oil in Ecuador and have exploration/production operations in Colombia, Malaysia and Zaire.[50]

Exxon has an interest but is not the operator of exploration activities in Gabon. The oil industry in Gabon is working with the government to develop guidelines for operations in tropical forest areas. In Indonesia, seismic and drilling activities are carried out in both open, cultivated forest areas and remote forested locations. In southern Trinidad, Exxon is gathering seismic data in heavily forested areas in partnership with the state oil company and others.

Exxon planned to drill exploratory wells in 1989 in a historic area of the Peten region of Guatemala but pulled out after a government agency rescinded permission for drilling. Rainforest Action Network claims "an angry coalition of Guatemalan environmentalists and archaeologists" forced Exxon out of its exploration site in El Ceibal, a historic Mayan site. While the exploration was to have taken place in an area of archaeological significance, "all appropriate permits were obtained from proper Guatemalan government officials," reports Exxon's Ball. Permission was rescinded because of an internal government dispute between two agencies rather than because of rain forest considerations or "the manner in which we conduct our operations," Ball says. The government excused Exxon from the contract, and the company ceased operations in the area.

MAXUS ENERGY CORP.: Maxus, based in Dallas, Tex., became operator of Conoco's Block 16 Ecuadoran concession after Conoco pulled out in October 1991. Maxus also holds the concession to Block 22, which is mostly in Yasuni National Park. Spokesman Douglas Graham says Maxus is committed to carrying out the environmental protection program prepared by Conoco and approved by the Ecuadoran government.[51] (See pp. 106-108 for details on Maxus's plans for Ecuador).

MOBIL CORP.: Mobil, based in Fairfax, Va., is active in oil and gas development in rain forest areas of Ecuador, Peru and Papua New Guinea. Mobil's tracts in the Oriente region of Ecuador include Blocks 18 and 19. In Peru, Mobil is committed to spending up to $100 million through 1995 to explore for oil in the Huallaga Basin in the northern part of the country. About 75 percent of the area is forested, and Mobil describes it as having "thick and jungle-like vegetation in the lower areas and less so in the higher areas." In Papua New Guinea, Mobil has licenses to explore for oil in a 1 million acre area northwest of Chevron's discoveries in the southern highlands.

Peru: Mobil will complete two studies of environmental impact in Peru's Huallaga Basin, one for the exploration phase and a second before field development. Shining Path guerrillas attacked Mobil's exploration base in the Peruvian Amazon in December 1990, killing two people and destroying millions of dollars worth of computers and communications systems. Mobil returned to the area in 1991 and drilled its first exploration well late in the year.

Mobil's exploration program involves collecting 1,000 miles of seismic data. Clearing will be done by hand; wheeled vehicles will be used only in unusual situations. Helicopters will require 30-by-30 foot landing pads. The cleared areas will be allowed to regenerate after two months. The first exploratory well that Mobil drilled in the Peruvian Amazon was dry, and company spokesman Thomas Cooney says the company is reviewing its options, including abandoning further exploration there.[52] If Mobil does find oil, it will be responsible for construction of links to an existing pipeline in northern Peru. Mobil says its policy is to go beyond existing laws and regulations when hazards are detected and to provide adequate protection for the environment.[53]

OCCIDENTAL PETROLEUM CORP.: Occidental Petroleum, based in Los Angeles, Calif., has significant oil finds in at least six wells in Block 15 in the Oriente of Ecuador and has begun extracting oil from the block. Occidental also has operations in forested areas of Colombia and Peru. The company says its environmental procedures in other countries are functionally equivalent to those it must follow in the United States.

Ecuador: Occidental's Ecuadoran block is in a more developed area of the Oriente, about 10 miles from the refinery at Shushufindi. Consequently, fewer roads need to be built than in more pristine areas to the south. One well has been drilled near the town of Limoncocha. Buried pipelines will tie the wells together and the company will place the main line under the Napo River. Occidental is reinjecting its formation (produced) water. "If you look at most South American oil operations, the biggest environmental problem is the way people handle produced water," says Charles Goodwin, Occidental's environmental manager for international operations.[54]

Because its Limoncocha well is in a floodplain, Occidental's consultants in Ecuador recommended elevating the well approximately 30 feet because of the danger of flooding. Occidental reportedly elevated it only part of the way, however. The area was later flooded, and pit waste was flushed into the Jivino River, where Quichua Indians fish and drink. The following week, residents reported digestive illnesses, according to Judith Kimerling, who spent 18 months in the Oriente and wrote the book *Amazon Crude.*[55]

In another incident, Occidental paid two families a sum of money for rights in perpetuity to mine for sand on their land. Later interviews confirmed that the Indians did not understand the meaning of perpetuity, according to Kimerling. Occidental returned a year later and paid the same family to dump pit wastes. After the first rain, balsa trees in the area died, and people who drank from water sources in the vicinity reported illnesses, Kimerling says.

Rainforest Action Network reports that a Quichua Indian community has asked Occidental to repair environmental damage caused by its operations and to prepare an environment management plan in cooperation with Confeniae, the Federation of Native Communities of the Ecuadoran Amazon. RAN says Occidental has turned down these requests.[56]

Colombia: Occidental's Cano Limon operation in Colombia is a state-of-the-art operation with raised oil wells, lined waste pits and pollution monitoring wells, Goodwin reports. The operation reportedly is not in a rain forest, although 20,000 trees were felled in developing the project. Occidental has planted far more trees than that—250,000 so far. In June 1991, Occidental announced a joint venture with the Spanish oil company **Repsol** to explore a 249,000 acre block in Colombia in the eastern foothills of the Andes mountains, about 100 miles northeast of Bogota. It plans seismic exploration and has permission to drill an exploratory well.

Peru: Occidental has had operations in the Peruvian rain forest for 20 years. Since 1988 it has drilled 10 wells in the blocks in the northern part of the country's rain forest, investing $25 million. In 1989, 60,000 barrels a day were being pumped from these wells. Occidental plans to drill a total of 24 wells.

ORYX ENERGY CO.: Oryx Energy, based in Dallas, Tex., is developing a 500,000 acre tract (Block 7) of degraded rain forest in the Oriente region of Ecuador. It has hired an Ecuadoran company to perform an environmental baseline study to monitor ecosystem changes as a result of its activities. Block 7 is colonized with Spanish-speaking settlers but no indigenous groups, reports Stanley Blossom, Oryx's director of environmental affairs. Many small plots have been cleared by colonists to grow coffee, bananas and palms. In the absence of comprehensive Ecuadoran environmental standards, Oryx says it has been operating under strict North American standards. Drilling operations for the first exploration well have required "minimal disturbances" in the form of drilling locations and short drill roads off existing main roads, Blossom says. Use of a geotextile fabric to cover roads is expected to reduce deforestation by 70 percent. The company seeks to prevent water pollution by lining all mud pits with plastic and requiring that water from the mud pits meet "purity standards" before it is discharged. All future drilling will utilize closed-loop systems, minimizing or eliminating the use of open pits.[57]

PENNZOIL CO.: Pennzoil, based in Houston, Tex., is involved in a joint exploration venture in Papua New Guinea with **Trend International**, **Union Texas** and a Japanese company, **Teikoku**.

PENTAGON PETROLEUM CO.: Pentagon, based in Baton Rouge, La., and **Valco International**, of Houston, Tex., have a four year license to explore for oil in a 260,000 acre area of Belize. (See box on p. 111 for details.)

PHILLIPS PETROLEUM CO.: Phillips Petroleum, based in Bartlesville, Okla., describes its activities in rain forest areas as "minimal." It says it is exploring in

Gabon and Papua New Guinea but not in rain forest areas. Phillips explored unsuccessfully in the Peruvian Amazon in the 1970s, according to Spda, a Peruvian environmental group.

SANTA FE SOUTHERN PACIFIC CORP: Santa Fe Energy Resources, a subsidiary of Santa Fe Southern Pacific, based in Chicago, Ill., is negotiating with Peru to explore for oil in an area exceeding 4 million acres. Company spokesman James Ford says Santa Fe has not worked previously in rain forest areas. Most of its prior production has been in California, where Santa Fe is the largest independent oil and gas company.[58]

TEXACO INC.: Texaco, based in White Plains, N.Y., has been involved in oil production in Indonesia for more than 40 years and has had significant operations in Colombia and Ecuador for 20 years. Its environmental record in Ecuador, where it operated from 1964 to 1992, has been the focus of sharp criticism by some environmental groups. (See pp. 100-103 for more details on its Ecuadoran operation.) In June 1991, Texaco announced a new exploration partnership in Bolivia with **Mobil** and **Shell** to explore a 5,700 square mile tract of the Amazon. Texaco also is exploring for oil in protected areas of Panama and is said to be negotiating with Honduras as well.

Indonesia: On the Indonesian island of Sumatra, Texaco operates 90 oil fields, pumping about 650,000 barrels a day from 3,000 producing wells. **Chevron** and its subsidiary company **Caltex Pacific Indonesia** are partners in Texaco's Indonesian operations.

"To explore and develop these oil fields, we had to clear forests to make way for the operations and its infrastructure, which includes well sites, roads, plant facilities, pipelines, terminals, gathering and storage facilities, offices, housing, medical facilities and schools," reports D.E. Six, Texaco's vice president for Middle East/Far East operations. "Due to the size and nature of these operations, the area's ecosystem is impacted; however, we conduct our operations in a manner such that it minimizes unfavorable impact on the environment," Six says. No large scale reforestation has been done where operations are ongoing. "When the operations cease, it is our practice normally to return our operating areas to its original state if practical and as required by the government of the host country," Six says.[59]

Bolivia: Texaco's Bolivian project involves oil exploration in the 3.7 million acre Madidi block in the northwestern part of the country. Texaco holds a 30 percent interest in the Madidi block, **Mobil** and **Shell Bolivia** each hold a 30 percent interest, and **Bolivia Andina Petroleum** holds a 10 percent interest.

Panama: In Panama, Texaco is exploring in two onshore and offshore blocks totaling 1,700 square miles. The blocks overlap three protected areas and the lands of two Indian tribes. About 28 percent of the exploration area is inside La Amistad International Park, on the border with Costa Rica, and 17 percent overlaps the Palo Seco protected forest area. Offshore, 87 percent of the Texaco tract overlaps Bastimentos National Marine Park, which consists of islands and coral reefs. The Guayme and Teride Indians oppose the Texaco operation, but they have limited influence because they have no formal title to the land. The operation also has been criticized in the Panamanian press. One article reports that the National Law College has asked Panama's attorney general to investigate whether the contract between the government and Texaco violates the law. The contract allows the government to expropriate private land if Texaco needs it and the owners refuse to sell it. The contract was signed without consultation with Panama's environmental agency, Irenare, the article says.[60]

TEXAS CRUDE EXPLORATION INC: Texas Crude, based in Houston, Tex., sought to explore for oil in the northern Amazon jungle of Peru, much of which was in a national reserve. It withdrew from the area in September 1991 after acrimonious discussions with environmental groups. (See pp. 108-109 for details.)

UNOCAL CORP.: Unocal, based in Los Angeles, Calif., explored for oil briefly in the Oriente region of Ecuador but abandoned its installations there in early 1991, when it could not find enough commercially exploitable oil. Unocal has continuing geothermal operations in Indonesia and in a rain forest area near Mt. Apo on the island of Mindanao in the Philippines. The Mt. Apo area is the ancestral land of Lumad and Moro peoples and is the habitat for the endangered Philippine eagle.

Ecuador: Unocal cleared 78 acres of land of a 500,000 acre block (Block 13) in Ecuador between June 1989 and March 1991, when it suspended drilling. "We cleared only land which was absolutely necessary for narrow trails, helicopter pads, drill sites and our base camp," reports D.L. Hanley, Unocal vice president for health, environment and safety. Each unsuccesssful well site was rehabilitated with topsoil and reseeded to start reforestation of the sites.[61] Unocal reportedly is continuing discussions with the Ecuadoran government. Part of the Huaorani community of Tiquino has moved to the abandoned Unocal camp.[62]

Indonesia: Unocal has drilled 13 geothermal exploration wells on the island of Java in Indonesia since 1983, resulting in forest loss of 230 acres, reports Hanley. The Indonesian government has retained another company to construct the geothermal power plants, which is expected to result in another 42 acres of forest clearing. Unocal will replace deforested land on a one-to-one basis with land purchased in areas adjacent to existing forest.

VALCO INTERNATIONAL CORP.: Valco International of Houston, Tex., and **Pentagon Petroleum** of Baton Rouge, La., have a four year license to explore for oil in a 260,000 acre area of Belize. (See box on p. 111 for details.)

OTHER U.S. COMPANIES: Other U.S. companies involved in rain forest areas include **Great Western Resources** of Houston, Tex., which wants to explore for oil in Peru; **Hunt Oil Co.**, of Dallas, Tex., which is exploring for oil in the rain forests of Guyana; and **Murphy Oil Corp.** of El Dorado, Ark., and **Nomeco Ecuador Oil Co.**, a subsidiary of **CMS Energy Corp.**, based in Jackson, Mich., which have a 20 percent stake and 14 percent stake, respectively, in Block 16 in the Oriente of Ecuador.

Brazil

PETROBRAS: Braspetro, the international subsidiary of Petrobras, the state-owned oil company of Brazil, is exploring for oil in Block 14 of the Oriente region of Ecuador with the French firm **Elf-Aquitaine** and **Britoil**. Braspetro is waiting for **Maxus** to develop sufficient operating structure in an adjacent block before it proceeds further with oil development, which has been halted by force majeure. The Braspetro block is in the center of the Huaorani protectorate. Three Huaorani communities in the Cononaco River area reportedly have moved as a result of noise and destruction.[63] Petrobras also is drilling in the Brazilian Amazon near the Urucu River, a tributary of the Upper Amazon. The company struck oil in the area in 1987.

Canada

PETRO CANADA: Petro Canada, formerly a state-owned company and now publicly traded, explored for oil in the Oriente region of Ecuador but left in July 1991. Petro Canada has agreed to pay for military guard posts for five years to protect the area south of the Tiguino River from encroachment by settlers. It extended the Auca Road approximately six miles during its time in Ecuador. The Sierra Club Legal Defense Fund maintains that "Petro Canada's withdrawal was partly due to the campaign held in Canada by groups concerned with human rights violations, whose protests reached international bodies."[64]

France

BASIC PETROLEUM: Basic Petroleum is a French company incorporated in the Bahamas. Basic has 14 oil fields in operation in the Peten region of Guatemala, two of which are within the protected Maya Biosphere Reserve. Production within the reserve is between 3,000 and 4,000 barrels a day, reports Rodolfo Sosa, Basic's manager of Guatemalan operations. Sosa says the company has deforested about 15 acres in the reserve for its operations. Basic uses low-yield explosives and portable seismic lines during exploration and has built only "a few hundred meters of" secondary dirt roads, according to Sosa. Basic relies mostly on government roads for transportation of oil to the coast.[65]

ELF-AQUITAINE: Elf-Aquitaine, the French oil conglomerate, is France's largest oil company and one of the 10 largest in the world. It has rain forest operations in Gabon and Nigeria, and in Ecuador in association with **Petrobras**.

Ecuador: In Ecuador, Elf-Aquitaine Equateur has drilled four wells in Block 14 and conducted 1,400 miles of seismic survey, and it is now building production facilities. When the drilling phase was completed, surface oil deposits were skimmed by mechanical devices and treated with a chemical bioremediation technology developed by Elf-Aquitaine (which was used in Alaska after the Exxon *Valdez* oil spill). Some have questioned the use of such chemicals in freshwater that may be consumed by humans, and Elf-Aquitaine reportedly has stopped the bioremediation treatment.[66] Reforestation of native species has begun on one of the sites and will be extended to the other sites eventually, reports Bernard Tramier, Elf-Aquitaine's vice president for environmental affairs.[67]

No access roads were constructed during the exploration phase; all drilling equipment was transported to the site by helicopter. However, a 15 mile road already exists, heading east from the Auca Road to the Tiputini River. The road eventually may be connected to another road being built by **Maxus**. During the production phase, Elf-Aquitaine plans to build access roads, a production station and a 15 mile pipeline.[68]

Gabon and Cameroon: Elf-Aquitaine is a partner in the Gabon oil field operated by **Royal Dutch Shell**. (See Shell summary below for details.) In Cameroon, Elf-Aquitaine paid for a scientific study of rain forest canopies using a unique tree-top rafting system.

The Netherlands

ROYAL DUTCH SHELL: Royal Dutch Shell is the world's largest oil company, with interests in 1 million square miles of concessions in more than 50 countries. Shell produces 5 percent of the world's oil and gas. The Royal Dutch Shell group of companies is a decentralized organization of approximately 2,000 companies. Operating companies are responsible for the performance and long-term viability of their operations. They do, however, adhere to a Group Statement of General Business Principles, which says the companies will "promote protection of environments which may be affected by the development of their activities and seek continuous improvement in efficiency of use of natural resources and energy."

Shell has oil operations or exploration underway in tropical rain forest areas of Brunei, Colombia, Gabon, Guatemala, Nigeria, Peru and Zaire, and in tropical dry forests in Burma, Madagascar and Thailand. Shell's U.S. subsidiary, **Pecten**, recently explored unsuccessfully for oil in Papua New Guinea and has left the country.

Brunei: Shell's operations in Brunei date back to 1927, when oil was discovered at the Seria field. Seria is in a coastal, cultivated area and is still producing oil. **Brunei Shell** has an ongoing exploration program that encompasses rain forest areas.

Burma: In Burma, Shell's exploration is in the Irrawaddy Delta, where there is a dry forest on the edge of a concession. Shell began exploratory drilling in mid-1991.

Colombia: Shell explored for oil in a rain forest area in the Putumayo Basin in southern Colombia in the mid-1980s, but those tracts have been relinquished. Shell subsidiary **Hocal SA** is producing oil in the Upper Magdalena Valley, a settled agricultural area. The wells there produced 72,000 barrels a day in 1990. A pipeline from Upper Magdalena to Vasconia was completed in 1990. A second pipeline to Covenas on the Caribbean coast was completed in 1992. Shell also has an interest in the Cano Limon field near Llanos, operated by **Occidental Petroleum**. Cano Limon produced 208,000 barrels a day in 1990.

Gabon: Shell has a major oil development in the rain forests of Gabon. The Rabi oilfield started operation in 1989 and is producing 140,000 barrels a day. Baseline ecological studies and an environmental impact assessment were completed before the field was developed. The World Wildlife Fund and the International Union for the Conservation of Nature were consulted in the development of an environmental management plan.

Guatemala: **Shell Exploration BV** (Guatemala) signed a production sharing agreement in 1990 to explore more than 2,000 square miles in the Lake Izabal area. Lake Izabal is a primary site for the rapidly expanding ecotourism business in Guatemala. Wetlands near the lake support a diverse range of flora and fauna, howler and spider monkeys, crocodiles and manatees and many species of birds. The wetlands zone is a nationally unique habitat and particularly vulnerable because of its small size and dependency on a fragile hydrological balance.

A detailed environmental impact assessment prepared by Shell Exploration BV was not approved by the national environmental agency, Conama, because the assessment did not meet the legal requirements for such a study, reports Hilda Rivera, the Central American representative of Conservation International.[69] Conama has requested that specialists complete a new study before seismic operations can begin.

The initial environmental impact assessment prepared by Shell Exploration BV was quite detailed. "Within the contract area," it explained, "there are a diverse range of habitats, some of which are extremely sensitive to seismic activities or other forms of disturbance and will therefore require the highest levels of environmental protection." Should seismic operations be required, a detailed plan will be discussed with environmental authorities to ensure "acceptability of the operation," the assessment stated. "Close liaison will be necessary to ensure that future exploration and possible oil field development plans are consistent with other long-term developments." Sustainable development and environmental protection projects are planned for portions of the contract area.

Hills bordering the Lake Izabal area are forested or partly deforested by slash-and-burn agriculture. Seismic lines are planned to be cut through 35 miles of forested areas. Clearance of vegetation for seismic lines, when necessary, will be kept to three feet wide. The cutting of trees is to be avoided wherever possible by adjusting the seismic shothole configuration. Clearance of seismic lines in or adjacent to wetlands or forest areas could allow post-operation access and encroachment of subsistence farmers. "Closure of access in these areas, impact controls and monitoring of these areas will be agreed with the authorities," the environmental assessment stated. No bulldozers or other earth moving equipment will be used except to maintain existing tracks.

The environmental assessment also said that complaints by local people will be dealt with swiftly, including those involved in agriculture, gaming, fishing and tourism. Liaison committees will be established to provide for regular consultation. About 300 temporary jobs will be available to local people for a projected six month period of seismic survey.

Shell Exploration BV has rehabilitated a village health center and will help it procure a water chlorination system. A well is set to be drilled in 1993, either in the lake or on shore. Studies of fish populations and flora and fauna are also planned. Finally, Shell Exploration BV has sponsored an archaeological study that has uncovered many important sites.

Madagascar: Shell is exploring in dry tropical forest in two blocks in Madagascar: the Karoo Corridor, where it drilled a well in 1991, and Majunga Central, where it has performed 3,400 miles of seismic testing. The company says it conducted a full environmental impact assessment before the operation began. The World Wildlife Fund reports that seismic surveys were "clearly carried out with the intention of causing as little damage as possible to the environment." The use of crooked line techniques allowed the flexibility of avoiding particularly sensitive areas by going around them. Any cutting of vegetation was done by hand.

Nigeria: Shell has been operating in Nigeria since the 1950s. Activity has centered in densely settled areas of southeast Nigeria, where vegetation is predominantly mangrove swamps. Pockets of rain forest in the area have been mapped, and special environmental and monitoring assessments have been carried out in vulnerable areas. The Ogoni, an indigenous tribe, have demanded compensation from Shell for alleged past environmental damage to their land. Eighty Ogoni were killed by Nigerian government soldiers during a protest in 1990 to press their demands. Shell spokesman Alan Jacobs says compensation for past environmental damage is a matter between the Nigerian government and its people. Shell operates the joint venture with the **Nigerian National Petroleum Corp.**, **Elf-Aquitaine** and **Agip**.

Peru: Shell invested $175 million in drilling for natural gas in the Camisea rain forest area in southeastern Peru, but it left the country in 1989 after talks over developing the resource broke down. **PetroPeru** has invited Shell to develop the huge field, but Shell has not decided whether to return. Survival International, an environmental group based in London, reported in late 1992 that Shell and PetroPeru had resumed negotiations to commence drilling in the fields. Shell declined to comment on these discussions.

An assessment by a World Wildlife Fund consultant of the impact of developing Camisea concluded that local people would be "severely affected" by the development and their needs would have to be addressed before the arrival of thousands of workers in the area, if the project continues. Major problems include epidemiological control to prevent spread of diseases, granting territorial rights to various native groups and providing compensation for the extraction of resources.[70]

Thailand: Shell's Sirikit field in Thailand is in an agricultural area, producing 22,000 barrels a day. It is also exploring the Khorat Plateau, a dry forest area.

Zaire: Shell has a joint venture with **Petrofina** as an operator in rain forest areas.

United Kingdom

BRITISH GAS: British Gas has operations in Ecuador and Gabon. It is also a partner in operations by **Enterprise Petroleum**, another British company, in Laos and Sumatra.

Ecuador: British Gas was the first petroleum company in Ecuador to release an environmental audit of its exploration activities. It became involved in Ecuador in 1986 when it purchased some of **Tenneco's** operations. It drilled three wells in 1986 and made one small discovery of oil. Its activities are now dormant while the company decides whether to develop the oil or drill more exploration wells, according to Steven Larcombe, the company's divisional manager. The company's exploration permit expired in April 1992.[71]

Luis Vargas, a representative of the Indian confederation Confeniae, told the *Financial Times* in August 1991 that British Gas has "done a lot of damage in our forest."[72] Vargas said the company called for and received military protection after armed tribesmen threatened British Gas workers. Larcombe confirms the incident.

Gabon: British Gas is exploring in rain forests in the 1.2 million acre Abanga block in the northeastern part of Gabon, not far from Shell's Rabi oilfield. It has drilled four wells in Gabon but has not yet made a major find. Larcombe says that Abanga is not as pristine a rain forest area as some in Ecuador. British Gas is using native trees from a nearby nursery to reforest areas where trees have been felled, and it is making special efforts to preserve topsoil.

BRITISH PETROLEUM: British Petroleum (BP) has interests in three rain forest projects for which production is planned or taking place: the Hides Gas project in the Western Highlands of Papua New Guinea, operated by BP; the Kutubu project also in Papua New Guinea, operated by **Chevron** (see pp. 110-112 for details); and the Sanagatta coal project in Indonesia, operated by Kaltim Prima Coal, a subsidiary of **RTZ Corp.** (see RTZ summary in the mining chapter for details). BP also is conducting exploration or seismic activity in Indonesia on the island of Sulawesi and in the Congo. It also has operations in Colombia, Malaysia, the Philippines, Singapore, Thailand and Vietnam but reportedly not in rain forest areas. BP has issued an internal environmental guidance document that contains guidelines for operations in rain forests.

Papua New Guinea: BP is developing the Hides gas project to produce electricity for the Porgera gold development project, operated by **Placer Dome Inc.** (See the Placer Dome summary in the mining chapter for more details.) About 37 acres has been affected by exploratory drilling at various sites and roughly 25 acres involved some forest clearance, according to BP spokesman Charles Nicholson. In addition to the Hides site, BP has drilled at five other sites in Papua New Guinea, but only Hides is in virgin rain forest. The other sites have been abandoned. No local people have been displaced as a result of the exploration program. At Hides, gas will be piped from a mountainous wellsite to a gas plant and turbine generator in the valley floor. A strip has been cleared down the mountainside for construction of the pipeline. Supplies for pipeline construction were dropped by helicopter, eliminating the need to construct an access road. Altogether, the construction project may clear up to 108 acres of forest, Nicholson estimates.[73]

Indonesia: In Sulawesi, BP has disturbed an estimated 37 acres of forest for seismic exploration of swamp forests. Helicopters were used for access into the area, requiring landing pads of 100 feet by 100 feet about every mile. Narrow, hand cut seismic lines were used with portable drilling gear and recording equipment.

Chapter 5

Mining in the Tropics

By the turn of the century, an estimated 100,000 square miles of the earth's surface—an area the size of Oregon—will have been disturbed by mining. Yet vast mineral wealth has just begun to be exploited in tropical countries like Brazil, Indonesia and Papua New Guinea. Mining can be especially lucrative—and destructive—in tropical forested nations. Multinational companies are expanding mining operations in the tropics because of vast untapped resources as well as the added attraction of comparatively low labor costs and less stringent environmental regulations.

Mining can be lucrative for host countries as well. Bolivia derived up to 70 percent of its export earnings from tin mining until the price of tin crashed in 1985, and it has since liberalized its investment policies to attract more foreign investment in mining. Papua New Guinea, from 1972 to 1988, derived 17 percent of its internally generated revenue, 45 percent of its export income and 12 percent of its gross domestic product from the Bougainville copper mine, partly owned by **RTZ Corp.**, the world's largest mining company.[1] But prosperity has its price. Philip Hughes, director of environmental science at the University of Papua New Guinea, describes the Bougainville mine as "an economic godsend—and an environmental disaster."[2] The mine was shut down in 1989.

The scope of environmental woes from mining in the world's developed nations is just beginning to be fully understood. Now environmental groups are pointing out that significant damage can occur from large-scale mining in developing nations as well, including irreparable damage to rain forests, human health and forest river systems and watersheds. Nevertheless, tremendous unexploited resource potential remains in tropical forested nations. On the Indonesian island of Irian Jaya, for instance, the mineral wealth is worth at least $100 billion, estimates Jim Bob Moffett, chairman of **Freeport McMoRan**, a multinational mining company based in New Orleans, La. If Freeport decided to walk away from its $1 billion investment there, "the Indonesian government would simply turn it over to someone else," Moffett believes. "They'd be standing in line to do it."[3]

Environmental Impacts of Mining

Many U.S., Canadian and European mining companies are grappling with the environmental challenges posed by mining in rain forest areas. These companies (profiled in the appendix of this chapter) include: **Alcan**, **Alcoa**, **Amoco**, **Brascan**, **Freeport McMoRan**, **RTZ** and **Royal Dutch Shell**. When carefully planned and executed, mining operations need not cause more damage than other kinds of development in the rain forest. In some instances, however, a lack of environmental planning and inadequate restorative measures can create a permanent blight on the landscape.

Large areas next to mines must be cleared to dispose of tailings. Heavy metals such as arsenic, cadmium, lead and zinc can leach out of these tailings and contaminate sources of food and drinking water. Consequently, mining areas often are associated with elevated rates of illness and death among humans in neighboring communities.[4] Waste ponds that prevent tailings from leaching into water supplies can still cause natural resource damage. If not covered, tailings with poisonous residues can kill birds and other animals that come to the ponds to feed.

Mining also brings social disruption to native cultures with the introduction of a cash economy, new diseases and a new social structure. Death and destruction caused by an influx of 50,000 migrant miners—"garimpeiros"—among the Brazilian Yanomami Indians is a case in point. Some 2,000 Yanomami—more than 15 percent of the tribal population—have perished since 1988, largely victims of malaria, yellow fever and hepatitis.[5]

Wildcat miners are not the only ones seeking to encroach on Indian lands, however; many large companies want to mine there as well. A 1987 study by Brazil's Ecumenical Center for Documentation and Information counted 560 mining permits in Brazil—34 percent of which were held by multinational companies. More than half of the permits were on lands recognized by presidential decree as Indian territory. Another 1,685 mining applications were pending on Indian lands, including 418 permits in the largely undisturbed state of Amazonas.[6] At the time of the study, most companies were still in the exploration phase of project development; only six had started to mine. Thus, the effects of mining—in the Amazon rain forest at least—are just beginning to take their toll.

(Two of the most active companies listed in the 1987 Brazilian study were the partners **Anglo American/Bozzano Simonsen**, with 117 permits, and **Brascan**, with 41 permits. Brascan, a large Canadian mining company, holds mining rights covering 179,000 acres in Brazil, including 140,000 acres in rain forest areas of Rondonia. **British Petroleum** sold its interests in the Brascan permits in 1990.)

Two mining research experts have summarized the international situation this way: "On every continent, sites of mining, smelting or other large scale waste-generating activities may be found with potential for creating highly contaminated primary waste deposits; secondary and tertiary contamination in soil, groundwater and surface water; and deleterious consequences for human health and ecosystems. The immense costs associated with historic sites of contamination in the western United States clearly point out the benefits of avoiding such problems elsewhere."[7]

The largest Superfund site in the United States is in fact a complex of abandoned copper and silver mines and a smelting complex in Montana. It has polluted an area one-fifth the size of Rhode Island as well as a 120 mile stretch of the Clark Fork River near Yellowstone National Park. Similar cleanup problems may result from large-scale mining operations in tropical forested nations, where the emphasis often is on getting out the ore now and dealing with the associated waste later. The social repercussions can be devastating. Four prominent examples follow.

Gold and Copper at Bougainville

Bougainville island is 500 miles off the coast of Papua New Guinea. **CRA Ltd.**, an Australian mining company, operated a huge copper and gold mine on the island from 1972 to 1989. (**RTZ** holds a 49 percent interest in CRA.) Bougainville islanders engaged in civil disobedience at the mine from the first day of prospecting there in 1969. Twenty years later, a bloody sabotage campaign led by a former mine employee, Francis Ona, caused the mine to close.

Controversy over the Bougainville mine galvanized the efforts of island separatists, who have long sought independence from Papua New Guinea. The Papua New Guinea government funneled only 1 percent of the mine's profits back to the islanders, while keeping 58 percent for itself. The sabotage campaign that led to closure of the mine in 1989 has deprived the government of these profits— and 40 percent of its export revenues. A subsequent military invasion in 1989 and 1990 by government forces reportedly destroyed thousands of villagers' homes on Bougainville island. Moreover, an economic embargo—still in force— reportedly has claimed the lives of thousands of islanders who lack the necessary medicine to treat illnesses.

Bougainville islanders have sought $11.5 billion for environmental, health and community damages purportedly caused by the mine's operation. About 11,600 acres of rain forest and agricultural land were disturbed, 800 people lost land rights in the mine tailings area, and 1,400 fishermen had their livelihood jeopardized by tailings dumped into the Kawerong and Jaba Rivers. The tailings contain heavy metals such as copper, zinc, cadmium, mercury and molybdenum, as well as sulfur, arsenic and mercury.

Hundreds of millions of tons of mine tailings and waste rock were dumped near the mine or deposited in the Jaba River Valley. Sediment has entered the Kawerong-Jaba river system, causing the Jaba River bed to rise more than 130 feet in some places. Leaching from the tailings has traveled 25 miles and spilled into the ocean at Empress Augusta Bay. Copper tailings with concentrations greater than 500 parts per million now cover approximately 50,000 acres of the ocean bay. Plant life near the shore has been destroyed, although ocean fish apparently have been spared.

The *Australian Financial Review* reported in 1988 that entire villages had been moved and rebuilt on tailings down river from the mine and that "crops grow only after heavy application of artificial fertilizer to the highly acidic soil."[8] During a 1988 visit to the Bougainville mine, Papua New Guinea's environment minister,

Perry Zeipe, pronounced the pollution "dreadful and unbelievable." The Jaba River was "full of all kinds of chemicals and wastes" and the people had been forced to abandon traditional fishing, he said in an account to the *Post-Courier* newspaper. A visiting scientist concluded that virtually "all aquatic life in the Jaba Valley has been killed" and that it would be impossible to restock rivers in the area until long after the mine's closure.[9]

For its part, **RTZ** says that it "has continually aimed to minimize the extent of environmental disturbance," as outlined in legal agreements, and that it is committed to stabilizing and revegetating all the waste areas "when possible." But with the mine now closed, no remedial work is being done, reports Roger Moody of PaRTiZans, a citizens group in London that monitors RTZ's activities worldwide.[10] While RTZ says the Bougainville operation complied with the relevant laws of Papua New Guinea, no environmental impact studies were performed before construction of the mine, because none was required.

There is talk of reopening the mine, but the question of royalties and compensation to Bougainville islanders has not been settled. It would take up to two years and $300 million to reopen the mine, *Multinational Monitor* reported in 1992.[11]

Iron Ore in Carajás

The Carajás iron ore operation in Brazil is another example of how mining can lead to tremendous environmental and social upheaval. In 1970, **U.S. Steel** joined with **Companhia Vale do Rio Doce**, a Brazilian government-owned mining company, to form **Amazonia Mineracao**. The joint venture sought to exploit the immense iron ore potential of the Carajás Range in the northern state of Para. U.S. Steel later bailed out (in 1977 before mining began), but the World Bank came through with a $304 million loan for the Carajás project in 1982.

The Carajás mining project was conceived as a part of a much larger development project called the Grande Carajás Project, which was designed to fund development of mining, metallurgy, cement production, logging, agriculture and ranching in the tropical forested region. **Alcoa**, among others, purchases minerals from this project. Most observers agree that the project has degraded the environment severely as well as the lives of indigenous people in the region. As the Carajás iron ore mine and railroad were built, thousands of unemployed people migrated from northeast Brazil, driving indigenous people off their lands. The Brazilian government was supposed to demarcate and protect the lands of about 10,000 Indians in the region, but by 1986 less than half of their lands had achieved such status.

Garimpeiros contaminated food and drinking water supplies of the Indians by dumping cyanide—used to separate gold from tailings—into rivers and streams. They also tangled with large landowners who had moved to the region to start cattle ranches. More than 1,000 murders have been recorded in the interior of Brazil since 1980, with no area accounting for more assassinations than the one around Carajás. In some towns, gunmen make price lists available for killings, offering different rates for union leaders, priests, lawyers and town and state legislators.[12]

The Carajás project has posed serious environmental consequences as well. Pig-iron companies fell vast amounts of forest to make charcoal as fuel for blast furnaces. Between 5 million and 7 million acres of land was deforested in the area around the Carajás project by 1986. One pig-iron company, **Cosipar** (part of the **Itaminas** group), consumes up to 123,500 acres of forest a year to make charcoal. Brazil's **Companhia Vale do Rio Doce (CVRD)**, which invested in Cosipar, now acknowledges a serious deforestation problem. A memo by the CVRD's Superintendent for the Environment states, "We know the companies building pig-iron factories are not taking any real steps for reforestation, and even if they have this intention, there still does not exist sufficient agroforestry knowledge to start large reforestation projects in the short term."[13]

Even if the full environmental cost of deforestation were included in the price of charcoal, a World Bank study concluded that "it is by no means clear that the (pig iron) plants would remain viable." In fact, such projects would be considered profitable only if the economic value of the forest is set at zero.[14] The Brazilian government originally planned to allow scores of smelters to operate on the edge of the Carajás project area. But now that the environmental and economic impacts of these facilities are being considered, only a handful are in operation. (A downturn in the economy has also slowed completion of the smelters.) As an alternative to charcoal-fueled smelters, the Brazilian government has considered converting some pig-iron smelters to use electricity—because of the abundance of hydroelectric power in the region. The dams themselves were created by flooding tropical forest areas, however.

CVRD has proposed a 10 year, $1 billion plan to reforest degraded areas and make the charcoal production process "sustainable" by creating plantations of quick-growing trees. Gustavo Bessa, CVRD's general manager for forestry, reports that the government-owned company expects to plant 1.7 million acres of eucalyptus and pine plantations to feed pig-iron smelters and the pulp industry, with 740,000 acres of natural forest remaining undisturbed. Toward that end, CVRD is experimenting with 250 species of exotic and native trees and plants to see which are best adapted to the area's soil and climate. The company has also signed contracts with the Japanese trading giant **Nissho-Iwai** and firms from Norway and Finland to reforest and harvest future plantation wood.[15] Altogether, CVRD has spent more than $65 million on conservation projects in the restricted region.

As for the garimpeiros, Brazilian President Fernando Collor de Mello ordered the army in 1990 to dynamite airstrips used by the interlopers. But there were so many areas where the miners could move undetected that only a fraction were forced off native Indian land.[16] Others fled and later returned to the mineral-rich area.

In 1992, just before the international "Earth Summit" in Rio de Janeiro, Collor decreed a 37,000 mile area as a Yanomami reserve, straddling the states of Amazonas and Roraima. Then, in early 1993, Collor launched a second effort to drive garimpeiros off the Yanomami's land. Brazilian police and military evacuated an estimated 3,000 miners (out of 11,000 present) in the first 10 days of March alone. Brazil's Air Force also closed the airspace over the Yanomami reserve to private planes and installed a radar system to monitor the area for violations.[17]

Critics of the evacuation say that garimpeiros will return to the reserve if they cannot find other sources of employment. Many tin and gold mining companies continue to purchase ore from garimpeiros as well, thereby contributing indirectly to degradation of the rain forest and the social problems caused by their activities. **Brascan**, for one, acknowledged in December 1991 that it had purchased cassiterite ore from garimpeiros "in the recent past."[18]

A recent report by Amnesty International, the human rights organization, offers a grim outlook for the beleaguered Yanomami. "As the pressure for minerals and timber increases," the report says, indigenous groups become more vulnerable to armed attack. These attacks are often carried out by private agents, including gunmen hired by land claimants, timber merchants or mining interests. They have gone almost entirely unpunished—in fact, state-level authorities have even colluded with them."[19]

'Trend Setting' in Irian Jaya

In Irian Jaya, **Freeport McMoRan** holds a mining concession totaling 6.5 million acres, or roughly 7 percent of the Indonesian island territory. It has operated a gold, silver and copper mine in Irian Jaya for more than 20 years. The Mt. Ertsberg mine, now nearly 2,000 feet deep, constitutes Irian Jaya's largest industry, with deposits of metals estimated to be worth more than $20 billion. Freeport also is investing $500 million for a new gold mine at Mt. Grasberg, where it expects to mine a record 57,000 to 66,000 tons of ore a day during the second half of 1993, increasing to 90,000 tons a day by 1996.

Freeport has publicized its plans for Irian Jaya in a full-page advertisement that appeared in *The New York Times*, *The Wall Street Journal* and other newspapers in early 1993. Under the ban-

Figure 12

Freeport McMoRan Advertisement About its Indonesian Concessions

ner headline, "Trend Setter," the company says: "Sometimes the best way to set a trend is to follow one. Our new exclusive contract of work in Indonesia...sits squarely on line with the New Guinea Mineral Trend—a trend that has already yielded massive finds and provided Freeport-McMoRan with the largest single gold reserve and one of the largest copper reserves of any mine in the world."

The Freeport concession area is home to many indigenous rain forest peoples, including the Dani, Hupla, Moni and Yali, many of whom had little contact with the outside world before the Mt. Ertsberg mine was opened. Freeport began its operations in Irian Jaya in 1972, clearing rain forests for a port, airport, 63 mile road and pipeline. It also created the company towns of Tembagapura, Timika and Kwami Lama. The company says it has promoted agricultural and economic development programs in the area and decreased the traditional slash-and-burn activities of local peoples. "We believe that the rain forest saved this way exceeds the area disturbed by our operations," remarks James Miller, Freeport's vice president for environmental affairs. The Mt. Ertsberg mine employs 680 Irianese people, 350 of whom are local. "We expect this number will increase dramatically with time as the company's job training programs continue," Miller predicts.[20]

Freeport's development of the Mt. Ertsberg mine has not been without conflict, however. The Amungme, an indigenous group whose traditional hunting ground overlaps part of the mining complex, sabotaged Freeport's operation in the 1970s, leading to government reprisals. Many mountain villagers who resettled away from Tembagapura (one of the company towns) reportedly became ill as they adjusted to a new lowlands climate and to an impoverished cash economy. Others who stayed near the mine allegedly were told to stop consuming sago (their staple food) and to drink only rainwater because of pollution from the mine. Freeport has provided barrels to some of these villagers to assist in the collection of rainwater.[21]

To compensate for any disruption to traditional hunting and gathering activities, Freeport has constructed schools, clinics, houses, markets and other facilities for some of the villagers. It provides free medical care to about 6,000 people a month and teaches people how to treat or avoid tropical diseases such as malaria. (One press account says 38 villagers died of malaria in one month after 1,000 residents of lower-Waa village were relocated to coastal lowlands.) Freeport purchases about 60 tons of fruits, vegetables and fish from local markets, and it has demonstrated ways to increase agricultural productivity by using high-yield farming techniques, better tillage techniques and natural fertilizer methods.

Some environmental groups maintain, however, that Freeport's mining operation is threatening the rain forest. Its dominant presence in the region attracts small businesses and an increasing population that cuts trees for housing, agriculture and firewood. In 1989, the company received permission to explore 6 million acres adjacent to the existing mine. This will lead to construction of new roads and other development measures that fell trees, environmentalists fear.

Their greatest concern, however, is the disposal of tailings and the residuals of solvents (used in the flotation process to extract ore) that are routinely released into a series of rivers that flow into the Arafura Sea on Irian Jaya's southern coast. Organic chemical solvents and metals such as arsenic, cadmium, copper, lead and mercury are contaminating these rivers. And as the new mine at Mt. Grasberg is developed, the volume of tailings and solvents disposal is likely to increase dramatically.

Freeport reportedly waited for 18 years before conducting a study of the impact of tailings disposal on neighboring water quality and aquatic life. In January 1991, it acknowledged in a meeting with environmental groups that tailings dumped in the Ajikwa River have increased its sediment load by two to three times. Freeport's own studies indicate, however, that the chemical and biological state of the Ajikwa River is nearly identical to two other nearby pristine rivers, although some consultants have criticized these studies as inadequate. Ann Maest, a staff scientist with the Environmental Defense Fund, fears that arsenic and lead could become mobilized after deposition in floodplain sediments, leading to further contamination of river and groundwater supplies.[22]

Rainforest Action Network says that Freeport has not opened its Irian Jayan operations to sufficient scrutiny from environmental organizations, a claim that Freeport disputes. In a June 1992 letter to RAN, the company said at least 40 site visits by more than 200 people had taken place since 1990. "Indeed, inspection of our operation by *responsible* and *reasonable* organizations has been ongoing." (Freeport's emphasis.)[23] Examples the company gave include representatives of the international news media, environmental groups, ambassadors, government and university officials, naturalists, development bankers, financiers and securities analysts.

Rainforest Action Network acknowledges that a site visit in July 1991 by the Indonesian Forum for Environment, an Indonesian environmental group, "was an encouraging start." But it says that further meetings with the group have been delayed and that one of two independent scientists approved by the Indonesian Ministry of Population and the Environment to be part of an inspection team has been turned down by Freeport.[24]

Is Ok Tedi OK?

Ok Tedi Mining Ltd. is the world's fifth largest producer of copper. **Amoco** owns 30 percent of the huge mine in central Papua New Guinea through its **Amoco Minerals** subsidiary. Other owners of the mine are Australia's **Broken Hill Properties**, with 30 percent; the Papua New Guinea government, 20 percent; and a German consortium consisting of **Metallgesellschaft**, 7.5 percent; **Degussa**, 7.5 percent; and the German government, 5 percent. A German parliamentary delegation has called upon the German government to sell its 5 percent stake in the Ok Tedi mine because of the pollution it has caused.[25]

Kennecott discovered copper at Ok Tedi in 1968 but never developed it. Soaring commodities prices led to the creation of the Ok Tedi Mining consortium in 1981. In recent years, copper output from the Ok Tedi mine has been approximately 25 million tons annually, with gross sales as high as $536 million and profits of $55 million.

"Weak [environmental] protection plans, coupled with a long series of ecological disasters, starting in 1984, have endangered the natural resources that sustain over 40,000 indigenous peoples living near the Ok Tedi and Fly Rivers," maintains David Hyndman, an Australian anthropologist who has studied the Wopkaimin people who live and work near the mine.[26] Hyndman reports that the Ok Tedi mine discharges tailings directly into waterways with extremely high pollution levels. The mine processes 130,000 tons of ore per day, resulting in 15 million to 20 million tons a year of increased sediment load into the Fly River. Pollution from suspended sediments and heavy metals exceeds U.S. standards by 10,000 percent and threatens subsistence staples such as fish, crustaceans, turtles and crocodiles as well as gardens and sago palms growing along riverbanks, according to Hyndman.

Mining operations at Ok Tedi are exempt from Papua New Guinea's environmental laws. Instead, the rules it must follow are set out in a series of special decrees between the mine and the government. One such agreement in 1980 required that tailings be maintained permanently in an on-site tailings dam. But in January 1984, a 50 million ton landslide dumped tailings piles containing cyanides, copper and other metals into the Ok Ma River. Another landslide in 1989 destroyed a temporary tailings dam that had prevented the release of waste rock into the Ok Tedi River. The mine's operators now contend that seismic activity and heavy rainfall in the mountainous region would make any new dam vulnerable to landslides. Moreover, the new dam's cost—$450 million—would be prohibitively expensive, they say. (A slightly less expensive alternative would be to transport wastes about 60 miles to flatlands and deposit them in swamps, at a cost of $360 million.) As a result, about 80,000 tons of sediment is dumped into the rivers each day.

Owners of the Ok Tedi mine say they are in compliance with a government agreement that sets limits of 940 milligrams of suspended sediment per liter and dissolved copper limits of 6 micrograms per liter. The problem is not with the sediment per se, according to the mine's operators, but with copper contained in the sediment. They believe the best option is to recover more copper from the sediment before it is released.

Discarded mine tailings from the Ok Tedi mine eventually flow into the Torres Strait, a body of water between Papua New Guinea and the northern tip of Australia. Torres Strait has a substantial prawn fishing industry, valued at $14 to $18 million annually. A 1989 Sydney University research survey concluded that cadmium and copper levels exceeded acceptable levels in prawns, seabed and sediments in the Torres Strait. The report further suggested that heavy metal pollution could be a serious problem and recommended further investigation to prevent damage to the food chain and marine environment.[27]

Another potentially serious environmental problem at the Ok Tedi mine concerns the release of large quantities of sodium cyanide into the water. In 1984, 2,700 15 gallon drums loaded with cyanide capsized on the Fly River, and only 117 were recovered. Five days after that incident, a bypass valve was left open at the mine site, allowing more than 1,000 cubic meters of highly concentrated cyanide waste to flow into the Ok Tedi River. Hyndman says operators were silent about the spill until dead fish, prawns, turtles and crocodiles washed up downstream.

A University of Papua New Guinea study commissioned by Prime Minister Namaliu concludes that it is unlikely that fish populations in the Fly River system will recover quickly following the cessation of mining at Ok Tedi and that, in fact, several generations of time may be required.[28] Environmental groups fear continued direct disposal of mining wastes could destroy traditional means of subsistence of rain forest peoples and force them into a poverty level cash economy. Operators of the Ok Tedi mine have offered a $3.7 million development package to assist villagers downstream of the mine.

In April 1991, the Papua New Guinea Ambassador to the United States, Margaret Taylor, said attempts at international oversight of the Ok Tedi mine by environmental groups would not be well received by her government. She suggested, however, that the mine's operators could brief indigenous groups about environmental problems at the mine. Mine officials now acknowledge that water in the Ok Tedi River is too polluted for human consumption, and they are trying to provide alternative water supplies.

In February 1992, the International Water Tribunal, an ad hoc adjudicatory body set up to mediate citizen disputes over transboundary water problems, found that the Ok Tedi mine has severely polluted the Ok Tedi and Fly River systems through its waste disposal practices. Among other things, the tribunal concluded that these practices have raised the level of the river beds, flooded plantations and food gardens and disrupted the entire river ecosystem. The tribunal also said the owners "should not, as it has done, use its foreign revenue earning power to influence the government to make exceptions in the application of the law in its favor and to the detriment of the local environment and the livelihoods of the local people."[29]

The tribunal also said that Ok Tedi Mining's foreign shareholders "should ensure that the company fulfills standards for environmental protection comparable to the ones that are enforced in their home countries and appropriate to the geographical characteristics of the Ok Tedi region." Finally, the tribunal recommended that the mining operation investigate a safe way to treat or store the mine waste dumped into the river and "if no such storage or cost-effective storage is feasible, the jury believes the externalized costs of the project grossly exceed the benefits and, consequently, the activities of the [mine] should be phased out." The tribunal's findings are advisory, however, and are not binding on the mine owners.

Reducing Environmental Impacts of Mining

While damage from mining can be severe, the ecological impact can be confined when development plans are well thought out and executed. Intensive mining generally involves substantially smaller areas than timber operations, for example, and reforestation can occur after mining has ceased. Sometimes materials can be transported to mine sites by aircraft and mined ores can be transported over water to avoid building roads into mine areas.

Nevertheless, surface and groundwater contamination from mine tailings and cyanide solutions remains a serious threat posed by most mining operations. Accordingly, containment and monitoring systems are necessary to prevent excessive rainwater from sweeping tailings and cyanide solutions into rivers and streams. Similarly, streams and runoff have to be diverted around mine areas to prevent silt from being washed into water supplies. Wildlife access to cyanide solution ponds also must be prevented. And the sometimes revolutionary social repercussions of starting mining operations in rural areas suggests that careful socio-economic and socio-cultural studies be performed before the projects begin.

After the mines are closed, reclamation of mine waste and revegetation and landscaping of abandoned mining areas is recommended to replicate original land contours. The Mineral Policy Center, a Washington, D.C., group that advocates reform of mining laws, also urges that site testing continue long after mine closure, with corrective action taken if surface or groundwater monitoring detects any leaks. Funding for such remedial measures should be guaranteed before mining is allowed, the center adds, so that the host government does not have to pick up the tab for cleanup.[30]

Chapter Five Appendix

Mining Companies With Tropical Forest Operations or Policies

United States

ALUMINUM CO. OF AMERICA: Alcoa, based in Pittsburgh, Pa., is the world's largest aluminum company, with more than 60,000 employees at 152 locations in 20 countries. The company mines bauxite (the principal raw material used in making aluminum) in Australia, Brazil, Jamaica and Suriname. In Brazil, Alcoa owns 65 percent of **Alcoa Aluminia SA**, which operates 13 plants for mining, refining, smelting, extrusion, chemical production and distribution purposes. Alcoa Aluminia recently acquired a 13.2 percent interest in the **Mineracao Rio do Norte** (MRN) bauxite mine, paying cash and giving **Alcan** a 10 percent interest in its Alumar facility in Sao Luis, Maranhao. (See Alcan summary below for details on the MRN mine.)

Alcoa Aluminia follows Alcoa's U.S. environmental policies to protect air, water, soil and natural resources. "It assumes that the industry can and should become an active part of the effort to contribute to improving the quality of life in the communities where it operates," says Marcelo Barreto-Vianna, environmental manager for Alcoa Aluminia.[31] Alcoa uses environmental auditing, monitoring and impact assessments to manage environmental risk. Brazilian environmentalists are concerned, however, about the environmental effects of a mine at Pocos de Caldas and the Alumar smelter, which reportedly displaced more than 20,000 local people.

Pocos de Caldas facility: Alcoa has had a growing presence in Brazil since 1970, when it opened a bauxite mine and alumina plant in Pocos de Caldas. Pocos de Caldas is south of the Amazon rain forest in the state of Minas Gerais. The area once was largely subtropical rain forest, but only a few patches of secondary forest remain, according to Donald Williams, Alcoa's mining manager at Pocos de Caldas. Mining leads to the removal of about 25 acres of forest a year and "leaves a moonscape effect on the surface," Williams says. Because Alcoa did not want to alter forever the scenic mountain landscape of the area, which attracts tourists, it began to rehabilitate and reforest mined-out areas in 1978. By 1986, Alcoa had restored 200 acres at a cost of $9,000 per acre (or 18 cents per ton of aluminum oxide mined). Mining is expected to continue at Pocos de Caldas for at least 15 years on approximately 600 acres of land.[32]

Alumar facility: In 1984, Alcoa started the **Alumar consortium** with **Billiton**, the metals sector of **Royal Dutch Shell**. The consortium is Brazil's largest aluminum producer; it has a port, refinery and smelting complex on the island of Sao Luis, Maranhao, off the northeast coast of Brazil. The consortium's $1 billion smelter went into operation in 1985, after the Brazilian government ceded approximately 25,000 acres of land. As such, it is one of the largest private investments in Brazil. The facility processes 950,000 tons per year of raw alumina and produces 330,000 tons per year of finished aluminum.

A Brazilian environmental group, SOS Mata Atlantica, claims that construction of the Alumar facility decimated miles of shoreline mangrove trees (a type of rain forest ecosystem). Alcoa responds that the smelter is not in a tropical rain forest area, although it does use subsidized electricity from the Tucurui hydroelectric dam, which was constructed by flooding rain forests. Most of the power produced at Tucurui is contracted at a substantial discount to American and Japanese aluminum plants operating in the region. The subsidy allows producers to make a profit when they export aluminum on the world market. The net result for the Brazilian public, however, is that they are providing a subsidy of more than $100 per ton of aluminum produced, according to a study by the Bank Information Center.[33])

One of the bauxite mines that supplies the Alumar smelter is in a rain forest adjacent to the Trombetas River (a tributary of the Amazon River), although Alcoa has no ownership interest in this mine. About 170 acres of rain forest are cut and burned each year to gain access to bauxite at the Trombetas mine site, which is part of the Grand Carajás Project. As of 1991, 2,200 acres had been leveled and 900 acres had been reforested.

AMOCO CORP.: Amoco, based in Chicago, Ill., owns 30 percent of **Ok Tedi Mining Ltd.**, a large coal and copper mine in central Papua New Guinea, through its **Amoco Minerals** subsidiary. In a 1990 filing with the Securities and Exchange Commission, Amoco reported that it had a nonoperating interest in the Ok Tedi mine and had "no effective control over its operations."[34] (See pp. 134-136 for details on the Ok Tedi mine.)

FREEPORT MCMORAN INC.: Freeport McMoRan, based in New Orleans, La., has mining concessions in Irian Jaya, Indonesia, totaling 6.5 million acres. It has operated a gold, silver and copper mine in Irian Jaya for more than 20 years. The Mt. Ertsberg mine constitutes Irian Jaya's largest industry, with deposits of metals estimated to be worth more than $20 billion. Freeport also is investing $500 million for a new gold mine at Mt. Grasberg—with the largest proven gold deposit in the world—where it expects to mine a record 57,000 to 66,000 tons of ore a day during the second half of 1993, increasing to 90,000 tons a day by 1996. (See pp. 132-134 for more details on Freeport's Irian Jayan operations.)

REYNOLDS METALS CO.: Reynolds Metals owns a 50 percent share of a bauxite mine in a rain forest area in Guyana, which is operated by the government; a 10 percent share of an aluminum smelter in Venezuela; and a 6 percent share of a bauxite mine in Guinea. It also owns a 5 percent share of Brazil's **Mineracao Rio do Norte** (MRN), which operates a bauxite mine on the Trombetas River in the Amazon jungle. (See **Alcan** summary below for details on the MRN mine.)

OTHER U.S. COMPANIES: **Newmont Mining Corp.** is involved in exploration in Papua New Guinea and Indonesia but is not actively mining. **Phelps Dodge Corp.** has mining operations in Mexico and Peru and is exploring for minerals in Mexico and Costa Rica. Phelps Dodge holds a 16.25 percent interest in **Southern Peru Copper Corp.** Phelps Dodge declined to tell IRRC whether any of its projects are in tropical rain forest areas.

Australia

BROKEN HILL PROPERTIES: BHP owns a 30 percent stake in **Ok Tedi Mining Ltd.** (See pp. 134-136 for details on the Ok Tedi mine.)

CRA LTD.: CRA Ltd. is the largest company within the British **RTZ** group. CRA is 49 percent owned by RTZ and operated the Bougainville mine in Papua New Guinea until it was closed in 1989. (See pp. 129-130 for details on the Bougainville mine.) CRA also operates the Kaltim Prima coal mine and Kelian gold mine in Indonesia. (See **RTZ** summary below for details on these mining operations.)

Canada

ALCAN ALUMINIUM LTD.: Alcan is Canada's largest multinational corporation and the biggest Canadian investor in Brazil, with $920 million committed to two smelters and nine other plants. Alcan began producing aluminum in Brazil in 1950 and mines approximately 300,000 tons of bauxite a year. Bauxite mined by **Alcanbrasil**, a fully integrated operation, comes from two mines in the southeastern state of Minas Gerais. Alcan holds an 11 percent stake in **Mineracao Rio do Norte** (MRN), the consortium that mines bauxite in tropical rain forest at Porto Trombetas. Alcan also has a 16 percent share in **Alunorte**, a planned alumina production facility in the northern Brazilian state of Para.

    Mineracao Rio do Norte bauxite mine: **Mineracao Rio do Norte** (MRN) is a Brazilian corporation that is the third largest producer of bauxite in the world, mining about 8 million tons a year. It operates in a rain forest adjacent to the Trombetas River, which itself is a tributary of the Amazon River. The Brazilian mining conglomerate **Companhia Vale do Rio Doce (CVRD)** owns 46 percent of MRN; **Alcoa** and **Alcan** are the major non-Brazilian shareholders, with combined holdings of 24 percent. Other owners of the MRN mine are **Billiton BV** (**Royal Dutch Shell's** Brazilian partner), **Billiton Metals**, U.S.-owned **Reynolds Aluminio do Brasil**, and Norway's **Norsk Hydro**. Each of these partners owns 5 percent of MRN. Alcan says MRN's direction "is determined by a board of directors of which we have a significant share, and hence we do have some influence."[35]

    MRN has built a modern urban infrastructure and bauxite loading terminal at Porto Trombetas, although the surrounding area is still mainly dense tropical forest. About 170 acres of rain forest are cut and burned annually to gain access to the bauxite. Since 1979, MRN has leveled about 2,400 acres of rain forest in the region. Topsoil is saved and used to reforest the ground after mining is complete. As of 1991, about 900 acres had been reforested at a cost of $6,000 per acre. (About 90 native species and 12 exotic species have been planted.)

The MRN reforestation project has been endorsed by Ghillean Prance, director of the Royal Botanic Garden. Writing in *New Scientist,* Prance argues that more rain forest will be saved by "collaborating with responsible companies and helping them to work with us than by driving them out of the region to be replaced by companies over which we have no control."[36]

Still, the bauxite mine has had its problems. Until 1989, MRN dumped tailings containing aluminum oxide silicates and iron oxide into Lake Batata, near Porto Trombetas. Progressive silting of the lake and concerns about toxic contamination—as detailed by Brazilian newspaper and television stories—prompted MRN to devise disposal alternatives. A $70 million washing plant has been built near the mine, and tailings are no longer dumped in the lake but returned to mined-out areas.

Representatives of Canadian environmental and human rights groups visited the bauxite operation in 1990 and learned that MRN had pioneered the construction of special ponds in mined-out pits, where red mud wastes are dumped and left to evaporate. "While such innovation is impressive," the groups' report stated, "concerns remain as to the ability of the evaporated ponds to support revegetation." (Eventually, the ponds are to be covered with topsoil and replanted.) The group also visited areas that had been reforested five years earlier with 70 percent native and 30 percent exotic species. Some of the growth was 18 meters high at the time of their visit.[37]

In 1989, **Alcan** and three other multinationals—**Alcoa, Billiton** and **Dow Chemical**—proposed a privately financed $1.2 billion, 1,300 megawatt hydroelectric dam at Serra Quebrada on the Toncatins River in Brazil, but the project has since been shelved.[38]

BRASCAN: Brascan's mining activities in Brazil are performed by its Brazilian holding company, **Cesbra.** Brascan owns 99 percent of Cesbra, having bought out **British Petroleum's** 49.5 percent share in August 1989. Cesbra consists of 37 mining companies and holds mining rights in 17 areas, totaling more than 500 square miles. Fifteen of its licenses are for tin, one is for diamonds and one is for gold. Only two of the areas have been mined, one of which is the Mineracao Jacunda mine, Brazil's second largest tin mine, located at Santa Barbara in the state of Rondonia. Altogether, Brascan holds mining rights to 145,000 acres in Rondonia in the western Amazon.

Brascan acknowledged in 1991 that it had purchased cassiterite ore "in the recent past" from Brazilian garimpeiros (migrant mine workers), but it has also been instrumental in a government decision to close down all garimpeiro activity in the area of the Bom Futuro reserves. The mining rights to this area have been granted to **Ebesa**, a Brazilian company in which Cesbra holds a minority interest. "The company's first obligation with the authorities is to start repairing whatever damage has been done to the environment," says R.P. Cezar de Andrade, President of Brascan Brazil.[39]

Mineracao Jacunda mine: The Mineracao Jacunda mine has been operating since the early 1970s. It has displaced more than 3,100 acres of rain forest, and the total area disturbed for roads and infrastructure totaled 4,791 acres as of 1991, reports Andrade. In 1984, Brazil created the 531,000 acre Jamari National Forest in a rain forest area that encompasses the mine site. Cesbra's mining rights overlap onto 24 percent of the park's territory, Andrade says, and 12 percent of this area has been disturbed by the mine.

The Mineracao Jacunda mine was the subject of a widely cited 1989 story in the *London Sunday Times* that claimed as much as 200,000 acres of forest had been disturbed. **British Petroleum**, which then owned half of the mine, strongly disputed the claim, insisting that only 4,500 acres, or less than 1 percent of the national forest, had been disturbed. The article painted a bleak image of bulldozers felling the forest, logs burned and giant holes carved 100 feet deep in the ground. "The destruction extends beyond the new sites being mined," the article said; "large amounts of soil are being dumped haphazardly, silting up one of the forest's main rivers." BP denied that areas were burned, maintaining they were instead cut down with the trunks left to decay and the stumps burned "in accordance with good practice."[40]

In 1990, the mine's operators began a seven year, $3.5 million restoration program of mined-out areas. Asked why the operators had just started a restoration program after 20 years of mining at the site, Andrade explained that mining had expanded through the 1970s and peaked in 1985, with 1,400 people working the mine. As long as the mined areas were still in operation, it did not make sense to start restoration, he said. In addition, the Brazilian government did not require restoration of mined-out land until 1988. Only in 1990—as most of the mineral reserves were depleted or became uneconomical as a result of falling mineral prices—did areas become free for restoration, according to Andrade.

GOLDEN STAR RESOURCES: Golden Star Resources, in a joint venture with **Cambior Inc.**, is constructing a $161 million gold mine and mill in secondary rain forest in Guyana, 100 miles south of the capital, Georgetown. The so-called Omai mine will cover 5.5 square miles, although less than that amount of land will be cleared, reports Golden Star President David Fennell.[41] The area around the Omai mine has been mined for 100 years. In addition, wood has been used as a primary fuel source, so the area is largely deforested. Golden Star's environmental impact statement has been accepted by the Guyanan government and includes a restoration program. Production will begin in 1993, with an estimated yearly average of 255,000 ounces of gold expected to be produced over the first three years.

Golden Star has also submitted a proposal to the Guyanan government for a second gold mine at Mahdia, another area with a history of mining. The Mahdia mine would exploit a gold-bearing channel on the Mahdia River that is five miles long and 1,000 feet wide. Two additional exploration activities may lead to mining operations in Guyana: Mazaruni, a diamond search on the Middle Mazaruni River floodplains, in a joint venture with **South American Goldfields** of Canada; and Aremu, a gold search in Guyana's Central Archaean Greenstone belt, in a joint venture with **Cambior**. Both searches are in rain forest areas.

Several small companies have already started mining on the Mazaruni and lower Potaro rivers, using missile dredges to pump water into alluvial deposits and then sucking the deposits out to process the minerals. Neighboring Indian communities report that silting has polluted water supplies and reduced fishing as far as 40 miles downstream. The silting also has blocked waterways, the main arteries for travel in the rain forests. Thousands of Brazilian garimpeiros also have moved across the border to mine in the headwaters of the Marazuni.[42]

INCO: Inco is the world's leading producer of nickel. It has nickel mining operations in rain forests in Guatemala and Indonesia and holds a share of a gold mine in Brazil. Inco's Indonesian mine is owned by **P.T. International Nickel Indonesia**, which is 58 percent owned by Inco, and about 7 square miles of forest have been cleared for the operation. In addition, about 50 miles of access roads have been cut in the area, as well as roads that are part of the mining operation, which employs about 2,200 people. Inco's Guatemalan operation has been inactive in recent years and has affected less than 1 square mile of forest.

In 1991, Inco completed a merger with **TVX Gold Inc.** of Canada. TVX holds a 49 percent share in the Brazilian Novo Astro mine, which is in a rain forest area in the northern territory of Amapa and operated by **CMP**, a Brazilian company, reports Inco executive vice president Scott Hand. [43]

Inco mines under "stringent environmental standards" in rain forests that are not relaxed in third world countries, even where national standards may be lower or nonexistent," according to Hand. Environmental impact studies are carried out before operations begin. Runoff, dust control and other environmental problems are addressed, and regular environmental audits are performed of mining operations. Hand says Indonesia is promulgating environmental standards for mining that are modeled after North American standards.

PLACER DOME INC.: Placer Dome is Canada's largest gold producer. It has two gold mines in Papua New Guinea in rain forest areas. The Misima mine is a gold and silver mine on Misima Island, about 130 miles east of the Papua New Guinea mainland. **Placer Pacific Ltd.**, a 75.8 percent owned subsidiary of Placer Dome, holds an 80 percent stake in **Misima Mines Pty. Ltd.**, which operates the mine. Engineering studies at the Misima mine started in 1977, but operations did not commence until 1989, after a metallurgical plant was completed. Misima Mines holds a lease covering 5,100 acres but estimates that only 540 acres will be disturbed by the operation. In 1989, the plant processed 11,000 tons of ore a day. Tailings are discharged into the ocean using a system that de-aerates tailings. The mine employs between 400 and 550 people in open pit mining and other operations.

Placer Pacific also operates the Porgera gold mine in the western highlands of Papua New Guinea. Gold production began in late 1991. About 1,200 of 5,400 forested acres leased to the company are expected to be cleared for mining and infrastructure activities. When in full operation, the Porgera operation will employ 1,200 people; 75 percent of them will be citizens of Papua New Guinea. Henry Brehaut, Placer's vice president for environment, says local people were involved extensively in planning for the mine. Many were relocated before the mine started operating, and "in all cases the people have been generously compensated on the basis of guidelines developed with the government," Brehaut maintains.[44]

Rehabilitation will be undertaken, where possible, at both of Placer's mines in Papua New Guinea as mining proceeds. Conceptual reclamation plans are in place and detailed plans will be prepared five years before cessation of mining. Brehaut says he expects "a high proportion" of the disturbed land will be returned to its original state.

Netherlands

ROYAL DUTCH SHELL: Royal Dutch Shell's mining company, **Billiton**, has numerous projects in rain forest areas. Billiton owns a bauxite mine in Guinea, an open pit nickel mine and ferro-nickel smelter in Colombia, an open pit gold mine in Ghana and holds a joint-venture interest in a bauxite mine and alumina refinery in Suriname. Billiton has a 70 percent interest in an underground gold and silver mine—the Lebong Tandai mine—in a tropical rain forest area of Sumatra, Indonesia. The mine is 80 years old, although Billiton acquired its interest less than five years ago. Billiton also owns the Lerokis open pit gold, silver and barite mine on the remote Indonesian island of Wetar. Billiton holds a 10 percent share in the **Mineracao Rio do Norte** (MRN) bauxite mine in Brazil (see the **Alcan** summary above for details). Finally, Billiton owns 40 percent share of a proposed bauxite mine adjacent to the MRN facility, which was to be operated in a joint venture with **Alcoa**. Alcoa decided recently not to proceed with development of the controversial mine, although it has retained its claims to the land for possible future use.[45] Alcoa owns 60 percent of the shares in the proposed mine, although Billiton was slated to operate it.

Proposed Brazilian mine: The proposed bauxite mine—originally scheduled to open in 1993 and now on hold—is in Amazonia near the Trombetas River. Native peoples who live near the site have objected to the mine, which was supposed to yield 2.5 million tons of washed bauxite a year. A group of descendants of freed black slaves, known as quilombos, told the Brazilian government that the mine would be on land they have claimed for their own hunter/gatherer activities. In 1990, state officials granted a provisional license to clear a 19,000 acre area for the mine, but the Brazilian environmental agency, Ibama, had to give further approval, because the site is in a national forest.

The quilombos say that the state government made no attempt to contact them or solicit their views before granting the provisional license for the new mine. In July 1991, representatives of 36 black communities and 23 nongovernmental organizations of the Trombetas River Basin met to discuss the new mine. They issued a joint statement demanding that the project be halted, that the initial environmental license given to Alcoa/Billiton not be renewed and that communal lands of quilombos be demarcated, as has been done for other indigenous people under the Brazilian constitution.

Representatives of Alcoa and Billiton reportedly met subsequently with the quilombos and offered to pay for the demarcation of their lands, reports Antonio Miguel Marques of Billiton's environmental staff. "We support the demarcation of their land and will give them legal assistance," says Marques.[46] The joint venture was expected to advance future taxes to the state of Para to pay for the demarcation. The nearest communities are 10 miles from the project, and no one would have been displaced by the mine, Marques says. He estimates that the operation would have employed about 700 people, including 100 quilombos.

Lucia Andrade of the Comisao Pro Indio, a group in Sao Paulo that defends the rights of indigenous tribes in Brazil, disputes that company officials actually met with the quilombos. She claims that the officials have dealt only with representatives from the state. Andrade also says that at least one community that was forced to move because of the existing Trombetas mine would have to move again as a result of the new Alcoa/Billiton mine. Moreover, the quilombos reportedly are not satisfied with the small area of land that the government wants to demarcate on their behalf. Only the immediate area around their homes and gardens is included—and none of the hunting or fishing grounds or areas used for gathering Brazil nuts, which is a major source of their income. In addition, poor pay and working conditions offered quilombos at the existing Trombetas mine are not attracting them to work at the new mine. Most quilombos reportedly still oppose the proposed Alcoa/Billiton mine project because of these factors.[47]

United Kingdom

RTZ CORP.: Formerly known as Rio Tinto Zinc, RTZ is the world's largest mining company, with 74,000 employees and more than 50 mines in 40 countries. Its reported rain forest mine holdings include the Kaltim Prima coal mine and Kelian gold mine in Indonesia; and Bougainville Copper, Hidden Valley and Lihir in Papua New Guinea. The company is considering a mine operation in Panama that could affect 15 Indian communities. RTZ reports it is also conducting mineral exploration in Bolivia, Brazil and Ecuador but not in rain forest areas. **Price Brothers**, an RTZ subsidiary, makes windows and doors, small numbers of which are derived from an African tropical hardwood, iroko.

Indonesia: In Indonesia, RTZ owns 49 percent of the Australian mining company, **CRA**, which operates three projects in rain forest areas. Two are described below.

In East Kalimantan, **Kaltim Prima Coal** is a 50/50 joint venture between **CRA** and **BP Coal**. The $550 million project entered full production in late 1991, with completion of a coal washing plant and export terminal. The project employs more than 1,000 people, almost all of whom are Indonesians. The Kaltim Prima Coal mining area has been designated as a production forest by the Indonesian government. Logging in the area (undertaken by a private Indonesian company) is nearly complete; the project will clear up to 32,000 forested acres. After mining is finished, the land will return to the jurisdiction of the Indonesian Forest Department. Mine infrastructure will be transferred to a state mining company that is a joint venture partner in the project.

CRA has completed an environmental impact statement outlining progressive restoration of the mining area. Mined-out land will be replanted with indigenous species as mining proceeds. The mine is north of the Kutei Wildlife Reserve but completely outside the reserve and will have not impact on it, the company says, adding that it is working with park authorities and the World

Wide Fund for Nature and "other industrial neighbors" to preserve and "develop" the park. (One of the mine's customers is **Applied Energy Services**, a U.S. power company involved in carbon sequestration projects, described in Chapter Seven. AES plans to buy coal from Kaltim Prima for its power plant in Hawaii.)

The **Kelian Gold** project is on the equator in East Kalimantan. It is 90 percent owned by **CRA** and will involve clearing about 1,700 acres of rain forest. An open pit mine and processing plant are expected to produce 6 million tons of ore and 264,000 ounces of gold a year through the end of the decade. A tailings dam, river port and access road also are being built. CRA says timber companies have logged much of the area already. CRA has prepared an environmental impact statement as well as a management and monitoring plan for rehabilitation of mined areas.

Papua New Guinea: In addition to the dormant Bougainville copper mine (see pp. 129-130 for details), RTZ is considering operations in Hidden Valley, a mountainous rain forest area, as well as on Lihir Island. An estimated 1,300 acres would be deforested for operations at Hidden Valley, but exploration has yet to reveal sufficient ore to sustain a mining operation. Lihir also is the subject of a feasibility study. About 20 percent of the island's palm plantations are in the exploration area. Some would be cut down and replacements would be planted elsewhere on the island if the project goes forward, according to RTZ.

Panama: In Panama, RTZ has been seeking since the early 1980s to develop a rich vein of copper ore known as the Cerro Colorado deposit. The planned mine and smelter, about 180 miles west of Panama City, would have serious impacts on the Guaymi indigenous people, according to several environmental and human rights groups. The project would force relocation of 15 communities for construction of the mine, dam and reservoir, affecting up to 70,000 Guaymi. The mine would dump 27 tons of rock tailings into rivers each year and the dam would flood 100,000 acres of agricultural land. The Guaymi have demanded that the Panamanian government respect their land rights and prohibit mining there. The Catholic bishops of Panama, the Catholic bishop of Liverpool and 50 members of the British parliament have rallied to their cause. The human rights group, Survival International, also has mounted a letter writing campaign, allegedly prompting an RTZ director to threaten to "squash Survival International like a fly" if it did not abandon its effort.[48] RTZ put the project on hold in 1982 because of low copper prices. Human rights groups considered that a victory, but RTZ has spent nearly $1 million a year since then to keep its options open on the project.

South America: In Brazil, RTZ is involved in the Gurupi project, south of Belem, in a joint venture with the Brazilian **Odebrecht** group. RTZ reports that the mining area was logged 50 years ago and contains some secondary forest growth. RTZ also has a 51 percent interest in the Morro do Ouro gold mine in Minas Gerais. The area consists of scrub and savannah vegetation, according to Dorothy Harris, a company information officer. She says RTZ also is exploring elsewhere in Brazil, Bolivia and Ecuador but not in rain forest areas.[49]

Chapter 6
Agribusiness in the Tropics

Corporate agriculture leads to tropical deforestation in two principal ways. Corporate interests can clear rain forests directly to grow cash crops such as bananas, cocoa, coffee, cotton, palm oil, sugar, tobacco or beef. Or they can take over prime agricultural land and prompt small farmers to migrate into rain forest areas, where they resort to slash-and-burn crop growing methods. In some instances, modern, capital-intensive farming degrades forest environments more severely than traditional slash-and-burn agriculture. Operations that clear the land by bulldozing trees uproot the thin layer of topsoil on which plants depend for nourishment. Heavily mechanized farming practices also promote erosion by altering traditional land contours. In addition, monoculture plantations often require liberal doses of pesticides to ward off pest infestations. Exposure to pesticides can adversely affect the health of farm workers, while chemical runoff contaminates rivers and drinking water supplies.

The extent of damage from agriculture to rain forest ecosystems depends largely on the crops grown on denuded land. Perennial crops like cocoa, coffee, palm oil and rubber do not cause major soil erosion and leave sufficient nutrients in the soil to ensure the crops' longevity. Bananas, on the other hand, exhaust the soil unless consistently fertilized. Cattle ranching is the most destructive farming activity, especially if undertaken on thin soils.[1]

In Latin America, the most productive farmland generally is owned by national elites and multinational corporations. Corporate plantations account for most of the commodity exports—bananas, coffee, cotton, sugar and beef—on which many of these countries' economies depend.[2] Subsistence farming generally occurs on hilly, marginal or previously forested lands not claimed by organized business interests. More than 100,000 farmers moved to the Brazilian Amazon, for instance, as corporate interests took over their lands in the northeastern and southern part of the country during the 1970s. In the southern state of Parana, the number of farms with fewer than 125 acres fell by 109,000 during the decade, while the number of farms larger than 2,500 acres grew by 450.[3]

While some large farms and cattle ranches are operated as profit-making enterprises, others are held for tax purposes or reasons not related to their agricultural potential. The U.S. Agency for International Development estimates that at least half of the farms larger than 125 acres in Central America are controlled by wealthy aristocratic landowners. "This, in essence, means that a vast amount of Central America's best agricultural land is controlled by owners who do not have the long term maximization of agricultural production as their primary interest," according to a study by the International Institute for Environmental and Development, a U.S. policy group.[4] While all forms of agriculture—regardless of ownership or production methods—can lead to tropical deforestation, those forms driven by tax incentives do perhaps the most to squander this vital natural resource.

Multinational food companies have cleared large forested areas in tropical countries, especially in Central America, since before the turn of the century. Minor Cooper Keith, a young railroad baron from Brooklyn, planted banana trees along the Atlantic coast of Costa Rica in the 1880s. The business Keith started is still the world's largest fruit producer, **Chiquita Brands International** (formerly United Fruit Co. and now owned by **American Financial Corp.**). Two other companies in addition to Chiquita dominate the tropical fruit market in Central America: **Dole Food** (formerly Castle & Cooke) and the Mexican-owned **Cabal Group**, which purchased **Del Monte Tropical Fruit Co.** from British-owned Polly Peck International in 1992.

In 1954, **Chiquita** (then known as United Fruit) achieved international notoriety when it encouraged the Eisenhower administration to use covert action to overthrow the elected government of Guatemalan President Jacobo Arbenz—after Arbenz expropriated some of United Fruit's land. Two decades later, in 1975, a U.S. federal investigation found that the president of United Fruit had authorized a $1.25 million bribe to officials in the Honduran government to rescind an increase in the banana export tax. During the investigation, the United Fruit president committed suicide by jumping from his 44th story New York City office window.[5] Chiquita Brands' involvement in Central American politics continues to this day. The company recently proposed investing $100 million in Panama if the government of President Guillermo Endara agreed to abolish a $14 million annual tax on banana exports and "liberalized" that country's labor laws. Chiquita's Panamanian subsidiary, **Chiriqui Land Co.**, grows two-thirds of Panama's banana crop and dominates its exports.[6]

Bananas

Bananas remain a potent force in the economies of many Central American countries. Because the industry is one of the three top earners of foreign exchange in the region, governments generally are willing to adjust taxes and labor laws to accommodate the requests of multinational exporters.[7] Since the 1950s, however, U.S. agricultural companies have scaled back their direct investments and used more local farmers as associate growers. Now more than one-third of the region's banana crop is grown by contract growers. While local farmers are bearing higher risks, the multinationals have been able to maintain effective control of contract land—without incurring the expenses and political liabilities of direct ownership. Today, when market prices are low, the multinationals simply reduce the volume they buy from contract growers to adjust supply to demand.[8]

Banana plantations—sometimes referred to as "green deserts"—take a heavy toll on the environment, and in ways other than razing tropical forests. Bananas are among the most pesticide-intensive crops grown in the world. Banana "fingers" are extremely sensitive—prone to scarring by insects, fungi and contact with human hands or even dust. The pesticide dibromochloropropane (DBCP) is commonly applied to bananas, and it has been associated with respiratory, skin, eye and reproductive problems among banana workers and nearby residents. Runoff from the pesticide enters networks of drainage ditches that run through banana plantations and empty into rivers that flow to the sea. A 1987 study of Costa Rica's Caribbean coral by the International Marine Life Alliance found that of all the activities "that have driven material, debris and wastes into the sea, none can equal the sheer tonnage of sediment that flows from the Atlantic-slope banana plantations."[9]

The marine environment off the Costa Rican coast now may be deteriorating more rapidly than the land. Chris van Arsdale, executive director of the Audubon

-Photo by Rocio Lopez - ABAS.

Plastic bags coated with pesticides protect banana "fingers" from pest infestation and hasten ripening of bananas. In Costa Rica, tens of thousands of these bags end up in rivers and the ocean, harming aquatic life.

Society of Costa Rica, estimates that pesticide runoff from banana plantations has killed 90 percent of the coral reefs along Costa Rica's Caribbean coast.[10] In addition, about 25 million blue plastic bags coated with pesticides and fertilizers are tied to banana bunches each year. Discarded bags often end up in rivers and the sea, where leatherback sea turtles mistake them for jellyfish and choke on them.

Back on land, banana cultivation can deplete soils of their nutrients in about 15 years—depending on the soil's quality and the amount of fertilizers used. Many companies prefer to move on and clear new land rather than perform maintenance to keep soils productive on existing plantations. Thus, "the banana plantation is a plantation in movement," explains Isabel Wing-Ching, a sociologist at the University of Costa Rica.[11]

A former United Fruit banana operation on Costa Rica's Pacific Coast offers a case in point. When production on the plantation declined in the 1950s, company scientists determined the banana plants' roots had been severely weakened by the accumulation of copper in the soil, apparently from heavy application of fungicides. **Chiquita Brands** later pulled out of the region in 1985 (after workers formed a union), leaving behind 16,000 acres of previously high-quality soils now contaminated with copper. As a result, the land is unsuitable for most agricultural production, reports the Audubon Society's van Arsdale.[12] Unsuspecting farmers bought the contaminated land from Chiquita, nevertheless. Altogether, 123,000 acres in Costa Rica have been contaminated with excessive copper, estimates Rocio Lopez, a biologist for the Environmental Association of Sarapiqui.[13] (Sarapiqui is a banana-intensive region in the Limon province on Costa Rica's Atlantic coast.)

Focus on Costa Rica Banana Plantations

Bananas are Costa Rica's number one source of foreign exchange. In 1991, bananas provided $441 million in export earnings and employed 32,000 people.[14] **Chiquita, Dole** and the Cabal Group's **Del Monte** unit comprise 96 percent of the nation's banana export production. No good data exist on the volume of Costa Rican forests cut specifically for banana plantations. Until recently, the government did not require a permit to cut forests for such purposes. Lopez of the Environmental Association of Sarapiqui estimates that 1.2 million acres in Costa Rica have been under banana cultivation at one time or another in the last century.[15]

Acreage used to grow bananas in Costa Rica has increased dramatically in recent years. In 1990 alone, banana companies expanded lands under cultivation by 10 percent, to a total of 78,000 acres, according to the Costa Rican Ministry of Agriculture. In the Sarapiqui region, foreign and domestic companies—including **Chiquita**—have purchased 24,000 acres of land for banana production, Lopez reports. Photographs by Lopez depict logging operations on lands where **Chiquita, Dole** and **Del Monte** allegedly operate together (although **Dole**, in communications with Lopez, has denied any involvement in this operation.)

The technical services director for **Chiquita** in Costa Rica, Gabriela Mena, acknowledges that a small amount of land that Chiquita has acquired for banana

-Photo by Rocio Lopez - ABAS.

Rain forest land being cleared for a new banana plantation near Puerto Viejo in the Sarapiqui region of Costa Rica. Chiquita, Del Monte and possibly Dole plan to expand their operations in the region, according to the Environmental Association of Sarapiqui, a Costa Rican environmental group.

production in the Sarapiqui and Siquerres regions of the Limon province has been deforested by the company. But she maintains that the majority of land purchased recently by Chiquita was deforested previously by cattle ranchers.[16] Environmentalists claim that some companies avoid the appearance of deforesting the land by inviting farmers and ranchers to clear the companies' land acquisitions and raise crops or graze cattle for three to five years. Then, when companies reclaim the land, they can say that others had deforested it. In some areas, wetlands are being converted to banana plantations. Wetlands play a vital role in flood control and provide critical habitat for many species, including migrating songbirds.

The land near Tortuguero National Park, a popular tourist attraction on Costa Rica's Atlantic coast, is one such area of banana company expansion. Lopez estimates that 40 percent of 10,000 acres purchased there recently by banana interests is forested. Environmentalists are concerned that deforestation of such lands will adversely affect the water quality of several rivers close to Tortuguero National Park and the Barra del Colorado Wildlife Refuge. Erosion

Box 6A

The Environmentally Friendly Banana Project

The Rainforest Alliance, an environmental group based in New York, and Fundacion Ambio, a Costa Rican environmental group, have launched a new effort to find solutions to the environmental problems posed by banana plantations—and forestall a possible boycott by environmental groups. "Banano Amigo del Ambiente," the Environmentally Friendly Banana Project, hopes to establish a code of conduct and product labeling program that covers all aspects of banana production, including worker safety, use of pesticides, reforestation and waste disposal. "Instead of resorting to a boycott, we offered the banana companies an opportunity to sit down with environmentalists and look for solutions," explains Diane Jukofsky of the Rainforest Alliance. "They have responded to this offer and, together, we are setting the standards for environmentally responsible fruit farming."[1a]

The guidelines, approved in early 1993, prohibit cutting of primary rain forest in new banana plantations. Clearance of secondary forests will require a government permit and an environmental protection plan. Participating companies have also agreed not to clear patches of forest in existing plantations if land use studies indicate that the land is better suited for forestry purposes than for banana cultivation.[2a] Buffer zones will extend for two miles around national parks and wildlife refuges and also will extend around watersheds, rivers and roads. Vegetation barriers will be required around employee living quarters. Worker housing for new plantations must be off the plantation site.

The guidelines also address pesticides and waste disposal issues. The use of pesticides will be minimized around sources of water, residential areas and packing zones. Participating companies will provide safety training and medical controls for employees working with agrochemicals and forgo the use of chemicals banned in the United States or by the European Community. Companies also will devise plans to recycle or treat the plastic bags doused with pesticides.

A proposal that one acre of land be preserved in its natural state for every five acres of land planted with bananas was dropped after opposition from industry. Instead, growers will reforest or maintain forest on those areas of their property that are deemed more suitable for forestry purposes than for banana cultivation.

Participating companies will have representatives of Banano Amigo visit their operations to determine whether they are in compliance with the guidelines. Growers who pass the inspection will receive a Banana Amigo seal that says, "ECO-O.K., Rainforest Alliance Approved." The seal will be placed on the fruit to alert consumers about their environmental benefits. The labeling program is expected to begin sometime in 1993.[3a]

Chris Wille of the Rainforest Alliance reports that at least one major grower and several smaller independent growers have expressed interest in the Banano Amigo project. These companies regard the guidelines as tough but achievable, and they are expected to seek certification. Significantly, however, **Corbana**, the group representing Costa Rica's major banana growers has not endorsed Banano Amigo. Corbana has created its own Banana Growers Environmental Commission, which espouses environmental goals that are more palatable to the growers.[4a]

of the land and silting of the water kills fish populations and has also contributed to the decline of the country's Atlantic coral reefs.

In 1992, the British company **Geest** was cited by the Costa Rican Ministry of Natural Resources for illegally cutting trees along creeks and streams near Tortuguero National Park, including 1,000 acres of protected land. Costa Rican law mandates that at least 33 feet of forest be left bordering its waterways (although the law has been widely ignored for years). A review of the records of the Forestry Ministry found that Geest had been given permission—errone-ously—to cut trees within the protected zone to establish a banana plantation. But that still did not permit Geest to cut trees so close to the waterways. Geest disagreed with the government's definition of creeks and streams. "For us, it was a depression where water was stagnating, it wasn't flowing," explains Eduardo de la Espriella, Geest's general manager in Costa Rica.[17] Nevertheless, the citation marked the first time that the Costa Rican government had fined a company for illegally cutting a rain forest to create an agricultural plantation.

The Costa Rican government has evidence that Geest clearcut trees on 1,750 acres of forest altogether. While Geest denies cutting primary or secondary forest, government forestry officials maintain that they saw a large number of tree stumps and commercial-grade timber stored on the site. Other wood reportedly was buried or thrown into rivers. The denuded habitat is home to monkeys, parrots and sloths, among many other tropical species. The state foresters who issued the logging permits to Geest were relieved of their duties and transferred to San Jose, Costa Rica's capital.

Religious and environmental groups are pressuring the Costa Rican govern-ment to control the banana industry more stringently. Before it fined Geest, the Costa Rican government had canceled plans to fund a study of the impact of banana plantations on deforestation and permitted the industry to expand rapidly. By some estimates, the area under production may increase by 50 percent over the next several years, covering a total of 115,000 acres.[18]

Meanwhile, **Corbana**, the national growers' cooperative in which **Chiquita, Dole** and **Del Monte** participate, has agreed to investigate pest-resistant banana strains to reduce the amount of chemicals that flow into the environment. The growers also are checking banana trees more carefully for pest problems, so spraying occurs as needed rather than on a set schedule. They also are experimenting with recycling the blue plastic bags that shroud the banana fingers as they grow—turning the recycled bags into flower pots, building bricks and prop-up poles for the banana plants.[19]

Palm Oil

Palm oil is used as a cooking oil and in margarine. Millions of acres of tropical forest have been felled to grow palm oil for export, including huge areas of Indonesia and Malaysia. In Ecuador, 49,000 acres in the Oriente region were being cultivated for palm oil production as of 1987, and the industry wanted to expand to more than 600,000 acres, or 4 percent of the region's total acreage. **Chiquita** and **Dole**, among others, have converted parts of their plantation holdings into palm oil estates.

While palm oil plantations do not affect soils as adversely as banana plantations, other environmental impacts are similar. Up to 15 pesticides—including aldrin, dieldrin, endrin and parathion—are sprayed on the trees at regular intervals, which drain off into rivers along with other wastes. Of these, endrin is of greatest concern. The chemical is highly toxic to fish, and eating game contaminated with endrin has caused brain damage and birth defects in humans.

"A prime example is found in the Cucaracha River, on the coastal side of Ecuador just west of Santo Domingo de los Colorados," says one report. "The waste dumped by palm oil extractors has covered this river with a lasting greasy film that makes its waters unfit for human consumption. The waste from palm oil extractors in some rivers in Malaysia has caused them to be compared with open sewers."[20] Fish kills have been reported downstream of existing plantations and sickness has occurred within communities that use river water for cooking and drinking.

Tobacco

The tobacco industry is considered a major deforester in tropical countries, but there are little reliable data about the extent of rain forest loss from tobacco cultivation, curing and wrapping. "Tobacco Control in the Third World," a 1990 report by the International Organization of Consumer Unions, claims the environmental impact of tobacco is "perhaps the most immediate problem" facing many governments in the developing world. "Being wrapped in paper and sold in packs, cigarettes are voracious users of paper and therefore of forest resources. A modern cigarette machine uses four miles of paper per hour," the report says.[21]

A less apparent but much greater cause of deforestation is the use of fuelwood in curing the tobacco leaf. About 19,000 acres of forest is consumed annually for tobacco curing in the Philippines, for example. A report by the group War on Want estimates that fuelwood curing of tobacco fells one tree for every 300 cigarettes produced. A separate study by the Economist Intelligence Unit claims that 80 percent of timber-generated fuel used in tobacco curing is "wasted."[22] Among tobacco processers, however, there is a wide disparity in the use and efficiency of fuelwood curing. Taken as a whole, production of one acre of tobacco leads to the felling of one acre of nearby forest, concludes an Earthscan report.[23]

Brazil is the world's third largest tobacco producer. The tobacco industry there is considered a significant contributor to tropical deforestation, mainly because of the amount of fuelwood used for tobacco curing. On the south Atlantic coast, where destruction of the rain forest is nearly complete, the tobacco industry has been cited as a main culprit.[24] **BAT Industries, R.J. Reynolds** and **Philip Morris** are the three largest tobacco companies operating in Brazil. But determining the responsibility of individual companies is problematic because most do not grow their own tobacco; rather, they purchase it through contractual arrangements with farmers or local companies, or purchase it at auctions.

The tobacco industry has commissioned the International Forest Science Conservancy to study tobacco's impacts on tropical forests. The conservancy's report concludes that the tobacco industry's total consumption of fuelwood represents only 0.7 percent of all fuelwood consumed in the 69 countries studied. The report notes, however, that the area of forest in most African and Asian countries is below the level at which they are capable of meeting current and future demand on a sustainable basis. "Tobacco growers, like other wood users, still tend to regard wood as a 'free good'," the report cautions, "though in some countries they have taken steps toward becoming self-sufficient. In other countries, most notably Thailand and Malawi,...inefficient use of fuelwood and only modest or nonexistent efforts to establish supplies for the future are contributing toward a generally serious national situation."[25]

The Earthscan report maintains that the tobacco industry could not survive without free or low-cost wood. "If they had to pay for their fuel, or bear the costs of planting trees to meet their needs, they would no longer be competitive in the international markets," the report says.[26]

Cattle Ranching

Cattle ranching often is a poor use of cleared rain forest land and can be especially damaging to rain forest soils. Immediately following forest clearing, the land typically will support one animal per 2.5 acres; within five to 10 years, the ratio drops to one animal per 12.5 acres. Cattle pulverize the soil into a hard surface, sometimes rendering it unusable for other agricultural purposes for many years. The degree of damage depends on the length of time an area is used for grazing and the number of cattle involved.

In Latin America, cattle ranching was a major cause of deforestation during the 1960s and 1970s. Rich and powerful land speculators opened up vast tracts of rain forest, partly to capitalize on tax incentives offered for clearing the land. Governments in Central America and Brazil, aided by the World Bank, promoted beef as an export for markets in North America and Western Europe.[27] Beef exports increased as a percentage of total beef production in the region from 34 percent in 1961 to 61 percent in 1986.

Government incentives drew a number of multinational beef producers to the Amazon in the late 1960s and early 1970s. In 1969, **Deltec International Ltd.**, a private investment bank, purchased **International Packers Ltd.**, a large meat packing firm that included **Swift-Armour Co. of Brazil**. Swift joined with **King Ranch of Texas** to establish a 176,000 acre cattle ranch under the government's fiscal incentives program. In 1972, Deltec sold its interests in the project to the Canadian mining firm **Brascan** and **Caemi**, one of the largest holding companies in Brazil.[28]

Also during the period, the Italian firm **Liquigas**, a major producer of industrial chemicals in Brazil, purchased a major share of the huge 1.3 million acre Suia-Missu ranch in the western Amazonian state of Mato Grosso. By 1976, Liquigas (which was said to have the Vatican as a principal shareholder) had cleared 168,000 acres for cattle raising.[29]

To the north, German automaker **Volkswagen** purchased a 56,000 acre ranch in Santana do Araguaia in the state of Para to produce meat, wood, cellulose and paper. In 1976, managers of the ranch received government approval to clear 21,000 acres by setting the forest on fire—but as much as 2.4 million acres burned accidentally. At the time, it was believed to be the largest manmade fire in a tropical rain forest. The Brazilian government later fined Volkswagen $6 million. Volkswagen had hoped to be grazing 110,000 head of cattle and exporting beef to markets in Europe, Japan and the United States by 1984. But like many other companies, it sold its business when huge tax concessions expired after 10 years. "Such speculation left behind huge waste-lands which are unfit for agriculture," according to a 1987 report by Brazilian ecologist Jose Lutzenberger, who became Minister of the Environment in Brazil during the presidency of Fernando Collor de Mello.[30]

In addition to burning the forest, ranchers used chemical methods to clear the land and maintain pastures in the Amazon. *Science* magazine reported in 1973 that the U.S. Air Force tried to sell 2.3 million gallons of the chemical herbicide Agent Orange—the same defoliant that the United States had used during the Vietnam War—to the Brazilian government. Two private companies, **Blue Spruce International** and **International Research Inc.**, reportedly sought to arrange the sale of the dioxin-containing chemical, which had been banned for such uses in the United States. The president of Blue Spruce told *Science* the herbicide could be diluted with gasoline and sold to ranchers for $5 a gallon to keep rangelands clear of unwanted growth and boost Brazilian beef production. A campaign by environmentalists persuaded the Brazilian govern-ment not to buy the herbicide, although its use was widespread among private farmers, according to government officials.[31]

All told, manmade pasturelands in Latin America have increased by two-thirds since the 1960s, almost all of which have been established at the expense of undisturbed rain forests, according to British researcher Norman Myers. In Central America, cattle production rose 160 percent from 1960 to 1980, and beef exports increased from 20,000 tons a year to 150,000 tons a year. Meanwhile, per capita consumption of beef declined 13.5 percent in the region, and tropical rain forest cover dropped from 280,000 square miles to less than 140,000 square miles.[32]

Pasture Regeneration

The Brazilian Amazon contains nearly 25 million acres of abandoned pastureland. If this land can be returned to productivity, it would reduce the pressure to cut more virgin rain forest. Scientists from various disciplines agree that small-scale cattle ranching, agriculture and logging of secondary forests is possible on abandoned pastureland, provided that appropriate steps are taken. Crop farming and cattle ranching requires that essential nitrogen-fixing legumes are planted with other vegetation and forage materials, for example. Improved management techniques that discourage the growth of weeds also could bolster the productivity of the denuded land. Many environmentalists believe, however, that cattle ranching should be confined to non-rain forest areas—where soils are more resilient—until these soil preservation methods are widely adopted on denuded rain forest land.[33]

Christopher Uhl, a plant ecologist at the Pennsylvania State University, has spent several years in Brazil studying pasture regeneration. He believes pastures in some areas are coming back more rapidly than previously thought. "Early on, it appeared that Amazon development was doomed and that the Amazon forest, once cleared, would never regenerate....But now, as one drives through the aging Amazon frontier, there are signs of prosperity—a nicely kept cacao grove here, a maracuja plantation there, and recently reformed pastures throughout," Uhl says.[34] While there are many abandoned ranches throughout the region, Uhl observes, more often than not they have turned into second growth forests, not deserts.

Part of the reason for the quicker recovery is new knowledge about the subsurface of tropical forests. The conventional wisdom was that the Amazon's trees got most of their nutrients from rainfall. Recent studies indicate, however, that far more of the moisture and nutrients of trees are obtained from roots than was previously thought. As a result, trees can come back swiftly, especially if cattle grazing was not intensive and rainfall patterns do not change. However, on land where cattle grazed heavily for many years, the creation of a healthy secondary forest might take 100 to 200 years.[35]

The 'Hamburger Connection'

Cattle in Central America are raised on grass rather than grain. This makes the beef very lean and suitable mostly for the fast food market as well as for luncheon meat, frankfurters and other processed meat products. Fast food restaurants deny they are using beef imported from Central America and say they use only domestic beef. But because meat imported into the United States is subsequently relabeled as domestic beef—making it difficult to trace its original source—buyers in this country may unknowingly be using imported beef.

A 1980 study for the U.S. State Department by Douglas Shane reported that **Burger King** (then a subsidiary of **Pillsbury** and now owned by **Metropolitan Foods PLC**), **Jack-in-the Box** and **Marriott** subsidiaries **Roy Rogers, Bob's Big Boy** and **Hot Shoppes** outlets all acknowledged using some imported beef.[36] Seven years later, Rainforest Action Network targeted **Burger King** for a boycott as the only company it could positively identify as using "rain forest beef." Burger King's sales reportedly dropped 12 percent in the month after the boycott was announced; in August 1987 it instructed its suppliers not to buy any more Central American beef.

In 1989, Rainforest Action Network contacted a variety of fast food outlets, and they all denied using beef from former rain forest areas. The activist group maintained that the denials were inconclusive because fast food companies claim to buy only from "domestic suppliers," who could import the beef and subsequently relabel it as domestic beef. In 1991, RAN supported a bill in Congress to require that beef products be labeled by the country of origin. The bill never got out of committee.

Box 6B

The Cocaine Connection

Legitimate corporate interests and local farmers are not the only agriculture-related causes of tropical deforestation. In Peru, illegal growth of the coca plant for the cocaine market has destroyed at least 500,000 acres of tropical rain forest, according to Peruvian conservationists. Throughout the Amazon basin, cocaine has directly or indirectly caused 1.7 million acres of deforestation—an area twice the size of Rhode Island.

Coca is, in fact, the largest crop under cultivation in the Peruvian Amazon. The number of plantations there has grown sevenfold in the last 15 years to meet increased demand for the drug in North America and Europe. Most of the coca is grown in the Upper Huallaga River Valley, a lush rain forest habitat in north central Peru. Farmers in the impoverished region find it hard to resist being paid up to eight times what they would receive for growing traditional cash corps, according to an account in *The New York Times.*[1b]

Coca cultivators clear all protective vegetation from the hillsides to grow coca, which is harvested four times a year. The forest clearing exposes more soil to pounding tropical rains and creates severe soil erosion. As a result, "superficial erosion is quickly transformed into furrows and deep gullies," explains Marc Dourojeanni, a former Peruvian forest engineer now with the Inter-American Development Bank. Coca growers also are polluting rivers by dumping huge amounts of toxic chemicals used to refine coca leaves. Dourojeanni estimated in a 1987 study that Peruvian coca growers each year dispose of 15 million gallons of kerosene, 8 million gallons of sulfuric acid, 1.6 million gallons of acetone, 1.6 million gallons of the solvent toluene, 16,000 tons of lime and 3,200 tons of carbide.

The coca growing areas are controlled by the guerrilla group Shining Path, which makes researchers, environmentalists and even the military fearful of attempting to intercede. American officials have been debating whether toxic defoliants should be sprayed on the plants. But major chemical makers like **Dow Chemical** and **Eli Lilly** have declined to sell defoliants for this purpose, because the chemicals may kill much more than coca plants and could lead to liability suits. The Peruvian government insists that developed countries must do more to stem the demand for cocaine within their borders.

Focus on McDonald's: McDonald's, the world's largest fast food chain, with more than 12,000 outlets worldwide, maintains that it does not purchase beef "raised on rain forest (or recently deforested rain forest) land." Pamphlets made available in its outlets—entitled "Our rain forest policy"—state that "It is McDonald's policy to use only locally produced and processed beef in every country where we have restaurants." The company has outlets in many countries with tropical rain forests, however, including Brazil, Costa Rica, Guatemala, Malaysia, the Philippines and Thailand.

McDonald's definition of "recently deforested land" refers to the date the company first opened a restaurant in that particular country. "Cattle must have been grazing on the land prior to our coming there," explains Mary Ann Lederer, McDonald's environmental affairs coordinator. The company requires its beef purchasers to certify quarterly that beef is not grown on recently deforested land. "We have dedicated beef suppliers and they know where the cattle have grazed," Lederer says.[37] Any supplier found to deviate from the policy is cut off immediately. Lederer was not able to say whether any suppliers have been removed for this reason.

McDonald's policy appears to allow the supplier to use land that may have been rain forest in recent years. If McDonald's plans to open an outlet in Honduras in 1995, for example, it presumably could obtain beef from land that was rain forest in 1992 and that is cut and burned in 1993 to make way for cattle grazing in 1994.

Chapter Six Appendix

Agricultural Companies With Tropical Forest Operations or Policies

United States

AMERICAN FINANCIAL CORP.: American Financial Corp., based in Cincinnati, Ohio, owns **Chiquita Brands International**, formerly known as United Fruit Co. and United Brands. United Fruit was formed in 1899 to grow and export bananas from Central America. United Fruit emerged as a powerful force in the region's economy and politics. Today, Chiquita Brands is the world's largest exporter of bananas, with 100,000 acres of owned land and 45,000 acres of leases in Costa Rica, Panama and Honduras. Most of the land is used for banana and palm oil production and related activities. Chiquita also exports bananas from the Philippines, Ecuador and Guatemala under contract from local suppliers.

In Costa Rica, the company has cleared a small percentage of secondary forest for banana plantations in the southern Limon province on the Atlantic coast. The majority of the land is "portrero," land that has already been cleared for cattle ranching, reports Gabriela Mena, technical services director for Chiquita's Costa Rican operations.[38] (See pp. 150-152 for more information on Chiquita's Costa Rican operations.)

THE COCA-COLA CO.: Coca-Cola, based in Atlanta, Ga., owns Coca-Cola Foods, the maker of **Minute Maid** orange juice. In 1985, Coca-Cola Foods and two Texas ranchers purchased 196,000 acres of land in the Central American country of Belize. The land was part of a former estate owned by the Belize Estate and Produce Co., a United Kingdom-registered company; part of it had been logged for more than 100 years, according to the company. Minute Maid made tentative plans to grow citrus on 25,000 to 30,000 acres of the land (and construct a citrus processing plant) to supplement its supply of Florida oranges, which are susceptible to fruit-killing winter freezes. The project raised concerns in Belize about the sale of territory to foreigners for business and agricultural purposes. Several environmental groups, including Friends of the Earth, also denounced the project and urged a boycott of Coca-Cola in Europe.

In 1988, Coca-Cola Foods shelved the Belize project, citing environmentalists' pressure, along with an inability to obtain political risk insurance and an improvement in the world market price for orange juice. "Our concern was that the most important asset Coke has is its name, its trademark," says Michelle Beale, senior vice president for human resources and public affairs for Coca-Cola Foods. "If that is in jeopardy, we decided the project was not worth it."[39]

Beale says that the land to have been cleared for citrus was classified as being on the border between subtropical moist and tropical dry forest. That distinction enabled the company to say that it would not be cutting down tropical rain forests (although the Texas ranchers had planned to fell about 5,000 acres to raise cattle). Lack of responsiveness by the company to the environmentalists' concerns aggravated the situation, the company now acknowledges. "We could have done a much better job about getting information out in a proactive way— which we didn't do," says Beale. Coca-Cola Foods subsequently donated 42,000 acres to the Program for Belize, a Belizean conservation group, for use as a nature preserve, and it gave $50,000 to assist in the group's efforts to raise money to buy additional parcels of land.

The fate of the rest of the land remains in doubt. Coca-Cola Foods retains 55,000 acres and does not rule out the possibility of planting citrus groves in the future. Another 90,000 acres have been sold to Belizean interests. A group of Mennonites have acquired 60,000 acres and deforested significant portions of their parcel for the development of farms and settlements. The remaining 30,000 acres have been sold to **New River Enterprises**, a Belizean logging company.

DOLE FOOD INC.: **Dole Food**, based in Westlake Village, Calif., is the world's largest producer and marketer of fresh fruits and vegetables. Dole, formerly known as Castle & Cooke, is also a major real estate developer in Hawaii. Dole owns nearly 130,000 acres of land in Hawaii, making it the third largest private landowner in the state. Its largest land holdings, approximately 88,700 acres, are on the island of Lanai; 12,250 acres are growing pineapples, 1,800 acres have diversified agricultural operations (including pasture land for livestock), and 1,300 acres are under resort and residential development. Dole also owns about 40,400 acres on the island of Oahu, 15,500 acres of which are growing pineapples and sugar cane, and another 11,600 acres of which are leased to 80 tenants.

In addition to the approximately 20,000 acres of pineapple cultivation on the islands of Lanai and Oahu, Dole owns a 30,000 acre plantation in the Philippines and owns 5,700 acres in Honduras and 5,000 acres in Thailand. It grows bananas on company-owned plantations in the Philippines, Honduras and Costa Rica, where it is known as **Standard Fruit Co**. Through its long-term leases, Dole owns or controls 23,100 acres of banana plantations in Costa Rica, 7,900 acres in Honduras and 2,000 acres in the Philippines. The company also owns a palm oil plantation in Honduras. An environmental group in Costa Rica claims the company has been involved in clearing tropical forests for new banana plantations, but Standard Fruit denies the allegation. The company did not respond to IRRC requests for further information about its activities in the tropical forest areas.

In 1992, the International Water Tribunal, an ad hoc adjudicatory group that mediates transboundary water disputes, cited Standard Fruit for cutting trees too close to riverbanks, causing soil erosion and water siltation, and contaminating waterways with large amounts of pesticides. The plaintiff, a Costa Rican environmental group, presented evidence that chemicals from Standard Fruit plantations had washed into rivers, leached into groundwater supplies and contaminated wells. Standard Fruit rejected the allegations and said it was in compliance with all Costa Rican environmental and worker safety laws. The International Water Tribunal recommended that the company replant denuded river banks and hydrographic areas to minimize erosion and flooding, phase out the use of hazardous chemicals and minimize the use of other pesticides, and establish a monitoring program to ensure the maintenance of water quality. Standard Fruit says it already applies pesticides in the smallest possible quantities and uses only chemicals approved by the U.S. and Costa Rican governments.[40]

From 1971 to 1978, Standard Fruit was among the banana growers that applied large amounts of the pesticide DBCP on its Costa Rican plantations. The U.S. Environmental Protection Agency banned the use of DBCP on all leafy vegetables and some fruits in the United States in August 1977. Dole allegedly pressured **Dow Chemical**, a manufacturer of DBCP, to continue shipments to Costa Rica until the government there banned the import and use of the chemical in 1979. "Unlike the competitor, **United Fruit**, which ceased to use DBCP [in 1977] and switched successfully to Furadan or Nemacur, Dole managers chose to use DBCP, placing priority on profit/production goals and disregarding the hazard," researcher Lori Ann Thrupp found in a 1990 study.[41]

Standard Fruit faces several lawsuits from workers alleging health problems related to exposure to DBCP. Thrupp estimates that at least 1,500 banana plantation workers in Costa Rica claim to be sterile because of exposure to DBCP. The U.S. Supreme Court has upheld a lower court ruling that will allow a lawsuit by these workers to be heard in a Texas court. In a separate lawsuit, workers at Standard Fruit's banana plantations in Honduras are seeking at least $30,000 indemnification each for exposure to DBCP, after rejecting Standard Fruit's out-of-court settlement offer of $4,000 each. The workers reportedly decided to take legal action after a fellow worker died of cancer, which they believe was caused by exposure to DBCP.[42]

THE GOODYEAR TIRE & RUBBER CO.: Goodyear, based in Akron, Ohio, is one of the world's leading manufacturers of tires and rubber products. It operates rubber plantations in Brazil, Guatemala, Indonesia and the Philippines. Most of the facilities have been operating for generations: the Indonesian plantation (Dolok Merangir estate) started in 1917, the ones in the Philippines (Mindanao, Pathfinder and Zamboanga) began in 1928, the one in Brazil (Marathon estate) opened in 1954, and the one in Guatemala (Las Delicias estate) opened in 1957. Today, only a small percentage of the rubber is used for tire production; most is sold on the open market for uses where synthetic rubber is inappropriate.

Goodyear provided IRRC with basic information about only one of its plantations, the Marathon estate in the Brazilian state of Para. The estate is 11,000 acres in size. Under Brazilian forestry law, Goodyear cannot deforest an area greater than half of its holdings. The company estimates, however, that it has already planted 6,100 acres there, which is more than 50 percent of its reported holdings. Goodyear is clearing another 592 acres for planting. Judy Kosmo of Goodyear investor relations says the company is in compliance with the law.[43]

McDONALD'S CORP.: McDonald's, based in Oak Brook, Ill., is the world's largest fast food company. It has operations in several rain forest countries but says none of its beef comes from recently deforested areas. The company says it monitors its beef suppliers for compliance. (See pp. 158-159 for more details on its beef purchasing policy.)

PHILIP MORRIS COS. INC.: Philip Morris, based in New York City, is the producer of the world's best-selling brand of cigarettes, **Marlboro**, and may be involved indirectly in deforestation. Its **Philip Morris Brasileira** subsidiary is one of the three largest cigarette companies in Brazil. Philip Morris also purchases tobacco from plantations in Costa Rica, through its **Tabacalera Costarricense SA** subsidiary, and in Ecuador, through its **Tabacalera Andina** subsidiary. In Bolivia, Philip Morris manufactures cigarettes under a licensing agreement with **Companhia Industrial de Tabacos**. It also has subsidiaries in the Dominican Republic, El Salvador, Guatemala, Mexico and Panama.[44]

RJR NABISCO: **R.J. Reynolds Tobacco Co.**, a principal subsidiary of RJR Nabisco, based in New York City, may be involved indirectly in deforestation. Its **R.J. Reynolds Tabacos do Brasil** subsidiary is one of the three largest cigarette companies in Brazil. In Ecuador, Reynolds trades through its **Fabrica de Cigarillos El Progreso** subsidiary. In Mexico, Reynolds brands are sold under a licensing agreement with **Cigarrera La Moderna**.[45]

Mexico

CABAL GROUP: Cabal Group owns **Del Monte**, one of three major banana companies operating in Central America. (The company, known as **Bandeco** in Costa Rica, used to be owned by Polly Peck International.) Del Monte did not respond to IRRC's requests for information about its activities in tropical regions. An environmental group in Costa Rica claims the company has been involved in clearing tropical forests for new banana plantations. (See pp. 150-152 for details.)

United Kingdom

BAT INDUSTRIES: BAT Industries is one of the largest companies in the United Kingdom, employing 200,000 people and operating in more than 80 countries. A U.S. subsidiary, **Brown & Williamson Tobacco Corp.**, is the third largest tobacco company in the United States. **British-American Tobacco** produces cigarettes for consumption in 40 countries in Europe, Australia, Latin America, Asia and Africa. BAT's affiliate in Brazil, **Souza Cruz**, is the country's largest cigarette manufacturer, and one of the world's leading exporters of leaf tobacco. Souza Cruz does not believe it is growing tobacco on former tropical rain forest areas because tobacco reportedly does not grow well there. It says it has programs in many countries to encourage farmers to replenish trees cut for tobacco curing.[46]

GEEST PLC: Geest is a British producer and marketer of fresh fruits and vegetables. Geest recently established banana plantations in the Caribbean Windward Islands and in Costa Rica, where it has been fined by the government for illegally cutting rain forest trees in its plantation development near Tortuguero National Park. (See p. 152 for details.) Geest plans to invest $42 million in its Costa Rican operation, which began in 1991. By the end of 1993, Geest expects to employ 2,000 workers, who are building employee housing facilities, 600 miles of drainage ditches and 20 miles of road. Geest says it has converted 7,500 acres of what it describes as "pasture" to plant 5.5 million banana plants.

METROPOLITAN FOODS PLC: Metropolitan's **Burger King** unit is the only fast food company in America to have admitted purchasing beef on deforested rain forest land. Burger King canceled its contracts with all such suppliers in 1987, following a boycott sponsored by the Rainforest Action Network. (See p. 157 for details.) Metropolitan Foods acquired Burger King when it purchased **Pillsbury** in 1989.

UNILEVER: Unilever is a British conglomerate involved in foods, specialty chemicals, personal products and agribusiness. It is one of the largest nonpetroleum industrial enterprises in the world, with annual sales of about $40 billion. Unilever adopted an Ecological Charter in February 1990 that prohibits rain forest destruction for plantation development. The specific wording of the charter raises some questions, however. It promises to avoid only "primary rain forests." Secondary forests and degraded areas may be targeted for future plantations.

Unilever has 190,000 acres of agricultural plantations in Colombia, Cote d'Ivoire, Ghana, India, Kenya, Malawi, Malaysia, Nigeria, Solomon Islands, Tanzania, Thailand and Zaire; all but Malawi include some rain forest areas. The principal crops grown are cocoa, coconut, palm oil, rubber and tea. Many of the plantations were established in the early 20th century. Those plantations developed in the last 20 years are on land already degraded by primitive farming methods, the company says.

The most recently established Unilever plantation is in Colombia (started in 1981), where about 15,500 acres have been planted with oil palm. Other oil palm plantations include Cote d'Ivoire (7,400 acres), Ghana (9,600 acres), Malaysia (53,000 acres), Nigeria (2,500 acres) and Thailand (14,000 acres). Unilever grows tea and coffee in India (15,000 acres), Kenya (18,000 acres), Malawi (1,000 acres) and Tanzania (5,400 acres). It produces rubber in three plantations in Nigeria (16,000 acres), and cocoa and cattle in the Solomon Islands (20,000 acres). Unilever also grows cocoa, coffee, oil palm, rubber, tea and cattle in Zaire.

Chapter 7
Nontimber Forest Products and Ecotourism

Tropical forests typically have not stood up well against commercial interests. While more care has been taken to protect them in recent years, businesses' gain generally has been the forests' loss. The very nature of commercial activities such as logging, mining, farming and oil production detracts from the forests' value as a vital ecosystem for the planet. As development pressures continue to mount, their survival may turn on the value society places on tropical forests above and beyond the value of the trees, the ground and the minerals they possess.

Tropical forests are brimming with nontimber products, some of which have commercial value already. Fruits, nuts, oils, resins and fibers have been harvested by tropical forest dwellers for at least two millennia. Marco Polo recognized the value of such nontimber forest products when he brought spices and other goods back from China to Venice in the 13th century. Further development of the trade in nontimber forest product markets, if done responsibly, may hold a key to preserving large tracts of rain forest—and provide ecologically minded investment opportunities as well.

The ultimate markets for nontimber forest products are never likely to match the revenues generated by other, more disruptive commercial activities in the rain forest. Yet they have already proven that they can generate significant income and support large populations while keeping the rain forest largely intact. In the Brazilian state of Acre, sales of renewable products like rubber latex and Brazil nuts contribute more to its rural economy—about 40 percent—than ranching, farming, logging or industry.[1] In Indonesia, an estimated 200,000 forest dwellers make a living by harvesting rattan (the stems of climbing palms that are made into furniture and basketry), an industry now employing three times as many people as that country's $3 billion logging industry.[2] The sale of nontimber forest products in Indonesia rose from 3 percent of total forest export value in 1973 to 15 percent in the mid-1980s.[3]

Leaving aside the unquantifiable ecological value of the rain forests, under the right conditions, these forests may be worth more standing than when cleared for other commercial purposes. At least that is the conclusion of a landmark botanical study by researchers Charles Peters, Alwyn Gentry and Robert Mendelsohn. Surveying one hectare (2.47 acres) of tropical rain forest near Iquitos, Peru, they found 72 species with commercial value. While 60 of these species produce commercial timber, 11 others provide food, and one—the rubber tree—produces latex. When the researchers compared the market value of the species cut for timber with the average retail prices for tree-derived foods and rubber, they concluded that the value of timber on the plot, measured over a 50 year period, would be less than half that of the nontimber forest products—$1,289 versus $2,761 per acre. If the same area were cut and cleared for pasture, they found, the revenues generated would be even less—about $1,198 per acre. While critics of the study maintain that not all plots contain so many valued nontimber forest products—and that market prices would fall if they do—the authors say the "results from our study clearly demonstrate the importance of non-wood forest products."[4]

The governments of tropical forested countries—often focused on the greater export potential of other commodities such as beef, oil, minerals and timber—have been slow to recognize the commercial value of nontimber forest products and have done comparatively little to enhance the export potential of these goods. Private groups such as Cultural Survival and Conservation International, which are dedicated to preserving rain forests and their peoples, have stepped into the void to promote expanded export markets for a range of nontimber forest products, including foods, fibers, cosmetics and apparel. At the same time, tropical forests are attracting a new import: so-called "ecotourists" who want to pay to see the rain forest in its preserved state.

This chapter focuses on the emerging markets for nontimber forest products and ecotourism. But first it examines another tropical forest resource that is hard to value in dollars but that money can buy: rain forest species that ward off illness and disease—and sometimes save lives.

A Natural Apothecary

Humid tropical forests are home to thousands of plants with medicinal properties. About one-quarter of the prescription drugs available today contain active ingredients derived directly from flowering plants. When antibiotics (which come from bacteria and fungi) are added in, practically half of today's drugs are derived from natural sources, with prescription and over-the-counter sales exceeding $40 billion a year.[5]

More than 120 clinically useful prescription drugs now on the market are derived from higher plant species. Of these, 39 originated in tropical forests, resulting in 47 marketed drugs.[6] Rain forest-derived medicines include quinine to fight malaria, reserpine (from the rauwolfia plant) for hypertension, ipecac as an emetic, quinidine (from the cinchona tree) as an antiarrhythmic for heart problems, and pilocarpine (from the jaborandi tree) to treat rheumatism and glaucoma. Curare—used originally by South American tribes as a poison for the tips of darts and arrows—now is used as a relaxant to control muscle spasms. And the rosy periwinkle, a rain forest flower, has provided two of the world's most powerful anticancer agents—vincristine and vinblastine. Vincristine is used to treat leukemia, the most common form of childhood cancer, and vinblastine is used as an effective treatment for Hodgkins' disease and testicular cancer. The two drugs account for about $100 million in sales each year, placing them among the largest plant-to-drug commercial successes of the last 30 years.[7]

In developing nations, traditional medicines, also derived from natural sources, form the basis of health care for approximately 80 percent of the population—and more remedies are waiting to be discovered. Not even 1 percent of 250,000 known plant species in the neotropics have been tested for their pharmacological value. Yet botanical research has shown that indigenous peoples and rural inhabitants of the tropics can—and do—manage myriad plant genetic resources in their environment. Steven King, vice president for conservation and ethnobotany at **Shaman Pharmaceuticals**, which is conducting research on rain forest-derived drugs, has observed that forest dwellers gather many medicinal plants from the wild and cultivate and maintain others as a natural apothecary.[8]

In 1992, ethnobotanist Michael Balick of the New York Botanical Garden's Institute of Economic Botany and resource economist Robert Mendelsohn of the Yale University School of Forestry and Environmental Studies published what may be the first study to quantify the value of tropical forests as a source of locally used traditional medicines. Balick and Mendelsohn traveled to the Central American country of Belize, where traditional practitioners minister to most of the primary health care needs of rural people, and conducted inventories of the plant material in two plots totaling slightly more than an acre. After harvesting everything in those plots considered to have medicinal value, they calculated what local pharmacists and healers would pay for the unprocessed materials. After subtracting farmers' expenses, they found that the value of medicinal plants on the land ranged from $228 to $1,236 per acre. These values, over the long term, compare favorably to management of the land for alternative uses such as agricultural crops and pine plantations.[9]

Yet despite the proven success and commercial potential of medicines derived from the rain forest, pharmaceutical companies have shown little interest in exploiting this market—until recently. **Merck**, the world's largest pharmaceutical company, invested $1.135 million in a Costa Rican research institute in 1991 to identify species that could lead to the development of new drugs. **Eli Lilly**, the giant U.S. pharmaceutical, invested $4 million in **Shaman Pharmaceuticals** in 1992 in an effort to market compounds that Shaman finds and proves effective. **Monsanto** added rain forest plants to its screening program in 1989, and **Bristol-Myers Squibb** recently bolstered a natural products screening program as well. Bristol-Myers has already licensed taxol, a substance found to treat ovarian cancer, which is derived from the U.S. Pacific yew tree. (A more complete list of pharmaceutical company screening programs, compiled by the World Resources Institute, appears in the box on pp. 169-171.)

There was a time before the 1950s when many drugs were developed from natural sources. Since then, however, the drug industry has scaled back its screening of higher plant species and made huge investments in biotechnology and synthetically derived drugs. Many pharmaceutical companies no longer have the patience or the background to search for plant-based drugs, explains pharmaceutical sciences professor Varro Taylor, because their past efforts mainly came up empty. Smith Kline & French (now **SmithKline Beecham**), for instance, supported a screening program for alkaloid-containing plants for more than a decade and did not obtain a single commercial product. Likewise, the National Cancer Institute could not identify a single agent in general use for the treatment of human cancer, despite 25 years of tests on 40,000 plants.[10] (The rosy periwinkle was not among the plants it screened.)

But the enormous costs of developing synthetic drugs and the fledgling success of medical biotechnology to date is prompting drug companies to search once again for medicinal products from natural sources. Drug companies are discovering that all drug research is basically a crapshoot, even as advances in biotechnology make genes from the entire world's biota accessible for testing. While industry and government researchers screen hundreds of thousands of chemicals routinely for useful biological characteristics, only about one in 10,000 screened chemicals shows any commercial development potential. And before a new drug is approved for commercial use, more than $230 million and 10 to 12 years of laboratory research are usually involved. Of the drugs that reach clinical trials, only one in four is ever approved for commercial use.[11]

Pharmaceutical companies are using new methods to replicate some of the more complex compounds found in nature. New bioassays and automated screening technology that make it possible to screen large numbers of molecules rapidly have led to faster, easier and more accurate means to identify prospective drugs from natural sources. Once a promising chemical compound has been identified, it usually can be replicated synthetically in the laboratory.

Sarah Laird of the Rainforest Alliance, who edited a 1991 study on natural products research by pharmaceutical companies, says the recent focus on drugs derived from nature represents a decided shift in plant research. High-volume, robot-controlled screening programs can check 50,000 samples a year and find up to twice as many promising drugs as can conventional synthetic chemistry research.[12] Indicative of the resurgent interest in nature-derived drugs, the National Cancer Institute—despite a lack of success in past efforts—has renewed an $8 million, five year contract with botanical gardens in New York, Missouri and Illinois to screen 10,000 natural substances for anticancer and HIV-fighting properties.

The European and Japanese pharmaceutical industries are getting into the act as well. German drug companies have had considerable success throughout the 1980s in introducing drugs with new plant constituents, and Japan recently launched a major biodiversity research program in Micronesia.[13] Meanwhile, two large British firms, **SmithKline Beecham** and **Glaxo Holdings**, have begun screening large numbers of plants, including rain forest samples, for potentially useful drugs. Smith-Kline has 25 people screening marine organisms, microorganisms and plants. It has one substance in clinical trials called campethecin that is an anticancer drug taken from an alkaloid derived from a tree grown in India and China. Glaxo has a natural products discovery department that is screening plants from South America. A third British firm, **Biotics**, is purchasing plants in developing countries and providing them to pharmaceutical companies which, in turn, pay for the samples and agree to make royalty payments to indigenous groups that knew of commercially valuable plants.[14]

(continued on p. 172)

Table 7

Drug Companies Active in Natural Product
Collection and Screening

Abbott Laboratories
Active since: 1950
Collectors: University of Illinois, independent collectors
Annual capacity: 20-50 primary screens
Therapeutic groups: anti-infective, cardiovascular, neuroscience, immunoscience

Boehringer Ingelheim
Active since: 1986-89
Collectors: University of Illinois, New York Botanical Garden (pilot program in 1986), independent collectors
Annual capacity: 8-12 screens; 5,000 compounds
Therapeutic groups: cardiovascular, respiratory, gastroenterology

Bristol-Myers Squibb
Active since: company established
Collectors: Scripps Institute of Oceanography, Oncogen (pokeweed protein), independent collectors
Annual capacity: proprietary
Therapeutic groups: anti-infective, anticancer, antiviral

Ciba-Geigy
Active since: 1989 (marine); 1992 (tropical plants)
Collectors: Chinese Academy of Sciences, Harbour Branch Oceanographic Institute, independent collectors
Annual capacity: 4,000 samples tested in 1991
Therapeutic groups: anticancer, cardiovascular, anti-inflammatory, CNS, respiratory, anti-allergy

Eli Lilly
Active since: active in the 1950s and 1960s
Collectors: now collaborates with the National Cancer Institute, Shaman Pharmaceuticals, independent collectors
Annual capacity: proprietary
Therapeutic groups: anti-infective, diabetes, cardiovascular, anticancer, CNS, pulmonary, antiviral, skeletal diseases

Glaxo Holdings
Active since: 1988
Collectors: Royal Botanic Gardens (Kew), Chelsea Physic Garden, Institute of Medicinal Plant Development (Beijing), Biotics Ltd. and University of Illinois/National Cancer Institute
Annual capacity: proprietary
Therapeutic groups: gastrointestinal, respiratory, anti-infective, cardiovascular, dermatology, metabolic diseases, anticancer, anti-inflammatory, infectious diseases

Inverni della Beffa
Active since: late 1950s
Collectors: in-house and independent collectors
Annual capacity: in-house screening of hundreds of samples a year
Therapeutic groups: cardiovascular, gastroenterologic, anti-inflammatory

Merck & Co.
Active since: 1991
Collectors: Inbio, New York Botanical Garden, MYCOsearch
Annual capacity: proprietary
Therapeutic groups: respiratory, anti-allergy, anti-inflammatory, anticancer, cardiovascu-
                       lar, anti-infective, antiviral, gastrointenstinal, prostate, bone disease

Miles Inc.
Active since: 1991
Collectors: contract companies, independent collectors
Annual capacity: proprietary
Therapeutic groups: CNS, anti-infective, cardiovascular, diabetes, rheuma diseases

Monsanto
Active since: 1989
Collectors: Missouri Botanical Garden
Annual capacity: 9,000 samples
Therapeutic groups: anti-infective, cardiovascular, anti-inflammatory

Pfizer
Active since: 1989
Collectors: Natural Product Sciences (now lapsed), New York Botanical Garden
Annual capacity: proprietary
Therapeutic groups: cardiovascular, anti-inflammatory, anti-infectives, psychotherapeutic,
                       diabetes, artherosclerosis, anticancer, gastrointestinal, immuno-
                       science

Pharmagenesis
Active since: 1990
Collectors: in-house experts in herbal medicine and more than 15 collaborating
                       entities
Annual capacity: 2,000-3,000 samples; 50 screens
Therapeutic groups: immune, endocrine, CNS, cardiovascular

Phytopharmaceuticals
Active since: 1992
Collectors: University of Sao Paulo, Brazil; Chinese Academy of Sciences,
                       independent collectors
Annual capacity: proprietary
Therapeutic groups: anticancer

Rhone-Poulenc Rorer
Active since: 1991
Collectors: University of Hawaii, Beijing Medical University, Shanghai Medical

University, Tianjin Plant Institute, independent collectors
Annual capacity: hundreds of samples; 9-20 screens
Therapeutic groups: cardiovascular, anti-infective, AIDS, CNS, respiratory, bone dis-
                      ease, anticancer

Shaman Pharmaceuticals
Active since: 1989
Collectors: in-house botanists and a network of collaborators
Annual capacity: 200 samples
Therapeutic groups: antiviral, antifungal, analgesics, diabetes

SmithKline Beecham
Active since: 1987
Collectors: Biotics Ltd., Royal Botanic Gardens (Kew), University of Virginia,
                     Scripps Institution of Oceanography, Morris Arboretum, University of
                     Pennsylvania, MYCOsearch, in-house collectors
Annual capacity: 2,000-3,000 samples, 10-15 screens
Therapeutic groups: anti-infective, cardiopulmonary, CNS, gastrointestinal, anti-inflam-
                     matory

Sphinx Pharmaceuticals
Active since: 1990
Collectors: Biotics Ltd., independent collectors
Annual capacity: 15,000 samples, 3 screens
Therapeutic groups: psoriasis, antifungal, anticancer

Sterling Winthrop
Active since: 1988
Collectors: Mississippi State University, Brigham Young University, New York
                     Botanical Garden (one shipment), independent collectors
Annual capacity: few hundred samples
Therapeutic groups: anticancer, anti-inflammatory

Syntex Laboratories
Active since: 1986
Collectors: Chinese Academy of Sciences
Annual capacity: 10,000 plant extracts, 10 screens
Therapeutic groups: anti-inflammatory, bone diseases, immunology, anticancer, gas-
                     troenterology, cardiovascular, antiviral, dermatology, oral contra-
                     ceptives

Upjohn
Active since: 1986-87
Collectors: Shanghai Institute of Materia Medica
Annual capacity: proprietary
Therapeutic Groups: CNS, cardiovascular, anti-infective, AIDS

NOTE: Some listed companies' screening programs are not in tropical forests.

SOURCE: World Resources Institute, *Biodiversity Prospecting*, 1993.

Shaman Pharmaceuticals

An American company taking a similar approach is Shaman Pharmaceuticals, a small, publicly traded company based in San Carlos, Calif. Shaman believes it has found an especially fast way to bring new drugs to market. It relies on "shamans"—medicine men among forest people—to identify rain forest plants that might make good commercial prospects. While Shaman has no drugs on the market now, its first candidate entered human clinical trials only 16 months after laboratory testing began. Such a short lead time is almost unheard of in the pharmaceutical industry.

Lisa Conte, president and founder of Shaman Pharmaceuticals, believes that rain forest medicine men are at an even greater risk of extinction than the forests themselves. As Western medicine penetrates tribal societies and young people reject their cultural traditions, fewer shamans are able to pass on their knowledge. Now Shaman Pharmaceuticals has ethnobotanists working on three continents, serving as apprentices to the medicine men.

Shaman Pharmaceuticals has identified two especially promising species to treat ailments for which few other commercial treatments are available. One is a South American plant used to make Provir, an oral antiviral agent that treats respiratory infections prevalent among children. A second drug, Virend, is a topical treatment for herpes I and II. Indians in Peru and parts of Mexico have used the native plant in Virend for generations to heal wounds and treat colds.

—Photo courtesy of Shaman Pharmaceuticals.

An ethnobotanist employed by Shaman Pharmaceuticals speaks with a medicine man about the healing properties of a rain forest plant.

Shaman Pharmaceuticals hopes to have both products approved for sale by the end of 1996. The worldwide market for these drugs conceivably could reach $500 million a year.[15] The fledgling company has two other drugs under development, an analgesic from Southeast Asia and an antifungal from North America.

In the fall of 1992, **Eli Lilly & Co.** announced that it was making a $4 million equity investment in Shaman Pharmaceuticals, commencing a four year, renewable development agreement. Under the agreement, Shaman Pharmaceuticals will identify and provide initial screening for plant extracts that show antifungal activity. Lilly will further investigate any promising compounds and have the option to obtain exclusive worldwide marketing rights for treatments that prove effective. Royalty payments to Shaman Pharmaceuticals will be determined on a case-by-case basis.[16]

Lilly is not the only pharmaceutical company that has expressed interest in Shaman Pharmaceuticals. Previously, **Inverni della Beffa SpA**, an Italian maker of plant-derived drugs, invested $500,000 in Shaman Pharmaceuticals and signed a licensing and manufacturing agreement. **Merck** has also entered into an agreement to screen compounds found by Shaman Pharmaceuticals for treatments of diabetes and analgesia. Individual and institutional investors are also getting into the act. In January 1993, Shaman Pharmaceuticals issued 3 million shares of common stock at $15 a share—which was 500,000 more shares and $1 higher in price than it had originally planned for its initial public offering.[17]

Shaman Pharmaceuticals hopes to share its commercial success with rain forest dwellers by creating a set of reciprocal obligations in which a percentage of its profits—reportedly 1 to 5 percent—is exchanged for conservation of forest habitat. Toward this end, it has created the nonprofit **Healing Forest Conservancy** to distribute profits to organizations that participate in plant collection and other collaborative activities. The conservancy also will work with local conservation groups to manage biological resources better and support sustainable production and marketing of rain forest products. The conservancy would like to provide reciprocal health benefits to indigenous peoples by making modern health care available to those who want or need it. Shaman Pharmaceuticals eventually hopes to employ 4,000 to 20,000 plant harvesters in tropical countries.

Merck/Inbio Agreement

Merck is taking a somewhat different approach to identify rain forest plants with medicinal value. In September 1991, it announced an agreement with the Instituto Nacional de Biodiversi-dad (Inbio), a nonprofit, private organization in Costa Rica, in which Merck will pay $1 million over two years to support Inbio's research on rain forest plants. The Costa Rican government established Inbio in 1989 to conduct a complete inventory of the nation's species. Costa Rica, a country only the size of West Virginia, is thought to possess 5 to 7 percent of the world's biodiversity.

Thomas Eisner, a biology professor at Cornell University who is credited with the idea of "biodiversity prospecting" in tropical forests, says that Inbio's field biologists will look for telltale signs from species with potential medicinal value. "A leaf on a forest floor that remains uncovered by mold may be the source of a new antibiotic," he explains, "as may certain insect eggs that remain untouched by microbes as long as the mother administers salivary fluids." Likewise, "A plant that is untouched by insect pests may contain a useful insect repellant."[18] Merck does not expect to find an active drug in the chemical samples extracted by Inbio, according to Lynn Caporale, a biochemist who oversees Merck's outside collaborations, "though I would love that to happen." Rather, she and her colleagues are looking for promising compounds that could be modified by Merck chemists.[19]

Merck had 30 people screening a variety of plants (some of which are rain forest plants supplied by the New York Botanical Garden) even before its agreement with Inbio. The Costa Rican group, which has indexed thousands of rain forest plants, now will supply up to 10,000 promising samples to Merck for testing. If Merck discovers any active ingredients from which it develops commercial products, it will retain all patent rights. Inbio may enter into similar contractual arrangements with other parties, but it cannot supply the same samples it gives to Merck without Merck's explicit permission.

Ten percent of Merck's initial $1 million payment to Inbio plus 50 percent of any royalties will be passed on to the Costa Rican Ministry of Natural Resources; the rest of the proceeds will used at Inbio's discretion to preserve the environment. Merck's payment, in effect, represents an up-front contribution of a share of the anticipated future royalties to cover the lag time between the identification and sale of new drugs, a period that can be 10 years or longer. The World Resources Institute estimates that if Inbio ultimately were to receive 2 percent of the royalties from sale of perhaps 20 commercial products that Merck might develop as a result of Inbio's survey, Inbio would take in more money than Costa Rica presently derives from the sale of bananas and coffee—two of the country's prime exports.[20]

In addition to its other payments to Inbio, Merck has donated equipment worth $135,000 to carry out the survey's chemical extraction process. Merck also has provided two natural products chemists to set up the extraction laboratories and train scientists in purification techniques. Eventually, Inbio hopes such training will aid Costa Rica in developing its own biotechnology industry and enable drug discovery to take place entirely within the country's borders.[21] Countries such as Indonesia and Kenya are establishing species inventory programs similar to Inbio's and have expressed interest in performing biodiversity prospecting in conjuntion with pharmaceutical companies.

Indigenous Knowledge and the Biodiversity Convention

Some anthropologists and environmentalists complain that drug companies still are not doing enough to protect the intellectual property rights of indigenous rain forest species, thereby undermining efforts to preserve those species and the forests in which they exist. Some warn that unregulated biodiversity prospecting could actually accelerate the destruction of certain species, if care is not taken to preserve samples in the field. As Lisa Conte of **Shaman Pharmaceuticals** sees the situation, most pharmaceutical companies "think they will be able to synthesize the active component of a plant-derived drug once it has been isolated, and they are not interested in developing sustainable industries."[22]

Anthropologist Darrell Posey insists that corporations have a responsibility to inform indigenous peoples fully about the value of commercial species growing on their land. He cites the case of two Kayapo Indians from the Brazilian Amazon, who traveled to Washington, D.C., in 1991 to express an interest in marketing medicinal plants to corporations as an alternative to minerals and timber extraction. Posey fears the Kayapo and other indigenous groups will be left with nothing but the "goodwill of companies that want to help them" if protections on intellectual property rights are not granted first. "Mining knowledge from the rain forest will be the last wave of neocolonialism," he predicts.[23]

Protection of intellectual property rights took center stage at the Earth Summit in Rio de Janeiro in 1992, when the United States refused to sign the International Convention on Biological Diversity supported by more than 150 other nations. Controversy arose because legal systems traditionally have not recognized a country's ownership of "unimproved genetic material"—wild species and traditional varieties of crops and livestock grown by farmers.[24] Innovations in biotechnology, particularly within the pharmaceutical industry, now make the potential economic returns to genetic information found in nature much greater than before—raising the stakes for the treaty's terms.

At the Earth Summit, representatives from developing countries argued that they should be entitled to a share of the proceeds from natural products "discovered" by traditional healers and sold by commercial interests in developed countries as well as products patented by agricultural and pharmaceutical companies derived from genes within their borders. The convention's planners originally considered giving a host country a royalty on any income derived from native material—a position that U.S. negotiators found objectionable. As finally drafted, the treaty calls for industrialized countries to provide funds for biodiversity preservation efforts of less developed nations—but does not specify a mechanism.

At Rio, the Bush administration expressed grave doubts about language in the treaty that gives developing nations "concessional and preferential" access to transfer of biotechnologies. Such language raises the specter of compulsory licensing of U.S. technology in nations where genetic information has originated. The Bush administration also said that patent rights of U.S. biotechnology companies would be weakened (although others maintained the language in the treaty could be seen as affirming those rights). The Bush administration decided in the end not to sign the Biodiversity Convention, arguing that private sector agreements—such as the one between **Merck** and Costa Rica's Inbio biodiversity institute—would facilitate the development of rain forest products and the transfer of technical knowhow.

"If the situation we have between Costa Rica and the United States was the same all over the world, the treaty wouldn't be necessary," acknowledges Rodrigo Gamez, director of Inbio. "But unfortunately, not all companies are like Merck, and not all countries are like Costa Rica."[25] The fact that Costa Rica already has a high level of dedication to preserving its biodiversity as well as a scientific collection system and technical expertise to process samples gives it a leg up in negotiating terms with multinational firms, Gamez says. Other developing countries may not be so fortunate.

Turning the argument on its head, the Biodiversity Convention should *not* preclude the kind of agreement that Merck has struck with Inbio, says Richard Wilder, an intellectual property rights lawyer in Washington, D.C., who is a member of the Association of Biotechnology Companies patent committee. Wilder says the treaty does not specify the creation of any particular contract between two parties. Rather, different parties are likely to interpret the treaty's vague language in different ways. Biotechnology and pharmaceutical companies will claim that the vague language supports strong intellectual property rights,

Wilder says, while developing nations take the opposite position. Ultimately, the parties will have to work out their differences over the bargaining table. (The National Cancer Institute, for one, is trying to develop "material transfer agreements" with tropical countries that provide for compensation, revenue sharing or both, in exchange for access to indigenous genetic resources.)[26]

In June 1993, the Clinton administration signed the International Convention on Biological Diversity over the objections of some U.S. pharmaceutical and biotechnology companies. The reversal of the American position represents a victory of sorts for tropical countries. It formalizes the principle that developing nations are the source of genetic material with promising biotechnological and biomedical applications and that these nations should share in the economic benefits arising from related research and development. The treaty also stipulates that industrialized nations must make good on their promise to provide funds to developing countries for biodiversity preservation—and share biotechnology with them—if they are to expect developing countries to live up to their end of the bargain. Future interpretation of the treaty might lead to the conclusion that a developing country is entitled to receive a percentage of royalties from sales of a product derived from its genetic resources, even if it does not acquire rights to the product itself.

Nontimber Forest Products from Extractive Reserves

As enthobotanists scour the rain forest for potentially life-saving medicines, other entrepreneurs are searching for markets for rain forest products grown in extractive reserves. Until recently, consumers and investors in the developed world have known little about these products. Sale of food, fiber, rubber and other materials from the rain forest has stayed mainly within local markets, employing a chain of subsistence farmers, middlemen and local retailers. "These decentralized trade networks are extremely hard to monitor and easy to ignore in national accounting schemes," observers Charles Peters, one of the botanists who studied nontimber forest products in the rain forests of Peru.[27]

Despite a paucity of research, available market studies suggest that expansion of markets for nontimber forest products could transform rain forest economies around the world. In 1990, three Harvard University graduate students traveled to the island of Borneo in the South China Sea to gather information on nontimber forest products that are collected and traded there. (Borneo is shared by Indonesia, Malaysia and Brunei and possesses the second largest area of undisturbed rain forest in the world after Brazil.) Of 90 products identified, they selected several as having the potential to be sustainably grown on Borneo and successfully marketed in the United States:

- keruing oil, collected from a tree sap and used as a base for perfume;
- illipe nut butter, a rich emollient for natural skin conditioners and a substitute for cocoa butter in chocolate confections;
- jamu, used in medicinal herbal teas; and
- a variety of mushrooms, spices and honey that are welcome additions in gourmet kitchens.

Combined sales of these products already generate millions of dollars a year, and promotion of such nontimber forest products now is part of the central government's forest development plans in Indonesia and Brunei, which own portions of Borneo.[28]

A more complete list of nontimber products from the rain forest, compiled by the Smithsonian Institution, includes many names more familiar to Western consumers (see Table 8 on pp. 178-179). Someday, these relatively obscure products may join the list of others now commonly found in kitchens, medicine chests, living rooms and lawns throughout the developed world. Still, the Harvard University students identified a number of formidable obstacles that stand in the way of bringing such products to market: The density of marketable species per acre of rain forest is relatively low; shifting cultivation among farmers and resettlement of landless peasants are constant threats to the resource; and large foreign debts compel central governments to promote high valued exports even when their effects on the rain forest may be devastating.

To foster sustainable development practices in humid tropical forests, environmental organizations like the World Resources Institute stress the need for "permanent forest estates" that provide secure, long-term land tenure for communities, concession holders and forest agencies.[29] In Brazil, where 4.5 percent of the landowners control 81 percent of the farmland, so-called "extractive reserves" are beginning to serve such a purpose. Today, 14 reserves covering more than 7 million acres of the Amazon have been established, conferring land rights to indigenous groups and squatters, some of whom have struggled decades to get them. While the fate of these reserves remains uncertain, their creation may lay the groundwork for expanded markets in nontimber forest products.

Plight of the Rubber Tappers

The establishment of extractive reserves in Brazil has been a turbulent and violent process, starting with the collapse of the Brazilian rubber boom in 1912 and ending with the life of Chico Mendes, a rural rubber tapper who died in 1988. After the collapse, rubber barons managed to keep the tappers under their control by using an exploitative patron/client relationship. Then the rubber barons got a boost when Japan cut off Allied sources of rubber from Asia during World War II. The United States financed the revitalization of Amazonian rubber estates as world rubber prices doubled. An estimated 50,000 peasants emigrated to the Amazon from other parts of Brazil during the war to form a "rubber tappers army." Many never left the rain forest. Today, an estimated 500,000 people earn a living extracting and selling native rubber latex in the Amazon.

In 1967, the Brazilian government ended the rubber barons' monopoly on selling rubber and allowed rubber tappers to market their products on their own. At the same time, however, the Brazilian government started to provide generous tax incentives to encourage wealthy businessmen from the south of Brazil to establish cattle ranches on the rubber barons' failing estates. This set up a confrontation between rubber tappers—who claimed title to the land after

(continued on p. 180)

Table 8

Familiar Products Originating...

FOODS AND SPICES

Spices	Fruits	Vegetables and Other Foods
Allspice	Avocado	Brazil nuts
Black pepper	Banana	Cane sugar
Cardamom	Breadfruit	Cashew nuts
Cayenne	Coconut	Chayote
Chili	Durian	Chocolate
Cinnamon	Grapefruit	Coffee
Cloves	Guava	Cucumber
Ginger	Jackfruit	Hearts of palm
Mace	Lemon	Macadamia nuts
Nutmeg	Lime	Manioc/tapioca
Paprika	Mango	Mayonnaise
Sesame seeds	Mangosteen	(coconut oil)
Tumeric	Orange	Okra
Vanilla	Papaya	Peanuts
	Passion fruit	Peppers
	Pineapple	Soft drinks (cola
	Plantain	Tea
	Rambutan	Vermouth
	Tangerine	(cascarilla oil)

PHARMACEUTICALS (partial list)

Item	Use
Castanaspermum australe	Research for potential AIDS cure
Annatto	Red dye
Curare	Muscle relaxant for surgery
Diosgenin	Sex hormones, birth control pills, steroids, asthma and arthritis treatment
Quassia	Insecticide
Quinine	Anti-malarial, pneumonia treatment
Reserpine	Sedative, tranquilizer
Strophanthus	Heart disease
Strychnine	Emetic, stimulant
Tuba root	Rotenone, flea dip

SOURCE: From the exhibition *Tropical Rainforests: A Disappearing Treasure*, Smithsonian

...in Humid Tropical Forests

OILS

Item	Use
Camphor oil	Perfume, soap, disinfectant, detergent
Cascarilla oil	Confections, beverages
Coconut oil	Suntan lotion, candles, food
Eucalyptus oil	Perfume, cough drops
Palm oil	Shampoo, detergents, food
Patchouli oil	Perfume
Rosewood oil	Perfume, cosmetics, flavoring
Sandalwood oil	Perfume
Tolu balsam oil	Confections, soaps, cosmetics, cough drops
Ylang-ylang oil	Perfume

FIBERS

Item	Use
Bamboo	Furniture, baskets
Jute/kenaf	Rope, burlap
Kapok	Insulation, soundproofing, life jackets
Raffia	Rope, cord, baskets
Ramie	Cotton-ramie fabric, fishing line

GUMS AND RESINS

Item	Use
Chicle latex	Chewing gum
Copaiba	Perfume, fuel
Copal	Paints and varnishes
Gutta percha	Golf ball covers
Rubber latex	Rubber products
Tung oil	Wood finishing

Institution Traveling Exhibition Service, Washington, DC.

working it for generations—and the new business interests who sought to clear the forests for ranching.

Union organizing in Acre, supported by an activist Catholic church, grew out of rubber tappers' resistance to eviction from the rubber estates. It was in this confrontational environment that a rubber tapper named Francisco Alves "Chico" Mendes Filho rose to international prominence and championed the idea that extractive reserves could serve as a way to save tropical rain forests.[30] Mendes was a union leader among 30,000 unionized rubber tappers in the rural state of Acre. Mendes recommended that former rubber estates be set aside as extractive reserves that could be run communally and owned by the government. Individual families would have the right to tap in areas where they had collected latex traditionally. While wholesale conversion of the land to nonforest uses would be prohibited, small clearings of up to 11 acres would be permitted for growth of subsistence crops.[31]

At the invitation of U.S. environmental groups, Mendes came to America in 1985 to discuss his proposal for extractive reserves. Two years later, Mendes attended the annual meeting of the Inter-American Development Bank (IDB), which had financed construction of a road from the Brazilian state of Rondonia into Acre. While Mendes and his followers did not ask that the road's construction be halted, they warned that lack of a coordinated plan would perpetuate the cycle of haphazard colonization and deforestation in the Amazon. To resolve the problem, they urged the IDB to require Brazil to demarcate Indian lands and those of established local communities as a condition of further bank lending.

Chico Mendes did not live to see the realization of his quest, however. Like 1,500 other rubber tappers, peasants and Indians in the Amazon, he was murdered by those competing for control of the forested land. After surviving six attempts on his life, Mendes was killed by cattle ranchers in December 1988. Soon after his death—which drew international attention—the Brazilian government established 14 extractive reserves, parks and study areas, covering 7.2 million acres in four states of the Amazon.

Much of the credit for the creation of these reserves goes to Mendes and his National Council of Rubber Tappers. Yet while the reserves are seen as a giant step toward legitimizing the rubber tappers' claims to the land, doubts remain about the economic viability of the reserves. Brazil's rubber tappers still depend on large government subsidies and a high import tariff in order to compete economically; rubber prices in Brazil are three times the international price. Given the nation's huge foreign debt, the subsidies cannot be expected to last indefinitely. Moreover, the reserves are not able to support a fast-growing population. Typically, one family manages 650 to 1,250 acres of rubber trees.

The biggest obstacle appears to be the underlying economic dimension of the latex rubber market. About 60 percent of Brazil's natural rubber now comes from plantations. The alternative is to make it synthetically. Such competing sources threaten the price-competitiveness of rubber from the extractive reserves.[32]

One Brazilian economist, Alfredo Homma, predicts that the reserves are doomed because of low productivity of the resource and the need for continuing government subsidies to compete with cheaper, plantation-grown rubber.[33] Amazon ecologist Philip Fearnside is also pessimistic about the rubber tappers' prospects. But he argues that traditional economic calculations must be discarded if such a sustainable use of forest resources is to be regarded as a viable enterprise. Even if the traditional products of extractive reserves do not measure up to other industries economically, Fearnside argues, the unique ecosystem harbored in the reserves justifies their continued existence.[34]

In any event, rubber tappers' financial interests would be served if markets are developed for nontimber forest products in addition to latex rubber and Brazil nuts (which rubber tappers harvest in the off-season) to increase the productive potential of the land. The long-term solution may not lie in more centrally planned government initiatives but in entrepreneurial efforts and creative marketing schemes that give local forest dwellers a critical stake in the success of their ventures.

New Marketing Efforts to Save the Rain Forests

Several socially minded entrepreneurs have launched rain forest marketing experiments to give more economic value to rain forest products and more political clout to forest inhabitants. Conservation and human rights organizations have set themselves up as temporary brokers of rain forest products to demonstrate to skeptical governments and investors that consumer markets for rain forest nontimber products can be established both domestically and internationally. These projects include exporting Brazil nuts and cashews to the United States for use in cereal and candies, tropical oils for cosmetics, tagua nuts for buttons on apparel and palm fronds for floral wreaths. One researcher is having success with using "iguana farming" as a means to save rain forest areas. (See the box on p. 188.)

Potential customers for these products are not all small marketers. **Safeway**, the largest food store chain in the United States, and the **Loblaw** chain in Canada have expressed interest in ordering large quantities of selected rain forest food products. **J.M. Smucker** and **Ben & Jerry's Homemade Ice Cream** already are purchasing rain forest food products such as Brazilian nuts and cupuassu fruit. **Patagonia** and **Smith & Hawken** are buying millions of tagua buttons for apparel. And **The Body Shop**, a fast-growing British marketer of natural cosmetics, is purchasing a variety of tropical oils for cosmetics.

Cultural Survival

The group that pioneered the concept of marketing rain forest products is Cultural Survival, a nonprofit organization based in Cambridge, Mass. Cultural Survival is dedicated to the preservation of indigenous peoples. It is convinced that the key to preserving their culture and habitat is to provide them with the means for greater economic and political power. "Without markets, people who want to expand their extractive activities have few incentives," says Jason Clay, who heads **Cultural Survival Enterprises**. "We define trade as a force for social change. Producers are stakeholders in the final product and have a right to share in the profits in areas above them on the marketing chain."[35]

The contracts brokered by Cultural Survival Enterprises require retailers of rain forest products to return a portion of their profits to local producers. Marketing rain forest products, of course, carries many business risks. Retailers are wary because consumers in developed countries usually are unfamiliar with rain forest products. In addition, arranging for a large-quantity, high-quality supply of products for high-volume marketing efforts can be difficult. Grants financed Cultural Survival's early marketing efforts. Now the group is hoping to secure loans instead. "Grants have the problem of no ownership, no incentive, no risk," Clay says. "With loans, forest residents learn marketing and financial principles that will someday make them self-sufficient."

One of Cultural Survival Enterprises' first marketing successes was conceived in a decidedly noncorporate setting, although it has paid real dividends in Brazil as well as the United States. In 1988, Clay met Ben Cohen, co-owner of **Ben & Jerry's Homemade Ice Cream**, at a Grateful Dead concert. Clay interested Cohen in producing a nut brittle using Brazil nuts and cashews imported from tropical rain forest areas. Rubber tappers harvest Brazil nuts in the off-season for rubber tapping.

Rubber tappers in Chico Mendes's hometown of Xapuri proposed building a nut processing factory that would be run by a cooperative and funded with the help of Funtac, the technical assistance agency for the Brazilian state of Acre. Funtac, in turn, invited the assistance of Cultural Survival. In 1989, Ben & Jerry's decided to create a new venture called **Community Products Inc.** to produce a candy brittle dubbed "Rain Forest Crunch." Cohen ordered a 15 ton container of nuts from Brazil initially to put in the brittle. Altogether that first year, Community Products sold $3.6 million worth of Rain Forest Crunch and shared $100,000 of profits with Cultural Survival. The shared profits were enough to finance the entire cost of building the Xapuri nut processing plant. The plant employs about 80 workers, each of whom earn at least $50 a month.

Today, Community Products imports about 300,000 pounds of nuts a year from Brazil and Bolivia, and Cultural Survival Enterprises still serves as the broker. The arrangement benefits Cultural Survival and rain forest dwellers in two ways. First, a 5 percent premium is added to the cost of all nuts sold through Cultural Survival Enterprises to help pay for its services. Second, Community Products pays an additional 20 percent of its after-tax profits (on a voluntary basis) to support rain forest-based organizations and their support groups. Through 1992, Community Products had shared nearly $500,000 in profits with these groups. Cultural Survival Enterprises still has a problem with obtaining a sufficient supply of nuts, however. In 1991, only 30 percent of the Brazil nuts supplied to customers of Cultural Survival Enterprises came from rubber tappers; the rest had to be purchased from commercial sources.

Cultural Survival Enterprises now accounts for about 10 percent of U.S. purchases of Brazil nuts, and its influence is felt throughout the commercial nut market. The Xapuri cooperative, for instance, has found that it could pay rubber tappers twice the going rate and still turn a profit. All nut collectors in Acre—not just those selling to the Xapuri facility—are demanding, and in most cases receiving, higher prices for their nuts than before Cultural Enterprises entered the scene. "We calculate that there was an increase of income to all collectors in the state of Acre totaling $600,000 in fiscal 1990, doubling to $1.2 million in 1991. You don't need 50 percent of the market to leverage this, just one honest broker," says Clay.

One of Cultural Survival's most successful ventures has been with **The Body Shop**, a fast-growing British cosmetics chain, which launched the first of its rain forest products in 1991. The Body Shop's products include a hair conditioner made from Brazil nuts harvested by Kayapo Indians in the Amazon and a lip balm made from babassu oil from the seed of an Amazonian palm tree. Other Body Shop products include a skin moisturizer called "mango body butter" that contains mango and avocado. (The Body Shop purchases Brazil nuts directly from the Kayapo; it works through Cultural Survival to obtain the other products.) The Body Shop also is investigating whether it can make products derived from andiroba, buriti, breu branco, copaiba, cupuassu, pequia and urucum. Some of these plant derivatives already have local uses. Andiroba is used as an ointment to ease muscle strain. Indians use copaiba as an antiseptic and healing agent.[36]

Another company buying from Cultural Survival is **Knudsen and Sons**, a division of **J.M. Smucker**, which uses the cupuassu fruit for its Rainforest Punch. **Rainforest Products**, a California company, markets Rainforest Crisp, a cereal available in health food stores that contains nuts from the rain forest. Cultural Survival has also held discussions with the makers of **Timex** watches to see whether the company would consider using tagua nuts (also known as vegetable ivory) as a replacement for ivory in some of its watches.

Other Product Ideas

Sales of rubber, Brazil nuts and other rain forest products, while increasing, still do not generate sufficient income for many forest dwellers. More commercially harvestable products will be needed to provide a diversified, sustainable resource base. One possibility is to plant a greater density of commercially valuable species such as Brazil nuts, cocoa, copaiba and acai. (Copaiba is used as a fixative in soaps and perfumes.)

The acai palm, a common tree in Brazil, has proven commercial potential if harvested carefully. Palm hearts from the acai are a delicacy in salads and have long been a valuable Brazilian export. The fruit of the acai also is used to produce a wine that is a popular drink in the Amazon. Extraction of acai palm hearts has been going on in the Amazon (particularly in an estuary near Belem) since the 1960s, when an overharvest of palm trees in southern Brazil created a shortage. Some families in forest areas near Belem generate 80 percent of their annual $4,000 income by harvesting an average of 15 acres of acai plants, according to Anthony Anderson, an ecologist who has worked in the Amazon for 15 years.[37]

Extraction of palm hearts, unlike other products, requires actual pruning of trees, however. Christopher Uhl of the University of Pennsylvania has found ample evidence of pressure on acai populations, including a declining number of acai stems cut per tree clump, a reduced dimension of harvested stems and a high frequency of dead trees. This, in turn, has led to a decline in work for employees in processing factories.[38]

Table 9

Marketing Projects of Cultural Survival

NUTS

Brazil nuts   From a tree species which grows only in primary rain forest. Virtually all brazil nuts are harvested from wild trees. Many uses in snacks, candies, nut mixes and baked goods. Samples available in a range of grades; price varies according to grades.

Cashew nuts   From a tree species widely grown on degraded soils in tropical regions. Cultural Survival is sourcing cashews grown on small-scale agricultural plots and reforestation projects. Many uses for snacks, candies, nut mixes and baked goods. Samples available in a range of grades; price varies according to grade.

FRUITS

Acai   The purple-colored fruit of an Amazonian palm. Widely consumed in fruit juice drinks, ice cream, chocolates and other confections. Samples of frozen açaí pulp cost $30.00 per liter.

Cupuaçu   The yellow-colored, highly aromatic fruit of an Amazonian tree closely related to the cacao plant. Cupuaçu fruit pulp can be incorporated into fruit drinks, ice cream and othe dessert items. One-liter samples of frozen fruit pulp cost $30.00 per liter.

Cashew fruit   Also from the cashew tree. Cashew fruits are eaten fresh, made into fruit drinks, jams and butters, and also dried to a date-like consistency. Samples of dried cashew fruit from Honduras available at $5 per lb.

HANDICRAFTS

Cuia   A gourd produced by a rain forest tree, cuias are crafed by indigenous peoples into pots, bowls, spoons, musical instruments, toys and other items. Cuia bowls available plain ($4 each) or painted with traditional indigenous designs ($8 each).

SOURCE: The Marketing Project, Cultural Survival Enterprises

At one point, Cultural Survival envisioned using latex from rubber trees to manufacture condoms—marketing them with the catchy phrase, "protect yourself, protect the rain forest." But the group discovered that latex from rubber trees is not durable enough to use in condoms if processed into solid form.

SPICES, FLAVORINGS

Honey   Cultural Survival is marketing two varieties of honey from Zambia. Both varieties are gathered by rural cooperatives from wild beehives. Samples cost $30.00 per liter.

Urucum   The small seed of a tropical American tree, it yields a brilliant red dye used by indigenous peoples as a body paint and to repel insects. Used widely under the name annatto to color dairy products and is also a common spice in Latin American cooking. Samples of ground urucum and whole seeds are $10.00 per 1/4 lb.

OILS

Babaçú   From the seed of an Amazonian palm. Many uses in soaps, shampoos, skin lotions and other personal care items, and also to make candles. Samples from Brazil cost $30.00 per liter.

Andiroba   From the seed of an Amazonian palm. Used in soaps, skin lotions and to treat insect bites and skin inflammations. Samples from Brazil cost $30.00 per liter.

Copaiba   A resin from a rain forest tree. Used in perfumes, soaps and a wide range of skin care items. Samples from Brazil cost $30.00 per liter.

ESSENCES

Cumaru   Derived from the seeds of a small rain forest shrub. Used to perfume tobacco, soaps, shampoos and other skin care items. Samples of cumaru essence cost $100.00 per liter.

Puxuri   Derived from the seeds of a rain forest tree. Potential uses include perfuming soaps, lotions and potpourris. Samples of puxuri essence cost $100.00 per liter.

Rubber tappers often heat liquid latex over a fire and form it into a solid ball to facilitate transport. If a way can be found to transport liquid rubber so that it can be made into high-quality latex, the condom factory idea might yet catch on in the Amazon.

In the meantime, Cultural Survival Enterprises is pursuing more conventional ideas in Brazil and other South American countries. It hopes to set up more nut processing cooperatives like the one in Xapuri throughout the Amazon. One of the facilities would be owned by Indians and rubber tappers in Rondonia. Another project would assist a cooperative of 1,600 cashew growers in the Brazilian state of Rio Grande du Norte who have already built a processing plant. The farmers there produce 12 million pounds of nuts a year but lack the expertise to process the nuts efficiently.

Cultural Survival is also looking at projects outside South America. In mid-1992, it began trading in Honduras, the Philippines, Tanzania and Zambia. The group imports dried fruit from Honduras, banana chips from the Philippines (for cereals and fruit mixes), and honey and beeswax from forest cooperatives in Tanzania and Zambia. Altogether, Cultural Survival supplies rain forest products to 40 companies and is in discussions with 80 others for possible project launches through 1995.

Conservation International

Conservation International, a nonprofit group dedicated to preservation of biologically diverse areas, is marketing another product to help conserve rain forests—tagua nuts. Tagua, found in the ripe fruit of tropical palm trees, sometimes is referred to as vegetable ivory because of its hardness and creamy color. Tagua once comprised 20 percent of the market for buttons, before plastic buttons took over the apparel market. Now Conservation International is hoping that apparel companies will return to tagua to support the efforts of forest dwellers to preserve tropical forest areas.

Unlike Cultural Survival, which serves as a broker and intermediary in the sale of nontimber forest products, Conservation International encourages companies to buy tagua nuts directly from producers. The group receives a licensing fee from the companies and uses the proceeds to further its research into ecologically sound harvesting techniques. Clothiers **Patagonia** and **Smith & Hawken** are purchasing tagua buttons, and at least nine other companies have explored the option and may sign on, reports Karen Ziffer, project manager for Conservation International.[39]

Patagonia pays 80 percent more for tagua buttons than for plastic buttons, but the company thinks the buttons are a good investment, nevertheless. "We do not perceive this as a marketing scheme," says Paul Tebbel, Patagonia's public affairs coordinator. "This is an opportunity to buy what we consider to be an environmentally proper product."[40] Patagonia has purchased several million tagua buttons since the program began. Amy Loucks, spokeswoman for **Smith & Hawken**, says her company bought 400,000 tagua buttons in 1991 and expected to buy 800,000 in 1992. Nearly all Smith & Hawken's garments use tagua buttons.

The tagua nuts themselves are harvested mainly by community cooperatives in northwestern Ecuador. Since less than 5 percent of the land in Ecuador has tagua growing on it, the price of tagua in producing areas has more than doubled since Conservation International's program began. (As of mid-1991, harvesters typically received $2.00 to $2.50 for each 100 pound bag of nuts.) The harvest provides a supplemental source of income for about 100 harvesters in a community of 20,000 people. The bulk of the community's income is derived from growing cocoa.

Conservation International is encouraging Ecuadoran forest peoples to diversify their products so that they are not wholly dependent on one product or market. "The history of tropical markets has been a series of boom and bust cycles, as in demand for rubber and gold," says Ziffer. "We are encouraging people to sell other rain forest products and we see good prospects for things like palm oil, fibers and dye."

Conservation International also is doing research on xate, an understory palm species that grows in shady areas, whose graceful green fronds are used in flower arrangements. Guatemala has exported xate fronds to North American markets for years. Conservation International is examining whether the 6,000 people who harvest xate in extractive reserves are managing the resource sustainably. Chicle (for chewing gum) and other spices are gathered and sold from these reserves at other times of the year.

Conservation International is especially excited about the prospects for tagua nuts, however. The organization hopes to popularize tagua as a substitute for ivory in jewelry and decorative carvings, not just for buttons. An indigenous group in the Choco region of Colombia is interested in harvesting tagua, and a new project there may lead to a marketing arrangement that is similar to the one in northwestern Ecuador.

Patagonia's Paul Tebbel reports that a number of customers have complained that tagua buttons tend to crack or split on garments laundered frequently in hot water and hot dryers. Patagonia has replaced tagua buttons on these garments with plastic buttons and is trying to determine if the tagua buttons can be coated to prevent breakage under harsh conditions. The larger challenge remains a socio-economic one. "This is really a process of social change that involves land use planning, calculating how much money to charge, how to spread social benefits at the same time that you have to meet the demands of an international market that plays by different rules," says Ziffer of Conservation International.

Agroforestry

Agroforestry offers another means by which forest dwellers can cultivate subsistence and cash crops while conserving forest cover. Agroforestry intersperses trees and shrubs with agricultural crops to encourage positive interactions between the two. Agroforestry has been used for generations in the humid tropical areas of Asia and Africa. In Latin America, it is practiced only among indigenous communities. Agroforestry offers a proven alternative to traditional slash-and-burn or shifting cultivation techniques that usually falter in the rain forest after two or three years.

In Senegal, farmers have doubled millet and sorghum production to 900 pounds an acre by planting acai trees in between the rows of crops. The trees

---

Box 7A

Iguanas: Chicken of the Forest

At first glance, it may be hard to see a connection between iguanas, farming and preservation of tropicals forests. Iguanas are scaly, prehistoric-looking lizards that have long thrived in rain forest areas. When cooked, however, iguanas taste a lot like chicken and offer a good source of protein. Unfortunately, years of deforestation is shrinking their habitat, and uncontrolled hunting is driving them toward extinction.

A German herpetologist named Dagmar Werner has hatched an idea to save the iguana as well as the rain forest. Werner has developed a method of breeding iguanas in captivity that increases their initial survival rate from 5 percent to 95 percent. She then releases young iguanas into the rain forest, where they feed on leaves for two years. Werner has discovered that iguanas grow much faster and gain up to twice as much weight when fed cheap protein supplements. A farmer using feeding stations in the forest to supplement the diet of iguanas can raise 100 six pound iguanas a year on 2.5 acres of land. The yield of low-fat meat is actually better than that on many cattle ranches.

Werner has been showing farmers in Panama and Costa Rica how to breed iguanas for nearly a decade. Through her efforts, 4,300 iguanas were reintroduced into areas of Panama (where they were virtually extinct) between 1984 and 1987. Werner has also established the Green Iguana Foundation to solicit financial assistance to continue her research on the genetics of iguanas and their dietary needs. She has identified more than 60 species of native plants that play a role in the feeding, resting and defensive behavior of iguanas. If her idea catches on, she envisions iguana farming replacing cattle ranching in some areas of Central America where only fragments of rain forest remain.[7a]

---

provide shelter from the wind and reduce soil erosion. The acai trees grow faster because they are exposed to more sunlight than in the dense forest and they replenish carbon dioxide more rapidly in their leaves. In Nigeria, farmers have quadrupled the production of corn to 1,800 pounds per acre in part by mulching crops with nitrogen-fixing leaves from trees.[41] And in Haiti, which has one of the most severe deforestation problems in the world, 110,000 farmers have benefited from planting more than 27 million tree seedlings. Improved nursery techniques, incentives for care of the trees and the creation of erosion control structures have contributed to the success of the Haitian agroforestry program.[42]

Indonesia's Social Forestry Project is an especially ambitious attempt to reforest degraded lands and raise the incomes of working poor people. Set on the tropical island of Java, one of the most densely populated areas on earth, the project offers landless farmers an opportunity to manage state-owned land indefinitely—as long as they take care of it. The project also addresses social problems that emerged in previous agroforesty projects, which pitted state forestry managers against farmers in a struggle over apportionments of what was to be grown. The Social Forestry Project plants timber species like teak and pine, alternating with food crops like cassava and corn. The trees are harvested by the state eventually for timber. Farmers get to keep and sell the crops they grow on the government land in return for caring for and protecting the timber species.[43]

Instead of relating to the state as individuals, farmers in the Social Forestry Project are encouraged to form groups and enter into forest management agreements on a collective basis. They also are allowed to plant fodder grasses and fuelwood shrubs along contour hedgerows for personal use and to plant previously forbidden crops like bananas and tobacco. By 1990, 2,300 forest farmer groups representing 50,000 households had been established on 500,000 acres of land. Another 50 million acres of degraded land could be reforested in the same manner in Indonesia.

The Indonesian State Forestry Corporation considers the Social Forestry Project a success. Survival and growth of timber species has increased significantly compared with traditional growing methods. Farmers are making more money as well; case studies show an 8 to 11 percent increase in income among project participants. The new approach also has formed more harmonious relationships between state forestry officials and farming communities. The project is so popular, in fact, that the state is having difficulty providing training for all those who wish to enroll in it.[44]

Ecotourism

"Ecotourism"—nature-oriented travel—is catching on among consumers as a means of doing more to preserve rain forests than simply buying nontimber forest products. The wanderlust can take low-impact vacations in tropical areas, where a portion of the proceeds from their trip may be donated to rain forest conservation efforts. Ecotourism can also bolster the economies of tropical countries and raise awareness about the importance of preserving rain forests. Haphazard development of ecotourism, however, can damage ecologically sensitive areas—leading to erosion, pollution and degradation of rain forest ecosystems. While tropical forested countries are beginning to realize the benefits of developing their natural areas for tourists, they are adopting different strategies based on their social and political climate.

In 1990, the World Wildlife Fund examined the economic and environmental impact of ecotourism in five countries: Belize, Costa Rica, Dominica, Ecuador and Mexico. The environmental group concluded that virtually none of these countries had promoted tourism actively in their protected areas, except for Ecuador's Galapagos Islands and Costa Rica's Monteverde Cloud Forest. While most of these countries have passed laws to encourage investment in tourism infrastructure, they are just awakening to the potential of ecotourism, the study found.[45]

The World Wildlife Fund study, *Ecotourism: The Potentials and Pitfalls,* delved into the pros and cons of ecotourism. On the positive side, ecotourism can generate significant amounts of income through fees charged to tourists for lodging, meals, park admission, guided tours and the like, according to author Elizabeth Boo. A portion of the fees often are used to preserve and protect natural areas. Ecotourism also can spur investment in infrastructure and services for tourists that provide jobs for local residents, the study found.

On the negative side, incursions into the natural resource can change its appearance and threaten the well-being of plants and animals. A tour operator who has led trips to the Brazilian Amazon reports, for example, that tourists have littered the rain forest with plastic bottles, trash bags, plastic nets and fishing lines. Tourists sometimes deliberately harass animals, swerve across roads to kill anaconda snakes and invade rookeries to photograph birds. "The people who run the hotels don't care because they're booked—everybody is making money," the tour operator says.[46]

From an economic standpoint, development of the tourism trade involves substantial promotional expenses abroad and imports of materials to provide tourist amenities. It also sometimes leads to expropriation of profits by foreign investors. The World Bank estimates that 55 percent of gross tourism revenues in developing countries actually "leak" back to developed countries.[47] In addition, local governments rarely have policies to ensure that a substantial amount of the money spent by ecotourists remains in the hands of local people, who are the most affected by development of the trade. Beyond that, tourism tends to be seasonal, which may leave local workers and their equipment idle for extended periods.

Success for some also can mean failure for others. The creation of wildife parks and preserves can cause hardship for local farmers, hunters and gatherers who no longer can perform their traditional functions on the land. Ecotourism can also raise the cost of living near a particular attraction and disrupt the local economy. In Madagascar, local people hired as guides and paid $2 a day quickly acquired more wealth, upsetting the social order of the ruling village elders.[48] In Costa Rica's Monteverde Cloud Forest Preserve (which is operated by American Quakers who settled in Costa Rica), the problem was that too few Costa Ricans were being hired as guides and that the operators were overly zealous in their effort to buy local farms to add acreage to the preserve. Local farmers staged a protest and shut down the preserve for a brief time in November 1990.

Focus on Costa Rican ecotourism: The ecotourism trade is well established in Costa Rica. This biologically rich, tropical country attracted many foreign scientists during the 1960s and 1970s to study its diverse rain forests. Now that rain forests have developed a mass-tourism appeal, Costa Rica is torn between those who favor a low-impact approach to tourism and those who seek high-rise hotels and paved roads to all popular destinations. Tourism already is one of Costa Rica's three top earners of foreign exchange—rivaling bananas and coffee.

Costa Rica is well-positioned to improve the infrastructure of its extensive park system, which consists of 13 national parks and five biological reserves. The government has obtained $50 million in funds derived from debt-for-nature swaps to educate and pay park personnel, develop visitor centers, protect park areas and develop buffer zones around the parks.[49] But the government does not intend to intervene in the business of catering to tourists, leaving that to private tour companies. As for the parks themselves, the Costa Rican government intends to keep them wild. While many visitors would like to stay in lodges within the parks, as they do on private reserves, no lodges will be built, according to the director of Costa Rica's National Parks Foundation, Inez Gallegos. Studies are being done to determine the "carrying capacity" of areas adjacent to the parks where lodging facilities may be built.

Some observers fear that the country's $4.5 billion foreign debt—one of the largest debts in the world on a per capita basis—will mean that the government cannot afford to pursue only small-volume, low-impact tourism. Anthropologist Carole Hill of Georgia State University believes that Costa Rica has already decided to cater to more upscale North American tourists by building more first class hotels and related amenities. In 1988, the government set a goal of bringing in $1 billion of tourism-related foreign exchange by 1995.[50]

Panama's Kuna Indians: One group of indigenous peoples who have managed to preserve their culture and the rain forest—while earning a little money on the side through ecotourism—are the Kuna Indians of Panama. The Kuna live within 150,000 acres of tropical rain forest on the north coast of Panama. Most of the land is untouched. The Kuna hunt, fish and grow crops near the coast. In the 1970s, a road was built on the western end of their reservation, and the Kuna realized that outsiders soon would be entering their land. To regulate the activity, the Kuna sought help from several environmental groups who assisted in creating the Kuna Wildlands Project.

The project divided the Kuna land into four distinct zones: one for Kuna agriculture, another for cultural and living space, one designated for tourism and research, and a restoration zone outside the reserve that provides a buffer around their land. Scientists or tourists who enter Kuna land are required to pay a fee. Researchers who study plants or animals in the area must be accompanied by a Kuna guide and leave a copy of their observations with the Kuna in case a species is discovered that is later made into a commercial product.

The Kuna opposed earlier efforts by the Panamanian government to develop tourism in their area. In the 1970s, the Panamanian Institute of Tourism tried to build a $38 million hotel complex near Carti, using private American investment dollars and funds from the Inter-American Development Bank. The Kuna themselves were to serve as tourist attractions, earning money by working at the hotel and selling artifacts to hotel guests. "Unfortunately for IPAT (the tourism agency), the Kuna did not see things through the same lens," recalls Mac Chapin of Cultural Survival. "After a good deal of questionable maneuvering by government officials, the Kuna rose up in unison, threatened the prefeasibility team with violence, and brought the program to an abrupt halt. Shortly thereafter, the entire project was abandoned."[51] American entrepreneurs who had planned to build resorts in the area also were flushed out. Now the Kuna themselves run several hotels in the town of Carti, on the edge of the reserve. Hotel operators are subject to Kuna laws, and the money earned remains in the region.

The Kuna appear to be a rare departure from the norm, where tourism transforms the local population into a servile class that caters to the needs of outsiders. Across the Pacific, the Toraja people of Sulawesi in Indonesia offer a more typical example. Anthropologist Kathleen Adams has observed the rising tide of tourism over the last 20 years that has completely transformed Toraja society. In 1972, only 650 tourists visited the Toraja. By 1987, the number of tourists had swelled to 179,000, making it the second most popular stop in Indonesia after Bali. It used to be that Toraja houses and cliff-side graves were known only to a few anthropologists and missionaries. Now local vendors set up souvenir shops on the porches of kindred houses, and even the tourists complain that the villages and limestone burial cliffs have become too commercialized.[52]

Chapter 8
Innovative Investment in the Rain Forest

S urvival of the remaining tropical forests depends on well-planned and -managed sustainable development projects that give value to the forest, provide indigenous peoples with the means to make a living and still preserve enough of the forest to allow it to perform its essential ecological function. Yet with an estimated 1 percent or less of tropical forests managed in a sustainable fashion, the challenge facing foresters and governments in tropical countries is indeed formidable.

Investors and lenders will play key roles in determining the fate of tropical forests. International lending institutions such as the World Bank and the U.S. Agency for International Development have adopted policies in recent years that prohibit financing for logging in primary tropical rain forests, although some recent loans by these agencies still raise the specter of tropical deforestation. So-called "debt-for-nature" swaps have emerged as another innovative way for the financial community to help preserve tropical forests, but these too are controversial; some critics say developing countries are trading away national sovereignty to reduce their debt burdens. In a more recent, untested innovation, several power companies in the United States and Europe have invested in large tropical forestry projects to offset emissions from their power plants that may contribute to global warming. And some individual investors are making direct investments in small scale sustainable forestry and agriculture projects in rain forest areas. A sampler of these projects appears at the end of the chapter, beginning on p. 207. Other investment mechanisms are examined here.

International Lending Institutions

The World Bank and other multilateral development banks are the largest public development lenders in the world, providing billions of dollars a year in financing for projects in agriculture, irrigation, rural development, electrification and road building in developing countries. Critics assert that many of these internationally funded projects have been poorly conceived and lacked proper environmental assessments. Regional development banks such as the African

Development Bank and the Inter-American Development Bank have been subject to similar criticism.

In the past, international lending institutions have financed such things as chemical and metallurgical plants without sufficient pollution controls, huge mining ventures that decimated the landscape and released toxins into the environment, and agricultural projects that encouraged heavy use of farm chemicals that contaminated water supplies and poisoned farm workers. Some of the banks' most controversial lending practices have been in rain forest areas, where roads have opened up previously inaccessible lands, and dams have inundated tens of thousands of acres and wiped out scores of indigenous communities.

World Bank lending reforms: In 1987, World Bank President Barber Conable conceded that the bank had "stumbled and...misread the human, institutional and physical realities of the jungle and the frontier."[1] He pledged to set up a new department within the bank to strengthen its environmental policy. The bank subsequently increased its environmental staff from four to more than 100 people and enacted a series of high profile measures to shore up its image. The bank granted a $117 million loan to Brazil, for example, to protect the Amazon forest, the Atlantic coastal forest and the Pantanal wetlands. Proceeds from the loan were intended to strengthen Ibama, the Brazilian environmental agency, and several state-level institutions responsible for environmental protection.

The reform plan also placed a great emphasis on the Tropical Forestry Action Plan (TFAP)—an internationally funded project that seeks to educate people about sustainable management of forest resources and increase technical assistance to tropical countries. Conable announced that spending on TFAP would increase more than threefold over a five-year period, from $138 million in 1987 to $800 million in 1992.[2] The bank's environmental department also announced key reforms to its forest policy in 1991. The most notable changes were that the bank would no longer fund logging activities or colonization schemes in primary tropical forests.

Some close observers of World Bank lending practices contend that the World Bank has flouted its own policy, however. The Environmental Defense Fund, the Natural Resources Defense Council, World Wildlife International and other prominent environmental groups have cited several questionable loans, such as a $23 million "forest management and protection" program in Guinea in which bank money was earmarked to build 45 miles of roads into 370,000 acres of pristine rain forest preserves.[3] The World Bank's management plan calls for two-thirds of the forested area to be logged. The World Bank had also planned to give a $167 million loan to Cameroon to build a highway in the southeastern part of the country that would have opened up 34 million acres of rain forest. That loan was scuttled after environmental opposition mounted.[4]

Global Environment Facility: A new source of international lending is the Global Environment Facility. GEF provides grants and concessional loans to developing countries for sustainable development projects under joint administration of the World Bank, the United Nations Environment Program and the United Nations Development Program. GEF was endowed with $1.3 billion in a three-year pilot program (through 1993) to finance projects in four areas of global concern: preventing climatic change as well as protecting biodiversity, oceans and the ozone layer. As such, GEF serves as a principal interim funding mechanism to implement the goals of the biodiversity and climate change treaties signed at the Earth Summit in 1992 as well as the Montreal Protocol to protect the ozone layer signed in 1987.

Many praise GEF for making bank lending decisions somewhat more open and democratic, but skeptics wonder whether it has really changed the direction of international lending policies. Elizabeth Barratt-Brown, a senior attorney with the Natural Resources Defense Council, believes that GEF—operating in the shadow of the World Bank—remains inclined to fund big, environmentally insensitive projects. "We think GEF should be independent," Barratt-Brown says. "There has been a lot of greening in the language of the World Bank. But what is really changing in the funding?"[5]

Korinna Horta of the Environmental Defense Fund agrees that some of the initial projects targeted by GEF for funding were as environmentally destructive as earlier projects funded by the World Bank. One $10 million GEF grant to establish protected forest conservation areas in the Congo, for instance, was tied to a $20 million loan to facilitate commercial logging in rain forest areas. Horta, an economist, says that the logging loan violates the spirit, if not the letter, of the World Bank's new forest policy and that components of the logging loan were shifted to GEF as "bait" to make the package more acceptable to the government of the Congo. The GEF portion of the loan included funds to build a 15 mile road and open up parts of a rain forest preserve to "rational forest exploration" by scientists and tourists. Wildlife density in the preserve is thought to be among the highest in the world because of the absence of human habitation.[6]

Ian Bowles, legislative director for Conservation International, thinks further lending reforms will come in time. "It is an inherently long-term proposition, but all of these things are continually advancing," he says. "The U.N. and the World Bank have been around forever, so it is hard to reform suddenly."[7] GEF's programs and directives will be reviewed at the end of the current funding cycle.

Multilateral Development Banks: Regional multilateral development banks have also made loans in recent years that, in the view of many environmentalists, will destroy rain forests even while appearing to protect them. The African Development Bank has financed construction of a road through one of the last intact blocks of rain forest in Côte d'Ivoire, which may facilitate large-scale logging operations there. Critics say the project could force the relocation of 250,000 people, in violation of the World Bank's policy of not funding resettlement projects. (Ironically, the World Bank has granted an $80 million loan to protect the same area, reports EDF's Horta.) And in the Central African Republic, the African Development Bank is weighing a $13.5 million loan that would build more than 200 miles of roads, some of which would enter the Danga-Sanha Forest Reserve, a protected rain forest area.[8]

International Finance Corp.: Multilateral banks also have private sector affiliates whose investments can affect the rain forest. The World Bank's affiliate, International Finance Corp. (IFC), is the world's largest source of direct project financing. (**Inter-American Investment Corp.** serves in a similar capacity for the Inter-American Development Bank.) IFC acknowledges that it has funded

logging projects in primary rain forests before. IFC has held an equity stake in
P.T. Astra, a large Indonesian logging company, which has proposed cutting
hundreds of thousands of acres of rain forest in Irian Jaya, for example. But it
says that the World Bank's new lending policy prohibits it from funding such
logging projects now.

IFC's financial stake in logging companies occasionally benefits the rain
forest. In 1991, IFC gained title to a 143,000 acre tract of undisturbed
subtropical rain forest in eastern Paraguay—virtually the largest undisturbed
tract of subtropical forest in all of Latin America—after the bankruptcy of a
logging company in which it had invested. IFC then sold the tract to The Nature
Conservancy and a Paraguayan foundation for $2 million—far below its esti-
mated market value of $5 million to $7 million.

U.S. Agency for International Development: The U.S. government's involvement in tropical forestry is largely through the U.S. Agency for International
Development. AID supports more than 100 tropical forestry projects each year,
offering traditional and innovative approaches to sustainable forestry management. Its 10 year, $40 million Forestry/Fuelwood Research and Development
Project seeks to develop multipurpose tree species in Asia and Africa and
encourage their socio-economic acceptance. AID got a major boost in 1992 when
President Bush pledged $150 million in additional assistance from the United
States each year to help tropical nations preserve their forests.

Congress passed legislation in the mid-1980s that has prohibited AID from
funding projects that could lead to tropical deforestation. The prohibition was
strengthened in 1991, when Congress added language barring the agency from
funding any project that involved timber cutting. AID officials think the amended
language went too far, however. "We felt this was overly stringent because it
prevented us from participating in projects that support sustainable forest
management," explains Jim Hester, chief environmental officer for AID's Latin
American bureau.[9] Part of AID's mission, Hester says, is to show farmers and
forest dwellers that tropical forests have value and should be used wisely. If a
forest cannot be touched, however, it loses its value in the eyes of those who are
responsible for caring for it. Congress subsequently worked out amended
language permitting AID participation in forestry projects that involve some
felling of trees, provided that three conditions are met: there can be no significant
loss of biodiversity, the natural function of the forest ecosystem must remain
intact, and the project must reverse a trend toward deforestation.

The Latin America/Caribbean bureau of AID has devised a $46 million,
decade-long strategy to promote forest conservation and biodiversity. The
agency works in collaboration with the Peace Corps and the U.S. Forest Service
in some areas. AID has also joined with the World Bank and other international
agencies to promote conservation in Madagascar, where rain forests are severely
depleted. AID also supports the Wild Lands and Human Needs Program of the
World Wildlife Fund, which seeks to integrate natural resource management and
grass roots economic development. One AID-supported sustainable logging
project, Dominica's **Cottage Forest Industries**, is described in the sampler at
the end of this chapter.

Debt-for-Nature Swaps

Huge foreign debt has compelled many developing countries to harvest tropical timber and plant other export-oriented crops as a means to pay down more than $1.2 trillion in exchange-related obligations. In recent years, some countries have retired portions of their debt in exchange for equity investments in their industries. American conservation groups have pioneered a variation of this debt-for-equity swap, investing in rain forests rather than industries. While these debt-for-nature swaps have the potential to do much good for the environment, they are complicated and often controversial transactions.

The man who came up with the debt-for-nature idea is Thomas Lovejoy. In 1984, when he first proposed it, Lovejoy was a biologist with the World Wildlife Fund. He later went to work for the Smithsonian Institution as the assistant secretary for external affairs. (He is now on loan from the Smithsonian to serve as science adviser to Interior Secretary Bruce Babbitt.) Lovejoy's idea was that a developing country could retire a portion of its foreign debt if it agreed to take certain measures to protect its tropical rain forests or other vital natural resources.

The transaction begins when a conservation group purchases debt from a commercial bank or other holder of foreign debt, usually at a deep discount from its face value. (Alternatively, the bank can donate the debt rather than sell it.) The conservation group then approaches the debtor country and agrees to convert the debt back into local currency, again at a discount, provided that the debtor government will support specified conservation activities. Usually the debt is converted into a bond, representing an "IOU," and a local conservation group takes title to the bond. The local group's participation assures the debtor government that the funds for conservation will remain under local control. Moreover, the local conservation group—typically underfunded—gets a large financial boost toward accomplishing its mission. While such swaps are not likely to make a significant dent in a country's overall foreign debt, they can free up considerable resources for conservation programs that many developing countries otherwise could not afford to fund.

Through 1992, debt-for-nature conversions totaling $122 million were transacted, generating about $75 million in conservation funds. The Nature Conservancy, a private U.S. conservation group that has participated in several swaps, estimates that each dollar invested in debt purchases has generated more than $3.50 for conservation projects.[10]

The first debt-for-nature swap took place in 1987, when Conservation International, a nonprofit environmental group based in Washington, D.C., purchased $650,000 of Bolivia's debt—paying only 15 cents on the dollar. Conservation International canceled the debt in return for the Bolivian government's agreement to take steps to protect and enlarge the Beni Biosphere Reserve, a unique rain forest region in northern Bolivia. The Beni harbors several endangered species and is home to the Chimanes Indians, a nomadic group of hunters and gatherers, but it is being threatened by logging and cattle ranching interests. The Bolivian government agreed to establish three conservation and sustainable use areas adjacent to the reserve, totaling 3.7 million acres.

Conservation International was designated an official adviser to the government on the design and planning of the protected areas.

The Bolivian swap ran into criticism because Conservation International did not consult with the Chimanes Indians before the transaction took place. Bolivian politicians and other local settlers also were not informed about the details of the swap, which, according to one report, ended up jeopardizing essential domestic support.[11] Conservation International did not enlist support from any local environmental groups, either, heightening concerns about outside interference in Bolivia's internal affairs.

Despite the problems encountered with the first swap, many others have since been transacted to protect rain forest areas. The World Wide Fund for Nature, The Nature Conservancy and the Missouri Botanical Garden worked out a $9 million swap to protect a rain forest in Ecuador, for example, and Conservation International engineered another $5 million swap to conserve forests in badly eroded Madagascar. The most active country in debt-for-nature swaps has been Costa Rica, which has swapped $78 million in debt for conservation projects to help pay for protection of its unique national park system.

Commercial bank involvement: Some commercial banks have discovered that they, too, can gain from participating in debt-for-nature swaps, particularly if the likelihood of eventual repayment of a developing country loan is small. Instead of writing off a bad loan, a bank can donate it to a conservation group and reap a public relations benefit as well as a charitable tax deduction. The first bank to donate debt in a debt-to-nature swap was **Fleet National Bank of Rhode Island**; it gave $240,000 in Costa Rican debt to The Nature Conservancy in 1987. **BankAmerica**, the holding company of Bank of America, announced in 1991 that it would donate about $2 million of debt a year over three years to the World Wildlife Fund, Conservation International and the Smithsonian Institution to promote rain forest conservation.

American Express, while not donating its debt outright, has cooperated closely with The Nature Conservancy in a $5.6 million swap of Costa Rican debt and a $3.6 million swap of Ecuadoran debt. American Express has also participated in a recent swap in Jamaica. "These transactions are hard to put together," says Geoffrey Barnard, chief of the Latin American division for The Nature Conservancy. "You need a lot of patience. You also need banks with an ongoing business interest in the country. For a lot of banks there is a sour taste in all this, because the countries are in default. American Express has used its debt very creatively in part because it has a credit card business in all these countries."[12]

In another instance, **Salomon Brothers** donated its services to arrange a $24 million debt swap for Costa Rica. Salomon's debt trader, Richard Kaul, was rewarded by grateful scientists who named a wasp in the rain forest after him—"Eruga kauli."

Enterprise for the Americas Initiative: President Bush included debt-for-nature swaps as part of his Enterprise for the Americas Initiative to assist the economies of Latin American nations. The Bush initiative—designed to reduce debt, liberalize trade and spur investment in Latin America—extended the debt-for-nature swap idea beyond commercial banks to include debt owed directly between nations. Congress authorized swaps under the initiative in 1990 to reduce $1.7 billion in debts incurred by Latin American countries through the sale of subsidized food by the United States. The first two debt swap agreements were signed with Bolivia and Jamaica in late 1991. Under the agreements, interest payments are made in local currency to support in-country environmental protection programs, while the remaining principal payments are still made directly to the U.S. government. The estimated accrued interest, to be paid out over 15 years, is $1.7 million in Bolivia and $9.2 million in Jamaica. Other nations have balked at strict conditions for the swaps, however, which include a requirement that fund dispersal be overseen by a board that includes private citizens nominated by the U.S. government.

Criticisms of the swaps: Some U.S. environmental and consumer groups have expressed the belief that debt-for-nature swaps smack of "industrialized country imperialism," as one put it. Michael Clark, the former president of Friends of the Earth, told the *Chronicle of Philanthropy* in 1991, "A lot of folks are having second thoughts. Many of us thought they would be a great way to transfer capital from the North to the South and to leverage resources for environmental conservation. But I think their attractiveness has declined as people know more about them." Clark believes some of the swaps create the impression that "here are wealthy governments or non-governmental organizations putting pressure on southern countries that are strapped for cash to make short-term decisions without looking at the long-term implications."[13]

Such critics maintain that debt-for-nature swaps often do not address the underlying poverty and land tenure policies that drive people to exploit rain forests. Evaristo Nugkaug, president of the Coordinating Body for the Indigenous Peoples Organization of the Amazon Basin (Coica), says the forest preservation programs tend to ignore the rights of indigenous peoples who had no role in creating the debt in the first place. "The environmentalists talk a lot about butterflies, fish, animals and trees. But in the view of the Amazon biosphere, they don't take human beings, indigenous peoples, into account. We are part of the ecosystem, and our ancestors are the ones who protect its resources. And if we're thrown out, who is going to defend the Amazon? National parks are not an answer. That's an outsider's solution." Instead of debt for nature, Nugkaug argues, "we should be talking about debt for indigenous control—creating large new extensions where Indians can live, to protect our culture while also protecting the land."[14]

Randall Hayes, director of Rainforest Action Network, agrees. "I would like to see a debt-for-Indian-land swap so that indigenous peoples can keep colonists from encroaching on their lands. These are the people (colonists) responsible for most of the slash-and-burn practices." Hayes also would like to see debt-for-land-reform swaps, whereby farmers would gain access to rich, fertile land so that they no longer need to engage in slash-and-burn practices in the rain forests to survive. But local environmental groups that advocate land reform policies generally are not allowed to participate in or administer debt swaps, Hayes points out.[15]

Aside from political and ethical questions about debt-for-nature swaps, the financial situation that made swaps attractive in the past has changed in recent years, reports Randall Curtis, director of conservation finance of the Latin American division of The Nature Conservancy. These factors include a rise in the secondary market price of debt, a tightening of conversion terms offered for the swaps and delays in approvals of swaps that lead to higher transaction costs.[16]

Still, Curtis and others believe that debt-for-nature swaps have resulted in lasting achievements. The swaps have focused government attention on the value of preserving rain forests, provided long-term sustainable sources of funding for conservation programs and helped conservation groups in Latin America achieve a status and degree of stability not known heretofore. Perhaps most important, the swaps have demonstrated that banks, government agencies and conservation groups can work together in ways that benefit all parties as well as the environment.

Carbon Offset Programs

Growing concern about the buildup of greenhouse gases in the earth's atmosphere has led to another investment idea to save the rain forests—planting and preserving trees in the tropics to offset carbon dioxide emissions from power plants elsewhere. Tropical forests play a vital role in regulating the earth's climate. They absorb and store large quantities of carbon while they are alive and growing, but they release the carbon when they are cut and burned. Trees left on the ground to decay release methane, an even more potent greenhouse gas.

While the greatest source of manmade carbon emissions by far is the burning of fossil fuels, scientists estimate that destruction and burning of tropical forests may account for 15 to 20 percent of the carbon released into the atmosphere from human activity. (Altogether, 6 to 7 billion tons of additional carbon accumulates in the atmosphere each year. Deforestation accounts for 1 billion to 2.5 billion tons of this amount; electricity generation accounts for another 2 billion to 2.5 billion tons. Most of the rest comes from industrial and transportation use of fossil fuels.) Slash-and-burn agriculture raises greater concerns than commercial timber operations from a global warming standpoint, because wood releases carbon immediately when burned while wood cut for lumber continues to store carbon for years or even decades.

Scientists believe that the atmospheric buildup of carbon dioxide may raise the earth's air temperature by 3 to 9 degrees Fahrenheit during the next century. Such global warming could have a major impact on commerce and agriculture by altering weather patterns and shifting the areas in which crops and forests thrive. More extreme weather events could also lead to extended drought and more severe hurricanes. A rise in sea level (resulting primarily from thermal expansion of the oceans) could inundate islands and low-lying coastal cities.[17]

Efforts are underway to promote reforestation as a means of addressing the global carbon imbalance. Because live trees absorb carbon as they grow, replanting deforested areas can sequester large amounts of carbon from the atmosphere and slow the trend toward global warming. Researchers believe that massive tree planting, while not a permanent solution, could act as a temporary "carbon sink" that gives industry more time to develop alternative energy sources and other means to combat the so-called "greenhouse effect."

Tropical areas are well-suited for reforestation. Scientists estimate that more than 3 million square miles of forest has been lost worldwide since pre-agricultural times. About half of the loss has come since 1850—and the loss has been mainly in the tropics. In percentage terms, the loss of forests worldwide equals 12 to 13 percent of the pre-agricultural worldwide total, an area roughly equal to the 48 contiguous states of the United States. A reforested area nearly the size of the United States west of the Mississippi River—about 1.15 billion acres—would be needed to sequester the excess carbon emitted into the atmosphere each year.

Most of the land available for reforestation is in the developing world, where deforestation, intensive agriculture and overgrazing have left an area about the size of China and India combined with moderately to severely diminished soils. Since virtually all prime agricultural land throughout the world is now under cultivation, taking the marginal land out of production and reforesting it would have relatively little impact on the future food supply. From a global warming standpoint, tropical forests would be best to replant because they are able to fix five to 10 times as much carbon per acre as temperate forests—owing to their higher rate of photosynthesis.

Beyond that, land acquisition costs and labor costs are lower in developing countries, making the economics of tropical reforestation more attractive. Roger Sedjo, a forest economist with Resources for the Future, an independent research group based in Washington, D.C., estimates that the price tag for reforesting 1.15 billion acres in a temperate zone would be $372 billion, whereas the same planting in the tropics would cost $250 billion.[18] Sedjo cautions, however, that reforestation costs could be driven up because some degraded tropical lands would likely require special care. Alternatively, more degraded acreage could be planted with a reduced amount of care. Mark Trexler of Trexler Associates, a forestry and carbon sequestration consulting firm, estimates that reforestation of 3 billion acres or more of degraded tropical lands would achieve carbon equilibrium in the atmosphere.[19]

Reforestation is not the only means by which trees can effectively limit the accumulation of carbon dioxide in the atmosphere. A second type of carbon offset is possible by improving forest management practices and calculating the reduction in carbon dioxide emissions that results. A third kind of carbon offset is to preserve standing forests rather than harvesting them, calculating the amount of carbon that remains stored instead of being emitted to the atmosphere. (In this third case, consideration must be given to the amount of carbon that would have accumulated over time in a replacement forest.)

The 1990 amendments to the U.S. Clean Air Act established a voluntary program by which power producers can buy and sell credits to offset carbon dioxide emissions from their fossil-fueled power plants (in a manner similar to that allowed for sulfur dioxide emissions under the act). Proponents of the legislation believe that international forest offsets may be one of the most cost-effective greenhouse gas mitigation strategies, costing between $5 and $7 per metric ton of carbon reduced. The Global Environment Facility associated with the World Bank also is looking to steer private cash in carbon offset programs.

AES Corp.: The company to pioneer the concept of carbon offsets through tropical reforestation is AES Corp., based in Arlington, Va. AES (formerly known as Applied Energy Services) is an independent power producer that specializes in the development of coal-burning cogeneration facilities. It earned $54 million in 1992 on sales of $400 million. The company has three projects underway for which it plans to offset carbon emissions over the life of its generating facilities. These projects are: AES Thames, a 180 megawatt plant in Montville, Conn; AES Barbers Point, a 180 MW plant near Honolulu, Hawaii; and AES Shady Point, a 320 MW plant in Poteau, Okla.[20] AES has also launched a consulting service to involve other energy companies, utilities and regulatory agencies in carbon offset programs.

The Thames project generated considerable publicity in 1989 when it was the first project of its kind to be announced. AES pledged to offset 15.5 million tons of projected carbon dioxide emissions over the 40 year life of the plant by donating $2 million in cash for a reforestation project in Guatemala. CARE, the international human relief organization, had started a reforestation program in Guatemala in 1974; it has planted more than 25 million tree seedlings there since 1979. CARE also is contributing $2 million toward the new reforestation project, which aims to plant 52 million trees in a 385 square-mile area of Guatemala between 1990 and 2000. The U.S. Peace Corps, the U.S. Agency for International Development and Guatemalan forestry extension agents are providing $10.5 million of in-kind support. Approximately 40,000 Guatemalan families are expected to take part in related agroforestry and forest and soil conservation initiatives.

AES's pioneering effort aims to address a severe deforestation problem in Guatemala's rich and highly diverse forests, which have shrunk by half in the last 35 years. A primary goal of the AES reforestation project is to take pressure off 47,000 acres of standing forest adjacent to the reforestation area. Half of the 52 million trees being planted are on 150,000 acres as part of the agroforestry program—enabling farmers to grow bananas, coffee and other cash crops as well as the trees. The other major portion of the project involves the development of new woodlots that can be harvested for poles and lumber within five years; about 25 million trees are being planted on 30,000 acres for this purpose.

Other elements of the project include installing 1,800 miles of "live fencing"—thorny shrubs that keep animals away from crops, constructing terraces to protect 5,000 acres of erosion-prone mountain slopes, and organizing forest fire brigades to protect both old and new forests from fires that normally destroy millions of trees each year. The fire brigades also are teaching new soil conservation techniques to Guatemalan farmers. Committees have been established among the farmers to develop agroforestry plans, assign responsibilities and coordinate management of community nurseries and woodlots.

The approach is similar for AES's second carbon sequestration project at Barbers Point in Hawaii. AES plans to offset emissions from the plant by donating $2 million to help The Nature Conservancy and the Moises Bertoni Foundation fund a major forest conservation project in Paraguay. In this case, The Nature Conservancy and the Moises Bertoni Foundation purchased a

142,800 acre tract containing dense subtropical forest from the **International Finance Corp.** in 1991. Over the first three years of the project, about $4.7 million will be required to pay for salaries, vehicles and other startup costs. Guard posts already have been built around the boundary of the reserve and seven patrolmen have been hired.

What distinguishes the Barbers Point offset program is that its primary goal is to preserve standing trees rather than plant new ones. The Mbaracayu region of Paraguay, where the tract is located, is home to 19 distinct plant communities and many unique and endangered species. It is also the historic home of an indigenous tribe of hunter-gatherers known as the Ache, who were not brought into contact with the outside world until 1976. They now live on the edge of the forest. By contributing to protection of the Mbaracayu forest (and the Ache who live nearby), AES says it will help prevent the release of much of the forest's millions of tons of sequestered carbon. (Loggers had sought to enter the forest before the acquisition by The Nature Conservancy and the Moises Bertoni Foundation.) In addition, the Nature Conservancy will create an economic development program for local communities that is based on sustainable use of natural resources.

AES's third carbon offset project, announced in the spring of 1993, is larger in scale, because its 320 MW Shady Point power plant in eastern Oklahoma will emit more carbon dioxide than the Thames and Barbers Points facilities—97 million tons over its projected 32 year lifetime. For Shady Point, AES conducted a competitive evaluation with a $5.5 million pool of funds available for carbon offsets, and it received more than 60 concept papers. The proposal it selected is by Oxfam America, an international relief and development group based in Boston, Mass., which has been funding initiatives for protection of indigenous Amazonian peoples and the rain forest since 1978.

The AES-Oxfam project has two main components. AES will provide a one-time grant of $600,000 to the Coordinating Body of Indigenous Peoples' Organization of the Amazon Basin (Coica) to help establish an endowment fund. (Oxfam and other groups will contribute an additional $400,000.) AES will disburse another $2.4 million over 10 years to fund projects in which indigenous peoples are trying to gain legal title to their traditional lands, develop sustainable land management plans and enforce laws against illegal resource extraction. Over the next five years, the AES grant will fund four projects designed and managed by indigenous peoples in Bolivia, Peru and Ecuador. AES estimates that the projects will preserve 1.2 million acres of rain forest and help indigenous peoples gain title to 3.7 million acres of land. By AES's reckoning, the projects funded over 10 years should offset 257 million tons of carbon dioxide emissions, almost three times the amount of emissions expected over the life of the Shady Point plant.[21]

New England Electric System: Several major electric utilities have followed AES's lead in establishing carbon offset programs. The first U.S. electric utility to participate in such a program involving tropical forestry is New England Electric System (NEES) of Westborough, Mass. NEES announced a goal in late 1991 to offset its carbon dioxide emissions by 15 million tons, or 20 percent of its annual carbon dioxide emissions, by the year 2000. In 1992, NEES contracted with **Innoprise**, a Malaysian logging company, to promote reduced-impact logging as a way to offset some of the utility's carbon dioxide emissions. Through the program, NEES estimates that it can sequester between 300,000 and 600,000 tons of carbon dioxide at a cost of about $2 per ton.[22]

Innoprise's timber concession is in the Malaysian state of Sabah on the island of Borneo, which contains the largest remaining contiguous lowland rain forest in Asia. The area is rich in biodiversity. At least 420 bird species, 90 bat species and 120 other land mammals have been identified. Innoprise's concession is 2.5 million acres—about four times the size of Rhode Island. The NEES-funded pilot project will carry out the new harvesting techniques on about 3,500 acres. Compliance will be monitored by an external environmental audit team. A study also will be undertaken by the Rainforest Alliance to estimate the net carbon dioxide saved from reduced-impact logging, reports Clive Marsh, the principal forest conservation officer for **Copec**, a California company that linked NEES with Innoprise.[23]

In Malaysia, as in many tropical countries, loggers seek commercially valuable trees that are scattered throughout the rain forest. Many other trees are lost, however, because of residual damage from felling trees and cutting trails through the forest. NEES is contributing $452,000 in an effort to improve forest harvesting techniques and reduce unnecessary losses on the 3,500 acre Innoprise tract. The funds will cover the additional expense and consultancy required to train Innoprise personnel to harvest timber according to the highest environmental standards. These standards include use of better-planned logging trails, directional felling of trees, cutting vines that would pull down neighboring trees, properly constructed and carefully planned skid trails and minimal use of bulldozers. Improved trail construction should reduce water runoff that impairs water quality.

Two botanists from the University of Florida, Francis Putz and Michelle Pinard, have made preliminary calculations of the carbon savings that may result from use of these reduced-impact logging techniques. With conventional harvesting, often as many as 50 percent of the trees are damaged and up to 40 percent of the acreage is crushed by bulldozers in the process of extracting three to six commercial-grade trees per acre. Thirty-four tons of carbon are released from storage in the process of harvesting timber that contains only nine tons of carbon. If the reduced impact logging results in only half as many trees being damaged and half as much forest being crushed by extraction equipment, Putz and Pinard estimate that the carbon savings works out to 19 tons of carbon at a cost of $54 per acre, or $2.80 per metric ton of carbon saved. In addition, the rate of carbon storage is expected to accelerate after the harvest because of reduced likelihood of vine infestations and retention of undamaged trees with the potential to grow very large.[24]

Dutch Electric Generating Board: The most ambitious carbon sequestration program announced to date comes from the Dutch Electric Generating Board. It announced a plan in 1990 to invest $10 million annually over 25 years to replant 60,000 acres of forest a year, about 80 percent of which will be in tropical forest areas. Funds for the project is being raised through a one guilder charge (worth about 58 cents) on every Dutch household. The program started planting trees in 1991 in Malaysia, Indonesia, Czechoslovakia and the Netherlands, with Latin American countries to be added in 1993.

The Dutch Electric Generating Board plans to offset emissions from a new 600 MW coal plant near Amsterdam that will emit an estimated 75 million tons of carbon dioxide over 25 years. The planting is being supervised by a foundation called Forestry Against Carbon Dioxide Emissions (Face), set up by the generating board. Hans Verwey, a forestry engineer with the foundation, says Face is concentrating on projects in the tropics because it is much cheaper to plant trees there. The cost of planting dipterocarps (a family of tall trees in Asia) is only $200 per acre, or less than one-twelfth the cost of planting trees in the Netherlands. Verwey says Face wants to work with companies that are well established, that can care for the trees over the long term and that will not disturb the activities of indigenous peoples.[25]

Like NEES, the Dutch have contracted with **Innoprise** of Malaysia to fund a $1.3 million enrichment planting of dipterocarps. About 3,500 acres will be planted during the pilot phase. If successful, Face hopes to plant 65,000 acres in the area over 25 years, the expected life of the coal plant. The project also includes research and training of Innoprise foresters by Britain's Royal Society and four Malaysian partner institutions.

The Los Angeles Department of Water and Power, the largest municipally owned utility in the United States, also is weighing proposals for tropical forestry programs to help meet its goal of cutting carbon dioxide emissions 20 percent (or 3.6 million tons) by 2010. The utility issued a request for project proposals in late 1991. "We're looking for creative, diverse proposals; they can be either afforestation or reforestation," says Mark Adams of the utility's research and development division.[26] The department hopes to sequester 300,000 tons of carbon a year through international forestry projects over a 10 to 20 year period.

Questions About Carbon Offset Programs

Carbon offset programs that rely on reforestation, afforestation and forest preservation may prove to be the salvation of many vanishing tropical forests. Yet questions remain about the efficacy of such programs: Will the carbon-sequestering tree plantations outlive carbon-emitting power plants? Will preservation of selected tracts of forest lead to accelerated deforestation of others? Will carbon offset programs come to be seen as a form of "green imperialism"— blocking industrial progress in tropical countries so that businesses in the developed world can continue to pollute?

Mark Trexler, who had a key role in planning the groundbreaking Guatemalan reforestation project for AES, acknowledges that it will be difficult to determine how much carbon such a program ultimately will store. He figures the Guatemalan forestry project could sequester as much as 18 million tons of carbon dioxide—or fall short of its goal of 15.5 million tons. "Projects that impose foreign concerns on local peoples by restricting access to resources without providing reasonable alternatives cannot be successful in the long term," warns Trexler, who adds that the World Resources Institute tried to address these issues in planning the AES project with CARE.[27]

Forces of nature add to the challenge. Forest fires and pest infestation pose a constant threat. When CARE decided to stop treating seedlings in Guatemala with a fungicide that may have harmful effects on humans, more than 50 percent of the seedlings in some areas succumbed to a fungus. Bad weather is another uncontrolled variable. A series of bad frosts killed 250,000 young trees in the Guatemalan planting program in 1990, and a later-than-expected rainy season reduced the transfer of seedlings from nurseries to plantations in 1991. As a result, actual seedling and tree plantings were 5 percent below their targets as of the spring of 1991.[28]

Such combination of socio-economic and environmental factors make it "impossible" to quantify the amount of carbon stored in the project over time, Trexler says. "This is inherently disturbing when you are trying to sell this idea on a ton-for-ton reduction basis." CARE project director Kirsten Johnson agrees that it may be difficult to tabulate carbon sequestration totals, but she says that an estimate can be made by recording the number of seedlings planted, the survival rates for the various species and their growth rates over time.[29]

In other instances where forest preservation (rather than reforestation or afforestation) is involved, a definitive calculation of carbon savings cannot be made because it is impossible to predict the fate of a forest had a company not stepped forward to preserve it. In the case of the Mbaracayu forest of Paraguay, for instance, a site study determined that a nearby forest had lost nearly three-quarters of its tree cover in the last 10 years. If the Mbaracayu tract met a similar fate, about 700 million tons of carbon dioxide would be released to the atmosphere. AES assumes for purposes of its Barbers Point carbon offset project that only 30 percent of the trees in the Mbaracayu tract would be lost were it not for its investment in preservation, resulting in the release of about 250 million tons of carbon dioxide. Yet the calculation does not consider how many additional trees may be felled elsewhere in the region now that the Mbaracayu tract is off-limits to loggers—or whether illegal logging may still occur in Mbaracayu itself.

Some environmentalists also question the value of the carbon offset plan for Barbers Point because coal for the 180 MW Hawaiian plant is being mined and shipped from a denuded rain forest area on the island of Borneo. AES has a 15 year contract to purchase the coal from **KPC Kaltim-Prima**, a joint venture of **CRA**, an Australian coal company, and **British Petroleum**. KPC Kaltim-Prima says the area is a valuable habitat for wildlife, such as orangutan, borbean gibbon, various species of deer, banteng and hornbills, yet the mining site itself contains relatively little timber because of forest fires and prior logging activities. KPC Kaltim-Prima says it is taking measures to minimize damage from the mining operation and will reforest the area after it is mined out. (The mining operation is discussed in more detail under **RTZ Corp.** in the mining company summaries of Chapter Five.) Sheryl Sturges of AES says the company chose to buy the coal from the KPC Kaltim-Prima because it was the cheapest source of low sulfur coal for the Barbers Point plant.[30]

Other U.S. power plants that burn domestic sources of coal avoid the delicate question of mining in rain forest areas. New England Electric's program to promote better forestry management practices in Malaysia also gets around questions regarding the survival rates of new forest plantations and the effects on unprotected forests when nearby tracts are preserved. All utility carbon offset projects raise a larger issue, however. Peter Hazelwood, CARE's deputy director for agriculture and natural resources, poses the question, "Should these power plants be built in the first place? If we got into carbon sequestration in a big way, we could be criticized for transplanting the problems of the North to the South. There is internal debate about it here."[31]

Despite such concerns, a number of things are certain about carbon offset programs. More trees are likely to be planted and remain standing with these programs than without them; hence, more carbon dioxide is likely to be sequestered from the atmosphere, ameliorating the trend toward global warming. Moreover, properly constructed carbon offset programs promote sustainable forestry and agroforestry management practices, cultural preservation, indigenous rights and economic development opportunities for regions in need of investment. As nations around the world search for ways to implement the goals of the climate change treaty signed at the Earth Summit in 1992, carbon offset programs involving tropical forestry seem destined to grow.

Innovative Investment Sampler

A variety of innovative investment options have emerged in recent years for small investors concerned about saving tropical forests. Such investors must be willing to bear a high degree of financial risk and possibly wait a long time for a return on their investment (if there is any return at all). A sampler of projects promoting sustainable use of tropical forests is provided below. IRRC does not endorse these projects, and it makes no warranty, express or implied, as to the accuracy, completeness or usefulness of this information. Changing circumstances may cause the information to be obsolete. Persons wishing to become involved in these projects should contact the project managers for additional information and consult with their own financial advisers.

Appropriate Technology International
Contact: Kenneth Locklin, senior adviser and director, Washington, D.C., 202-879-2900

Appropriate Technology International (ATI) demonstrates technologies and provides development assistance to Third World communities. ATI has helped to develop improved ceramic jiko stoves in Kenya that use 25 percent less charcoal and increase combustion efficiency relative to traditional stoves. If 80 percent of Kenyan households used the improved stove, ATI estimates, more than 220,000 acres of trees would be saved each year because of reduced demand for fuelwood. ATI also is working with conservation groups to increase the value and marketability of spices and other nontimber rain forest products in Africa and Central America. ATI generally seeks grants from public and private sources. It is soliciting private loans to help provide financing for its projects.

Conversion Tourism Limited
Contact: Norman Fast, chairman, Wellesley, Mass., 617-239-3626

Conversion Tourism Ltd. constructs open-air aerial tram systems to view the canopy of rain forests. Donald Perry, a pioneer in the study of rain forest canopies and author of *Life Above the Jungle Floor*, regards the rain forest canopy as the "unexplored continent" because it has been accessible only to a few scientists yet harbors a wealth of plants and animals that cannot be seen from the ground. Conversion Tourism is in the process of building a $2 million tram in Costa Rica that is scheduled to open in early 1994. Conversion Tourism is seeking further investments ($50,000 minimum). A portion of the tram's profits will go toward forest canopy research.

Cottage Forest Industries
Contact: Randall LaRonde, project director, Dominica, 809-448-4488

Cottage Forest Industries is a purchasing and marketing cooperative for rural woodcutters on the Caribbean island of Dominica. Dominica has 65 percent of its area under tropical forest cover but is heavily dependent on agriculture. Cottage Forest Industries seeks to provide a stable market for sawyers who practice sustainable forestry on Dominica. Members agree to abide by harvesting, utilization and silviculture guidelines, participate in training programs and volunteer 40 hours a year to reforest harvested areas and improve existing timber stands. A reforestation fund has been established; 4 cents from each board-foot sold by the group is deposited into the fund.

The Dominican government is shifting away from large-scale timber extraction to environmentally sound extraction as practiced by this cooperative. The island has many independent sawyers who convert logs to boards without the use of logging roads. Because these rural sawyers tend to operate independently, however, their individual output is low, and they have not been able to compete with mechanized operators for large lumber contracts.

Cottage Forest Industries, consisting of more than 50 sawyer groups (each with four to five men) markets lumber to local furniture makers. The cooperative wants to build a larger, more efficient lumber processing and marketing facility on the dry west coast of the island, which is more accessible to customers. Successful implementation of its development plans could create as many as 120 new jobs, making the cooperative one of the largest employers in the country.

Additional investment is required to efficiently process sustainably grown wood into furniture. The group's startup activities have been supported by the World Wildlife Fund and the John D. and Catherine T. MacArthur Foundation.

Ecological Trading Co. PLC
Contact: Herbert Kwisthout, chairman, United Kingdom, 44-52-250-1850

Ecological Trading Co. imports timber from local cooperatives and sources of sustainably grown timber in Honduras, Peru, Papua New Guinea and the Solomon Islands. It is a consultant to **B&Q**, the largest do-it-yourself home improvement store in the United Kingdom, which has committed to selling only sustainably grown timber by the end of 1995. Ecological Trading says that one of its goals is to benefit the people who harvest sustainably grown timber by offering them higher prices than conventional timber traders. Ecological Trading's annual sales are around $250,000. It plans to raise additional capital ($150 minimum investments) through a public offering in England in the fall of 1993.

Ecos Management Ltd.
Contact: Ernst Brugger, managing director, Switzerland, 41-58-211-750

Swiss billionaire Stephan Schmidheiny founded Ecos Management Ltd. in 1990. Schmidheiny is a leader of the Business Council for Sustainable Development, which seeks to integrate environmental values and concepts into ordinary business practices. Ecos Management offers consulting services to corporations to further its environmental objectives. Ecos Management also manages The Ecos Fund—endowed with more than $15 million in equity capital—to fund ecologically and economically feasible projects sponsored by local business people in Latin America.

Managers of the fund believe that underdevelopment and poverty inevitably lead to overuse and destruction of natural resources in developing countries. The Ecos Fund seeks to invest in agriculture, forestry, water purification and other environment-related projects that can offer a competitive return on investment. One funded project in Costa Rica is establishing a plantation of macadamia trees on denuded land.

EcoTimber
Contact: Eugene Dickey, Jason Grant, Tony Lent or Aaron Maizlish, San Francisco, Calif., 415-864-4900

EcoTimber imports timber from community-run cooperatives in Mexico, Papua New Guinea and East Africa that use responsible, conservation-oriented management practices. The company promotes the use of lesser known tropical timber species to divert pressure from overexploited ones. A private placement stock offering is seeking to raise $250,000 in operating capital.

Environmental Enterprises Assistance Fund
Contact: Brooks Browne, president, Arlington, Va., 703-522-5928.

The Environmental Enterprises Assistance Fund, a nonprofit investment fund, promotes the spread of commercially viable renewable energy technologies in developing countries. It estimates that 50 percent of wood waste from sawmills in tropical countries typically is thrown away. The waste could be used to power small boilers connected to steam turbines and replace diesel fuel as a source of electricity in remote areas. Alternatively, the wood waste could be converted into charcoal. One of the fund's recent projects was to replace diesel-fueled generators at a rain forest lodge in Costa Rica with a small-scale hydroelectric generator.

Foundation for People of the South Pacific

Contact: Bruce Grogan, project director, San Diego, Calif., 619-279-9820

The Foundation for the People of the South Pacific is supporting distribution of a portable sawmill—the "Wokabout"—which allows forest dwellers to mill timber without the use of heavy machinery. The Wokabout can be operated by four men in a forest. The mill is light enough to mill a log right where it falls— eliminating the need for bulldozers, roads and trucks traditionally used by logging companies. The foundation has sponsored the placement of these portable mills in several native communities in Papua New Guinea and the Solomon Islands. In the Solomon Islands, most of the timber felled using the Wokabout is sold locally to build schools, churches, community centers and houses. Some native landowners have greatly increased their income. The Rainforest Action Network—usually critical of logging in tropical forests—has endorsed the Wokabout.

Pilar del Cajon Forest Cooperative

Contact: Ian Hutchinson, Catie project manager, Costa Rica, 50-65-566-431

The Pilar del Cajon Forest Cooperative, a small sawyers cooperative in Costa Rica, has approached the Inter-American Institute of Agricultural Sciences (Catie) in Turrialba for a joint project to promote sustainable forest management. The cooperative, which faces a diminishing supply of forest wood for its sawmills, has obtained a nine year lease on 440 acres of tropical forest, with an option to renew. The tract consists of secondary forest logged in the late 1950s, which regenerated naturally after cattle grazing fields were abandoned.

The cooperative believes that the reforested area can yield profitable resources immediately, while guaranteeing natural regeneration of wood for its sawmills. In 1988, relying on Catie's expertise, the cooperative implemented a selective cutting program, taking precautions to ensure diversity and conservation of tree species on the site. No heavy machinery is used during the harvest. Either oxen or tractors with rubber tires keep forest disturbance to a minimum. No replanting occurs, either. All regrowth is from natural regeneration over a rotation cycle of approximately 35 years. About five acres in the tract will be left undisturbed as a wildlife refuge, according to Ian Hutchinson, a Catie tropical silviculturalist.

Hutchinson estimates that up to $500,000 is needed for better sawmill machinery and to acquire and properly manage 5,000 acres of land, which would keep the mill operating year-round. (The present supply lasts only a few months out of the year.) Some of the funds would be earmarked for technical assistance and education of cooperative members in the management of natural forests. "The land—much of it logged over—could be purchased very cheaply," Hutchinson says. "We could then aim our product at export markets." Hutchinson believes that further development of the project would represent a reversal of unsustainable logging activities elsewhere in Costa Rica and make the cooperative's mill perhaps the only permanently self-sufficient mill in the country.

Prewood Ltd.
Contact: Roman Jann, president, Switzerland, 41-17-154-917.

Prewood Ltd., chartered in the British Virgin Islands, owns 2,560 acres of denuded land in the Guanacaste province of Costa Rica. Swiss investor Roman Jann wants to reforest the land, planting teak and pochote for a timber operation that he says will attain the highest environmental standards. **Macori**, the company managing the Costa Rican project, and owned by Prewood, expects to plant 1,900 acres of trees in 1993. The first controlled harvest of trees will occur in 25 to 30 years. Macori hopes to obtain an agreement with the U.S. Food and Agricultural Organization for technical assistance to ensure that the reforestation is conducted properly. Jann estimates that each acre of land can be reforested for about $2,000.

Jann spent $200,000 to establish the Costa Rican Foundation School of Reforestation—Central America's only school to teach forestry students advanced concepts of reforestation. The failure of many reforestation projects, in Jann's view, is the result of a shortage of experienced forestry technicians. Jann also hopes to offer many jobs to women in the Macori project.

Prewood raised $840,000 through a private offering of 7,000 shares in 1991. Prewood is planning a second private offering in the United States in the fall of 1993 and has a public offering in Europe. Jann wants to raise $15-$20 million in investment capital to buy another 7,500 to 12,000 acres of degraded pasture land. No dividends will be distributed until after the first harvest occurs. Prewood imputes the rising value of plantation wood into each share held. Jann believes a possible shortage of precious woods in coming decades may increase prices by several hundred percent during the growth period of the trees.

Vitoria Amazonica Foundation
Contact: Carlos Miller, director, Brazil, 55-92-642-1336

Vitoria Amazonica Foundation, a recently created nongovernmental group based in Manaus, wants to promote ecotourism in the Brazilian Amazon as a means to raise the standard of living of traditional Amazon river dwellers, known as "ribeirinhos." According to Carlos Miller, director of the foundation, "There is no real ecotourism in the Amazon basin. The businessmen want to use nature to bring tourists to Manaus but the money goes in their pockets. Ecotourism should bring benefits to the people living in the rainforest areas that tourists visit."

A true rain forest tourist experience, in Miller's view, should involve a three or four day trek through forested areas, where plants and animals can be viewed in the wild. Toward that end, the group is raising money to build rain forest lodges in the Anavilhanas Ecological Station and Jau National Park, both of which are two days upriver from Manaus. Italian businessmen reportedly have invested $1 million toward the construction of a lodge at the Anavilhanas Ecological Station. Miller also hopes to build observation towers that overlook the forest canopy.

The Jau National Park, in the Rio Negro Basin, features the world's largest fresh water archipelago. Because the government lacks the necessary resources, the park and the ecological station mainly exist on paper, with no infrastructure. Miller believes a majority of the revenues raised through investments in ecotourism would stay in the community, with river dwellers serving as tour guides and working in other tourist-related jobs.

Yanesha Forestry Cooperative
Contact: Gary Hartshorn (World Wildlife Fund), Washington, D.C., 202-293-4800

Members of five Indian communities living near the base of the Peruvian Andes formed the first native forestry cooperative in the Amazon in 1985 to promote natural forest management. The Yanesha Forestry Cooperative operates in an area where 75 percent of the primary rain forest remains intact. The Yanesha Indians, who recently obtained title to their land from the Peruvian government, are involved in all levels of production—from harvesting to processing to marketing.

The cooperative has achieved natural forest regeneration using an innovative "strip shelterbelt system." The process involves clear cuts of narrow strips of forest about 20 to 50 yards wide, spaced well away from other cuttings. The strips create gaps in the forest canopy, allowing sunlight to penetrate to the ground and stimulate the growth of commercially valuable native species.

The U.S. Agency for International Development provided initial start-up funds totaling $22 million, but AID left in 1989 after the Shining Path guerrilla group stepped up its activity in the area. The Yanesha have apparently repelled the Shining Path from the area and are renewing efforts to develop markets for their products. The cooperative is trying to develop local and national markets for telephone poles and charcoal as well as an international export market. It made its first export shipment to the United States in 1990 to **Luthier's Mercantile**, a California mail order company for woodworkers. The John D. and Catherine T. MacArthur Foundation has supported the cooperative with a long-term, low-interest loan.

Appendix

Contacts for More Information on Tropical Forests

The following list provides a brief summary of some of the major U.S. nonprofit organizations involved in tropical forest research and preservation efforts.

Conservational International
Washington, D.C., 202-429-5660

Conservation International seeks to preserve critical tropical forest habitat and promote scientifically based, economically sound and culturally sensitive alternatives to deforestation. It negotiated the first ever debt-for-nature swap in 1987 and has been a key player in several others. It now hopes to establish a conservation trust fund to promote long-term financing of conservation projects in Guatemala and Madagascar and has worked with the Global Environment Facility to promote endowments in Peru and other countries. It has helped to create U.S. markets for nontimber rain forest products.

Cultural Survival
Cambridge, Mass., 617-495-2562

Cultural Survival seeks to preserve indigenous cultures in tropical forests throughout the world. A marketing arm of the organization, Cultural Survival Enterprises, finds buyers for nontimber rain forest products in the United States and Europe. It brokers deals with retailers so that a portion of the profits are shared with indegenous communities.

Environmental Defense Fund
Washington, D.C., 202-382-3500

The Environmental Defense Fund conducts extensive research on corporate activities in tropical forests and closely monitors the lending policies of the World Bank and other multilateral development agencies for their effects on tropical forests. The fund was a key promoter of Brazilian rubber tappers in their quest to secure extractive reserves in the Amazon rain forest.

The Forest Partnership Inc.
Burlington, Vt., 800-858-6230

The Forest Partnership, previously known as The Timber Source Inc., promotes sustainable forestry in temperate as well as tropical nations. It maintains a comprehensive database of tree species—the Forest Resource Information System—highlighting alternatives to tropical hardwoods, and it is compiling a list of buyers and sellers of sustainably harvested forest products. Forest Partnership hopes to market a supply of sustainable wood products under a "forest friendly" label.

Forest Stewardship Council
Richmond, Vt., 802-434-3101

The Forest Stewardship Council is an international body now being formed to encourage sound stewardship of forest resources. An organizing convention is planned for October 1993 in Toronto to establish a widely accepted set of principles for "good forest management." The council will accredit certification programs for products harvested from forests worldwide, furthering the efforts of several retailers to introduce supplies of timber that are labeled as well-managed or sustainably grown.

Green Cross Certification Co.
Oakland, Calif., 510-832-1415

Green Cross is a division of Scientific Certification Systems, a for-profit company, which provides certification of a range of consumer products, including tropical and temperate timber.

Greenpeace
Washington, D.C., 202-462-1177

Greenpeace, an international environmental group, has conducted extensive research on the tropical timber trade, including imports into the United States. It has advocated consumer boycotts of certain timber corporations and staged numerous public events to draw attention to its cause.

International Hardwood Products Association
Alexandria, Va., 703-836-6696

IHPA is the trade association for U.S. tropical timber importers. It sponsors voluntary rain forest conservation and awareness programs for its members and publishes a directory that lists the majority of U.S. tropical timber importers. It successfully fought a bill in Congress in 1990 that would have required the labeling of U.S. tropical timber imports by the country of origin.

Natural Resources Defense Council
Washington, D.C., 202-783-7800

NRDC has conducted extensive research on tropical forests, particularly with respect to energy development. It published the first detailed study on the effect of oil development in the Ecuadoran rain forest as well as a book on the status of U.S. rain forests in Hawaii and Puerto Rico.

The Nature Conservancy
Arlington, Va., 703-841-5300

The Nature Conservancy purchases threatened ecosystems in order to preserve them. The group has been involved in numerous debt-for-nature swaps in the tropics to further its conservation objectives, including in Costa Rica, Ecuador and Paraguay. The Nature Conservancy has also purchased rain forest tracts in Hawaii, assisted in the establishment of reserves in Panama and helped to preserve the Peten tropical forest ecosystem in Central America.

Rainforest Action Network
San Francisco, Calif., 415-398-4404

Rainforest Action Network is an advocacy and direct-action environmental group devoted to saving rain forests. It conducts extensive research on corporate activities in rain forest areas and has launched several boycotts and publicity campaigns against companies with controversial ties to the tropics; some companies subsequently severed those ties. RAN promotes sustainable timber extraction by indigenous peoples and has published a book on alternatives to tropical timber.

Rainforest Alliance
New York, N.Y., 212-941-1900

The Rainforest Alliance is an international group that promotes economically viable and socially desirable alternatives to tropical deforestation. It has established the Smart Wood program for well-managed tropical timber and the Banano Amigo program in Costa Rica to encourage more environmentally sound management practices for banana plantations. Its Periwinkle Project is working with scientists and native peoples to investigate and utilize medicinal plants from tropical forests. The Rainforest Alliance has published a report on natural products research by pharmaceutical companies. Another project is studying the effects of reduced-impact logging on emissions of carbon dioxide to the atmosphere.

Tropical Forest Foundation
Alexandria, Va., 703-838-5546

The Tropical Forest Foundation is a nonprofit educational foundation created by the International Hardwood Products Association, which represents U.S. tropical timber importers. The foundation provides information on the means and benefits of conserving tropical forests. It is considering a program to monitor sources of tropical timber.

Woodworkers Alliance for Rainforest Protection
Easthampton, Mass., 413-586-8156

WARP, as this nonprofit group is known, is a grassroots organization of North American woodworkers who formed to address wood harvesting issues in general and tropical rain forest issues in particular. WARP publishes a newsletter that features information on tropical timbers that woodworkers can use to take pressure off overharvested species. WARP also was a key player in the creation of the Forest Stewardship Council.

World Wildlife Fund
Washington, D.C., 202-293-4800

The World Wide Fund for Nature, an international environmental group, and its American counterpart regard tropical forest preservation as a top conservation priority. The fund supports scores of projects in developing countries in an effort to improve land use management practices, species conservation and use of local resources by indigenous communities. Among many other activities in the rain forest, the fund has promoted the creation of extractive reserves in Brazil, participated in debt-for-nature swaps in Costa Rica and Madagascar and advised oil companies on protective measures for oil exploration and development activities in Papua New Guinea. Its Wild Lands and Human Needs program encourages the integration of natural resource management techniques and grass roots economic development.

Footnotes

Chapter 1: Tropical Forests in Trouble

1. A summary of recent estimates regarding tropical forest cover appears in the report by Nels Johnson and Bruce Cabarle, *Surviving the Cut: Natural Forest Management in the Humid Tropics*, World Resources Institute, Washington, D.C., February 1993, pp. 5-7.
2. A reference discussion on the dynamics of the rain forest appears in Arnold Newman, *Tropical Rainforest*, Facts on File Inc., New York, N.Y., 1990, pp. 52-59.
3. Robert M. May, "How Many Species Inhabit the Earth?", *Scientific American*, October 1992, p. 44.
4. Edward O. Wilson, "Threats to Biodiversity," *Scientific American*, September 1989, p. 108.
5. See note 3, pp. 45-46.
6. See note 4.
7. Walter Reid and Kenton Miller, *Keeping Options Alive: The Scientific Basis for Conserving Biodiversity*, World Resources Institute, Washington, D.C., 1989, p. 15.
8. William Booth, "Tropical Forest Loss May Be Killing Off Songbirds, Study Says," *The Washington Post*, July 26, 1989.
9. Jake Page, "Clear-cutting the Tropical Rain Forest in a Bold Attempt to Save It," *Smithsonian*, April 1988, p. 107.
10. See note 4, and W.V. Reid, "How Many Species Will There Be?", *Tropical Deforestation and Species Extinctions*, T. Whitmore and J. Sayer, editors, Chapman and Hall, London, U.K., 1992.
11. Mark J. Plotkin, "The Outlook for New Agricultural and Industrial Products from the Tropics," *Biodiversity*, E.O. Wilson, editor, National Academy Press, Washington, D.C., 1988, p. 106.
12. "Rain Forest Worth More If Uncut, Study Says," *The New York Times*, June 29, 1989.
13. Norman H. Farnsworth, "Screening Plants for New Medicines," *Biodiversity*, E.O. Wilson, editor, National Academy Press, Washington, D.C., 1988, p. 83.
14. David Lenderts, "Plants that Give Life," Rainforest Alliance, New York, undated pamphlet.
15. Conrad MacKerron, "Will Drugs Die with the Trees?", *Chemical Week*, March 28, 1990, p. 58.
16. Walter V. Reid *et al.*, "A New Lease on Life," *Biodiversity Prospecting*, World Resources Institute, Washington, D.C., 1993; and Timothy B. Wheeler, "Deal Shows Biodiversity's Possibilities," *The Baltimore Sun*, June 16, 1992.
17. World Resources Institute, *World Resources 1990-91*, Oxford University Press, New York, N.Y., 1990, pp. 101-102.

18. Ernest Lutz and Herman Daly, "Incentives, Regulations, and Sustainable Land Use in Costa Rica," Environment Working Paper No. 34, World Bank, Washington, D.C., July 1990.
19. Robert Repetto and Malcolm Gillis, *Public Policies and the Misuse of Forest Resources*, Cambridge University Press, New York, N.Y., 1988.
20. Robert Goodland, "Tropical Deforestation: Solutions, Ethics and Religions," Environment Working Paper No. 43, World Bank, Washington, D.C., January 1991.
21. See note 19.
22. Hans Binswanger, "Brazilian Policies That Encourage Deforestation," Environment Working Paper No. 15, World Bank, Washington, D.C., April 1989.
23. Marguerite Holloway, "Sustaining the Amazon," *Scientific American*, July 1993, p. 93, citing Stephan Schwartzman of the Environmental Defense Fund.
24. Tom Barry and Deb Preusch, *The Central America Fact Book*, Grove Press, New York, N.Y., 1986, p. 129.
25. Julio Centeno, Venezuelan forestry researcher, personal communication, July 1991.
26. James Brooke, "Brazilian Moves To Rescue Tribe," *The New York Times*, March 27, 1990; and Julia Preston, "Brazil Grants Land Rights to Indians," *The Washington Post*, Nov. 16, 1991.
27. See note 23, and James Brooke, "Rain Forest Indians Hold Off Threat of Change," *The New York Times*, Dec. 5, 1990.
28. Wade Davis, "The Apostle of Borneo," *Outside*, January 1991, p. 87.
29. "WWF Focus," World Wildlife Fund newsletter, September/October 1990, p. 1.
30. Tim Burt, "Unlikely Champion for the Amazon's Forgotten People," *Financial Times*, Aug. 22, 1990.
31. Report of the Independent Review Committee, Tropical Forestry Action Plan, Kuala Lumpur, Malaysia, May 1990.
32. Bruce Rich, "The Emperor's New Clothes: The World Bank and Environmental Reform," *World Policy Journal*, Spring 1990.
33. Letter from U.S. environmental groups to World Bank President Barber Conable, quoting Martin Colchester, Aug. 21, 1987.
34. For the quote, see the article by Gwen Robinson, "Development Too Fast for Environment," *International Herald Tribune*, Dec. 5, 1990.
35. "TFAP? TFLOP!," *Bank Check*, September 1990.

Box 1A: Colonizing the Rain Forests

1a. Dennis J. Mahar, "Government Policies and Deforestation in Brazil's Amazon Region," World Bank, Washington, D.C., 1989, p. 33-36.
2a. For the quote and a summary of the analysis, see the article by William K. Stevens, "Loss of Species Is Worse Than Thought in Brazil's Amazon," *The New York Times*, June 29, 1993.
3a. James Brooke, "Homesteaders Gnaw at Brazil Rain Forest," *The New York Times*, May 22, 1992.
4a. Mark Collins, *The Last Rainforests*, Oxford University Press, New York, N.Y., 1990, p. 41, and Roger J. Stone, "The Global Stakes of Tropical Deforestation," *USA Today* magazine, March 1988, p. 74.

Box 1B: Rainforest Action Network

1b. Randall Hayes, Rainforest Action Network, personal communication, November 1991.

Chapter 2: Early Efforts to Tame the Rain Forests

1. Susanna Hecht and Alexander Cockburn, *The Fate of the Forest,* Verso, London, U.K., 1989, p. 61.
2. *Ibid.,* pp. 66-72.
3. *Ibid.*
4. See note 1, and Richard Bourne, *Assault on the Amazon,* Victor Gallancz Ltd., London, U.K., 1978, p. 30.
5. See second citation of note 4, pp. 30-31.
6. Shelton H. Davis, *Victims of the Miracle: Development and the Indians of Brazil,* Cambridge University Press, New York, N.Y., 1977, p. 153.
7. See note 1, pp. 85-6.
8. Gwen Kinkead, "Trouble in D.K. Ludwig's Jungle," *Fortune,* April 20, 1981, p. 102.
9. Philip M. Fearnside and Judy M. Rankin, "Jari and Development in the Brazilian Amazon," *Interciencia,* May/June 1980, p. 147.
10. See note 8.
11. Philip M. Fearnside, "Jari at Age 19: Lessons for Brazil's Silvicultural Plans at Carajás," *Interciencia,* January/February 1988, p. 22.
12. See note 6, p. 42.
13. *Ibid.*
14. Dennis J. Mahar, "Government Policies and Deforestation in Brazil's Amazon Region," World Bank, Washington, D.C., 1989, p. 33-36.
15. *Ibid.,* p. 4.
16. *Ibid.,* p. 46.
17. Michelle Beale, Coca-Cola, personal communication, June 1991.
18. Penny N. Sass, Scott Paper, undated printed manuscript addressed to Scott consumers.
19. For the quote, see the article by Robert Weissman, "Scott Surrenders," *Multinational Monitor,* October 1989; and Penny N. Sass, Scott Paper, personal communication, November 1989.
20. "New Partner for Former Scott Project in Irian Jaya," *World Rainforest Report,* Rainforest Action Network, April/May 1991, p. 4.
21. "Indonesian Logging Conglomerate Buys Astra," *World Rainforest Report,* Rainforest Action Network, January/March 1993, p. 10.
22. "IFC Link in Astra Pulp Project," *Independent,* London, U.K., April 21, 1991.

Chapter 3: The Tropical Timber Industry

1. United Nations Food and Agricultural Organization and United Nations Development Program, *Tropical Forestry Action Plan Joint Interagency Planning and Review Mission for the Forestry Sector: Cameroon Mission Report,* Vol. 3, Main Report, New York, N.Y., 1988.
2. Jeffrey R. Vincent, "The Tropical Timber Trade and Sustainable Development," *Science,* June 19, 1992, *op. cit.*
3. Alan Grainger, "The Future Role of Tropical Forests in the World Forest Economy," PhD dissertation, Department of Plant Sciences, University of Oxford, 1986, cited in Kathleen Reilly, "The Tropical Timber Trade: With an emphasis on the United

States," Workshop on the U.S. Tropical Timber Trade, Rainforest Alliance, New York, N.Y., 1989.

4. Nels Johnson and Bruce Cabarle, *Surviving the Cut: Natural Forest Management in the Humid Tropics*, World Resources Institute, Washington, D.C., February 1993, p. 42.

5. A more complete discussion appears in Jan G. Laarman, "Export of Tropical Woods in the Twentieth Century," in *World Deforestation in the Twentieth Century,* edited by John F. Richards and Richard P. Tucker, Duke University Press, Durham, N.C., 1988.

6. Norman Myers, "Deforestation in Tropical Forests and Their Climatic Implications," Friends of the Earth, Washington, D.C., 1989, p. 77.

7. See Reilly in note 3, and Cathleen Fogel, "Tropical Wood Imported into the United States (1989)," citing U.S. Department of Commerce statistical data, Sierra Club International Program, San Francisco, Calif., February 1991.

8. Michael Hicks, personal communication, U.S. Commerce Department, September 1991.

9. Robert Repetto and Malcolm Gillis, editors, *Public Policies and the Misuse of Forest Resources*, Cambridge University Press, New York, N.Y., 1988, p. 132.

10. See note 4, p. 15.

11. See note 2, p. 1651.

12. Nels Johnson, Bruce Carbarle and Dexter Mead, "Development Assistance, Natural Forest Management, and the Future of Tropical Forests," World Resources Institute, May 1991, p. 6.

13. For the quote, see note 9, p. 167.

14. See note 6, p. 40.

15. Malcolm Gillis, "Multinational Enterprises and Environmental and Resource Management Issues in the Indonesian Tropical Forest Sector," in *Multinational Corporations, Environment, and the Third World*, edited by Charles S. Pearson, Duke University Press, Durham, N.C., 1987, p. 65.

16. See note 5, p. 155.

17. See note 9, p. 119.

18. John Laird, "South-East Asia's Trembling Rainforests," *Our Planet,* Vol. 3, No. 4, 1991, United Nations Environment Programme, Nairobi, p. 8.

19. Greenpeace press release, Washington, D.C., Sept. 11, 1991.

20. Lim Keng Yaik, Malaysian Minister of Primary Industries, before the Malaysian Timber Industry Development Council, printed manuscript, Jan. 10, 1992.

21. Paul Senior, Pat Brown Lumber Co., personal communication, January 1992.

22. Ivan Ussach, Rainforest Alliance, personal communication, November 1991.

23. Meg Ruby, Greenpeace, personal communication, October 1990.

24. Russell Stadelman II, Russell Stadelman & Co., personal communication, October 1991.

25. Robert Waffle, International Hardwood Products Association, personal communication, December 1992.

26. "Indonesia: Forest, Land and Water: Issues in Sustainable Development," World Bank, Washington, D.C., 1989, pp. 2-3.

27. See note 15, p. 54.

28. See note 26, p. xviii.

29. *Ibid.*, p. 2.

30. Carol Stoney, "Forest Resources in Indonesia," Winrock International, April 1991, p. 37.

31. Indonesia Tropical Forestry Action Programme, Executive Summary, Indonesian Ministry of Forestry, Jakarta, Indonesia, August 1991.

32. See note 30, p. 2.
33. See note 26, pp. 10-11.
34. See note 4, p. 39.
35. "Last of Great Teak Forests Vanishing," *Journal of Commerce*, July 26, 1990.
36. Gwen Robinson, "Development Too Fast for Environment," *International Herald Tribune*, Dec. 5, 1990.
37. See note 4, p. 18.
38. Greenpeace USA, "Estimated Top 10 Tropical Wood Importers in 1990," citing *Journal of Commerce* reporting service statistical data, Washington, D.C., 1991.
39. George Draffen, "Weyerhaeuser: The Tree Whackers," *Multinational Monitor*, October 1992, p. 30.
40. *Ibid.*, and Lowell Moholt, Weyerhaeuser Corp., personal communication, June 1993.
41. Francois Nectoux and Yoichi Kuroda, "Timber from the South Seas," World Wildlife Fund International, Gland, Switzerland, 1989, p. 79.
42. *Ibid.*
43. Robert M. Orr Jr., "From the Land of the Rising Sun: The Private Sector and Japanese Official Development Assistance," *Japan Economic Journal*, Jan. 27, 1990, *op. cit.*
44. For the quote, see the article by David Minkow and Colleen Murphy-Dunning, "Assault on Papua New Guinea," *Multinational Monitor*, June 1992, p. 8.
45. "Indonesia Suspends License for Marubeni Logging Work," *Japan Times*, Oct. 24, 1990.
46. Joe Rinkevitch, "Destruction of an Internationally Important Wetland in Irian Jaya, Indonesia for Woodchipping Exports to Japan," *Japan Environment Monitor*, Japan Tropical Forestry Action Network, June 30, 1990.
47. "Mitsubishi Actions Span the Country," *World Rainforest Report*, Rainforest Action Network, January-March 1993, p. 3.
48. Tomoo Aoyagi, "Knocking on Wood," *Look Japan*, July 1990.
49. See note 8.
50. See note 5, p. 157.
51. See note 15, p. 299.
52. Virginia Luling and Damien Lewis, "The Scramble for African Timber," *Multinational Monitor*, September 1992, p. 11.
53. See note 15, p. 306.
54. See note 52, p. 11.
55. *Ibid.*, p, 10.
56. *Ibid.*
57. *Ibid.*, p. 11.
58. See the article by Korinna Horta, Environmental Defense Fund, "The Last Big Rush for the Green Gold," *The Ecologist*, May/June 1991.
59. Nigel Dudley, *Transnational Companies and Tropical Rainforest*, Earth Resources Research Ltd., London, U.K., June 1989, *op. cit.*
60. See note 58.
61. Virginia Luling and Damien Lewis, "Cameroon's Road to Ruin," *Multinational Monitor*, September 1992, p. 12.
62. David Thomsson, Brookside Veneers, personal communication, October 1991.
63. See note 59, p. 10.
64. *Ibid.*, p. 14.
65. See note 9 for the chapter written by John Browder, "Public Policy and Deforestation in the Brazilian Amazon," p. 247.

66. Campbell Plowden and Yuri Kusuda, "Logging in the Brazilian Rainforest," Rainforest Alliance, New York, April 1989; and Marguerite Holloway, "Sustaining the Amazon," *Scientific American*, July 1993, p. 96.

67. U.S. Department of Agriculture, Foreign Agricultural Service, "U.S. Trade Data Collection," Washington, D.C., March 11, 1992.

68. *World Rainforest Report*, Rainforest Action Network, January/February 1991.

69. Danilo Remor, The Maginco Group, personal communication, December 1990.

70. "Brazil Alters Forest Policy," *The Wall Street Journal*, Feb. 10, 1993.

71. Bruce Larson, Larson Wood Products, personal communication, September 1991.

72. World Resources Institute, *World Resources 1990-91*, Oxford University Press, New York, 1990, p. 102.

73. David Dudenhofer, "Deforestation and Forest Protection in Costa Rica," August 1990, unpublished manuscript.

74. Ernst Lutz and Herman Daly, "Incentives, Regulations and Sustainable Land Use in Costa Rica," *Environmental and Resource Economics: 1*, Kluwer Academic Publishers, 1991, p. 179.

75. Henry Tschinkel, "Natural Resource Management in Costa Rica: A Strategy for U.S. AID," U.S. Agency for International Development, San Jose, Costa Rica, December, 1987.

76. Quote appears in the article by David Dudenhofer, "Lumber Industry One Victim of Deforestation," *Tico Times*, San Jose, Costa Rica, March 9, 1990, p. 9.

77. Luis Villalobos, Forestry Director, Costa Rican Ministry of Mines and Natural Resources, personal communication, November 1990.

78. David Dudenhofer, "Forestry Laws Easily (and Frequently) Flouted," *Tico Times*, San Jose, Costa Rica, Feb. 23, 1990, p. 9.

79. Keister Evans, forest industry consultant, personal communication, September 1991.

80. "Consensus Statement on Commercial Forestry, Sustained Yield Management and Tropical Forests," co-sponsored by the Smithsonian Institution and the International Hardwood Products Association, January 1990.

81. D. Cassells, "ITTO Develops Criteria for Measuring Sustainable Forest Management," *ITTO Tropical Forest Management Update* newsletter, 1992.

82. Robert Goodland *et al.*, "Tropical Moist Forest Management: The Urgency and Transition to Sustainability," World Bank, Washington, D.C., Sept. 9, 1990.

83. Duncan Poore *et al.*, *No Timber Without Trees: Sustainability in the Tropical Forest*, Earthscan Publications, London, U.K., 1989, p. 5.

84. See note 82.

85. Bruce Cabarle, World Resources Institute, personal communication, October 1991.

86. See note 4, p. 41.

87. "Proposed Ban on Tropical Timber Forestalled!," *Import/Export Wood Purchasing News*, August/September 1991.

88. See note 4, p. 18.

89. Press release, World Wildlife Fund, Washington, D.C., May 28, 1991.

90. "Timber Conservation Elusive," *The Wall Street Journal*, May 21, 1993.

91. See note 80.

92. *Ibid.*

93. Wendy Baer, International Hardwood Products Association, personal communication, October 1991.

94. Donald Schramm, Georgia-Pacific Corp., personal communication, October 1991.

95. Howard Steinberg, Ply-Gem Manufacturing Co., personal communication, October 1991.

96. Mark Baker, forest industry consultant, personal communication, September 1991.

97. See note 4, p. 47.
98. Gary Hartshorn, World Wildlife Fund, personal communication, December 1992.
99. George Wilmont, The Knoll Group, personal communication, October 1991.
100. See note 4, p. 49.
101. *Ibid.*, p. 51.
102. Sonny Koontz, Thomasville Furniture Industries, personal communication, December 1991.
103. See note 21.
104. Edward Clem, Champion International, personal communication, November 1991.
105. See note 71.
106. See note 94.
107. Phyllis Austin, *Maine Times*, Feb. 23, 1990, p. 9.
108. Michael Vidan, Georgia-Pacific, personal communication, August 1991.
109. Carol Stoney, "Forest Resources in Indonesia," Winrock International, April 1991, p. 35.
110. See note 107.
111. See note 38.
112. See note 94.
113. Robert Johnston, Herman Miller, personal communication, June 1991.
114. See note 99.
115. See note 71.
116. See note 38.
117. Bruce Chaffin, Liberty Woods International, personal communication, February 1992.
118. See note 95.
119. Donald MacMaster, Plywood Panels Inc., personal communication, October 1991.
120. Richard Newman, Plywood Tropics USA, personal communcation, October 1991.
121. Samuel Robinson Jr., Robinson Lumber Co., personal communication, October 1990.
122. James Nations, Conservation International, personal communication, August 1991.
123. Theodore Clayton, Scott Paper Co., personal communication, October 1990.
124. Jon Walker, Simpson Paper Co., personal communication, October 1990.
125. See note 24.
126. Paul Howell, Stone Container Corp., personal communication, November 1991.
127. "Stone Plans Massive Chip Mill in Costa Rica," Rainforest Action Network, Action Alert #84, San Francisco, Calif., May 1993.
128. Lowell E. Moholt, Weyerhaeuser Co., personal communication, October 1991.
129. Robert Lowery, Weyerhaeuser Corp., personal communication, May 1991.
130. See note 52.
131. See note 58.
132. Keiichi Ohashi, Honshu Paper, personal communication, February 1992.
133. Colleen Murphy-Dunning, Rainforest Action Network, personal communication, September 1991.
134. "C. Itoh Sets Up Environment Office," *Japan Times*, July 25, 1990.
135. Fukashi Furukawa, Marubini Corp., personal communication, October 1991.
136. See note 41.
137. Joseph Rinkevich, "Destruction of an Internationally Important Wetland in Irian Jaya, Indonesia, for Woodchipping Exports to Japan," *Japan Environmental Monitor*, Vol. 3, No. 3, June 30, 1990.
138. See note 134.

139. Dick Shinohara, Mitsubishi International Corp., personal communication, November 1991.
140. As reported by Norman Altstedter, Shell Oil Co., personal communication, July 1990.
141. Guillermo Castillega, World Wildlife Fund, personal communication, February 1992.
142. Alan Knight, B&Q, personal communication, June 1993.
143. M.E. George, Unilever, personal communication, December 1991.

Box 3A: Weyerhaeuser: An Indonesian Case Study

1a. Norman Johnson, Weyerhaeuser Corp., personal communication, October 1991.
2a. Robert Lowery, Weyerhaeuser Corp., personal communication, May 1991.
3a. Malcolm Gillis, "Multinational Enterprises and Environmental and Resource Management Issues in the Indonesian Tropical Forest Sector," in *Multinational Corporations, Environment, and the Third World,* edited by Charles S. Pearson, Duke University Press, Durham, N.C., 1987, p. 89.
4a. *Ibid.,* p. 85.

Box 3B: Mitsubishi Man to the Rescue!

1b. Untitled article in the *Asahi Shimbun,* June 5, 1991.
2b. Peter Hadfield, "Superhero Defies Logic To Defend His Company," *Daily Yomiyuri, April 23, 1991.*

Box 3C: National Forest Policies and Tropical Deforestation

1c. Robert Repetto and Malcolm Gillis, editors, *Public Policies and the Misuse of Forest Resources,* Cambridge University Press, New York, N.Y., 1988, *op. cit.*
2c. Jeffrey R. Vincent, "The Tropical Timber Trade and Sustainable Development," *Science,* June 19, 1992, *op. cit.*
3c. See note 1c.
4c. *Ibid.,* p. 1.
5c. Paul Senior, Pat Brown Lumber Co., personal communication, January 1992.
6c. Mark Baker, personal communication, September 1991.
7c. "Lost in the forest," *The Economist,* Aug. 31, 1991.

Box 3D: Natural Forest Management Practices

1d. Mario Barrenechea, Portico Co., personal communication, November 1990.
2d. Gary Hartshorn, World Wildlife Fund, personal communication, October 1991.
3d. Matthew A. Perl *et al.,* "Views from the Forest: Natural Forest Management Initiatives in Latin America," World Wildlife Fund, March 1991. This publication contains summaries about the Yanesha project and 14 similar attempts to move toward sustainable forestry in Latin America.
4d. Edgar Londono, Smurfit Carton de Colombia, personal communication, October 1991; and Nels Johnson and Bruce Cabarle, *Surviving the Cut: Natural Forest Management in the Humid Tropics,* World Resources Institute, Washington, D.C., February 1993, pp. 32-33.

Chapter 4: Oil Production in the Tropics

1. Paul Driver, International Union for Conservation of Nature, personal communication, November 1991.
2. Charles Goodwin, Occidental Petroleum, personal communication, November 1991.
3. The section on environmental impacts of oil production draws on previous work by Judith L. Kimerling and Dirk W. McDermott. Kimerling is the principal author of *Amazon Crude*, published by the Natural Resources Defense Council in New York, N.Y., in 1991. Kimerling also wrote a draft manuscript in 1989, entitled "Petroleum Development in Amazonian Ecuador: Environmental and Socio-Cultural Impacts," and published a review article in the Hastings Law Review, entitled "Disregarding Environmental Law: Petroleum Development in Protected Natural Areas and Indigenous Homelands in the Ecuadorian Amazon," Volume 14, 1991, pp. 849-963. McDermott drafted a study regarding development of a natural gas field in Peru, entitled, "Technical Concerns and Recommendations for the Camisea Gas Field, Peru," published by the World Wildlife Fund in Washington, D.C., in August 1990.
4. Environmental Guidance Document, American Petroleum Institute, Washington, D.C., 1989, p. 35.
5. "Oil Industry Operating Guideline for Tropical Rainforests," E&P Forum, London, U.K., Report No. 2.49/170, April 1991.
6. For a more detailed history of the oil boom in Ecuador, see the book by Judith Kimerling, *Amazon Crude*, written with S. Jacob Scherr, J. Eugene Gibson, Glenn Prickett, Jennifer Gale and Lynn Fischer of the Natural Resources Defense Council, New York, N.Y., 1991.
7. J.F. Sandoval Moreano, "Oil and Environment in the Ecuadorian Amazon," published in Spanish in the Ecuadorian journal "Ediciones ABYA-YALA," Quito, Ecuador, March 1990, pp. 79-89.
8. For the quote, see the transcript by Damien Lewis, "BBC Wildlife," London, England, Aug. 1, 1991.
9. See note 6, p. xii.
10. *Ibid.*, p. xiv.
11. Decision of the International Water Tribunal, "Corporation of Legal-Ecological Investigation and Defense of Life (Cordavi) vs. Petroecuador, Texaco Petroleum Co. and City Investing Co.," Amsterdam, The Netherlands, Feb. 20, 1992.
12. D. York LeCorgne, "Texaco Petroleum Co. Response to Cordavi's Case Document," White Plains, N.Y., Feb. 7, 1992.
13. *Ibid.*
14. For the quote, see the article by James Brooke, "New Effort Would Test Possible Coexistence of Oil and Rain Forest," *The New York Times*, Feb. 26, 1991.
15. For the quote, see the transcript by Sandy Tolan, *All Things Considered*, National Public Radio, Washington, D.C., Sept. 3, 1991.
16. "Setting the Record Straight," Texaco, Westchester, N.Y., undated manuscript (obtained by IRRC on Jan. 29, 1993).
17. Michael Trevino, Texaco, personal communication, September 1991.
18. Judith Kimerling, personal communication, June 1993.
19. Michael Gallagher, Texaco, personal communication, February 1993.
20. See note 14.
21. Alex Chapman, Conoco, personal communication, July 1990.
22. Judith Kimerling, personal communication, October 1991.

23. For a summary of recent developments, see the petition by Lauri J. Adams, Adriana Fabra Aguilar and Karen Parker, "Supplemental Report to the Petition Submitted to the Inter-American Commission on Human Rights of the Organization of American States by Confeniae and Onhae on Behalf of the Huaorani Nation Against Ecuador," Sierra Club Legal Defense Fund, San Francisco, Calif., January 1993.

24. *Ibid.*

25. S. Jacob Scherr, Natural Resources Defense Council, minutes of meeting with Conoco, New York, N.Y., Feb. 5, 1991.

26. S. Jacob Scherr, Natural Resources Defense Council, "NRDC's Actions on Conoco's Proposed Oil Development in Ecuador," printed manuscript, New York, N.Y., July 1991.

27. Martha M. Hamilton, "Forest's Fate Splits Environmentalists," *The Washington Post*, May 15, 1991.

28. C.L. Blackburn, Maxus Energy Corp., personal communication, October 1991.

29. See note 23, p. 35.

30. "Drillers Are Adapting to the Rain Forest," *The Wall Street Journal*, Jan. 5, 1993.

31. See note 23, p. 6.

32. *Ibid.*, p. 43.

33. Actualidad Economica, Peruvian Environmental Law Society, Lima, Peru, July 1991.

34. *Ibid.*, p. 25.

35. Letter from Texas Crude Exploration-Peru Inc. to the Peruvian Society of Environmental Law (Spda), June 14, 1991.

36. "Oil Boom Exploding in the Western Amazon," *World Rainforest Report*, Rainforest Action Network, January/March 1993, p. 5.

37. Charles McCoy, "Chevron Tries to Show It Can Protect Jungle While Pumping Oil," *The Wall Street Journal*, June 9, 1992.

38. Bruce Bunting, World Wildlife Fund-U.S., personal communication, October 1991.

39. See note 37.

40. Colleen Murphy-Dunning, Rainforest Action Network, personal communication, September 1991.

41. See note 37.

42. *Ibid.*

43. Harry Partlow, Amoco Corp., personal communication, July 1991.

44. D. Chamberlain, Arco, personal communication, November 1991.

45. David Munro, "Oil in Ecuador," Fact Sheet #25, Rainforest Action Network, San Francisco, Calif., 1992.

46. See note 44.

47. See note 23, p. 13.

48. Scott McCreary, G. Mathias Kondolf, Joe R. McBride and Robert Twiss, "Independent Review of Environmental Documentation for Petroleum Exploration in Block 10, Oriente, Ecuador," Center for Environmental Design Research, University of California at Berkeley, June 17, 1992.

49. C.R. Ball, Exxon Corp., personal communication, August 1991.

50. Susan Meeker-Lowry, "Who Is Destroying the Rainforests?" *Z Magazine*, May 1993, p. 37.

51. Douglas Graham, Maxus Energy Corp., personal communication, October 1991.

52. Thomas Cooney, Mobil Corp., personal communication, June 1993.

53. R.R. Graves, Mobil Corp., personal communication with Stewart Hudson, National Wildlife Federation, March 1990.

54. Charles Goodwin, Occidental Petroleum Corp., personal communication, November 1991.

55. See note 6.
56. See note 45.
57. Stanley Blossom, Oryx Energy Co., personal communication, November 1991.
58. James Ford, Santa Fe Energy Resources, personal communication, October 1991.
59. D.E. Six, Texaco, personal communication, October 1990.
60. Carlos Camarena Medina, "Texaco Viola la Ley Le Recursos Naturales," *Correo Economico*, August 1991.
61. D.L. Hanley, Unocal, personal communication, March 1992.
62. See note 23, p. 14.
63. *Ibid.*, pp. 13-14.
64. *Ibid.*, pp. 14-15.
65. Rodolfo Sosa, Basic Petroleum, personal communication, August 1991.
66. See note 18.
67. Bernard Tramier, Elf-Aquitaine, personal communication, March 1992.
68. See note 23, p. 12.
69. Hilda Rivera, Conservation International, personal communication, August 1991.
70. Dirk W. McDermott, "Technical Concerns and Recommendations for the Camisea Gas Field, Peru," World Wildlife Fund, Washington, D.C., August 1990.
71. Steven Larcombe, British Gas, personal communication, January 1993.
72. Ken Warn, "Ecuadoran Tribe Attacks British Gas over Forest Use," *Financial Times*, Aug. 16, 1991.
73. Charles Nicholson, British Petroleum, personal communication, November 1991.

Box 4-A: Building Better Corporate-Environmental Relationships

1a. Jeff Sayer, International Union for Conservation of Nature, personal communication, November 1991.
2a. Arnold Brown, Program for Belize, personal communication, November 1991.

Chapter 5: Mining in the Tropics

1. Information supplied by RTZ Corp.
2. For the quote, see Roger Moody, "Plunder, People Against RTZ and its Subsidiaries Campaign Against Foreign Control of Aotearoa," (PaRTiZans/Cafca), London, U.K., 1991, p. 68.
3. Bill Collier, "Freeport Taps Global Controversy," *Austin-American Statesman*, Austin, Tex., Sept. 1, 1991.
4. Johnnie N. Moore and Samuel N. Luoma, "Mining's Hazardous Waste," *Environmental Science and Technology*, No. 24, 1990, American Chemical Society; reprinted in Clementine, *The Journal of Responsible Mineral Development*, Washington, D.C., Spring 1991.
5. "Yanomami in Peril: An Interview with Davi Kopenawa Yanomami," *Multinational Monitor*, September 1992, p. 23.
6. "Mining Enterprises and Indigenous Lands in Amazonia" (in Portuguese), Ecumenical Center for Documentation and Information, Sao Paulo, Brazil, 1987.
7. For the quote, see note 4.
8. For the quote, see note 2, p. 69.

9. *Ibid.*, p. 68.

10. *Ibid.*

11. David Minkow and Colleen Murphy-Dunning, "Assault on Papua New Guinea," *Multinational Monitor*, June 1992, p. 8.

12. "Funding Ecological and Social Destruction: The World Bank and the International Monetary Fund," Bank Information Center, 1990, Washington, D.C., *op. cit.*

13. For the quote, see Adrian Cowell, *The Decade of Destruction*, Henry Holt & Co., New York, N.Y., 1991.

14. See note 12, p. 17.

15. Gustavo Bessa, Companhia Vale do Rio Doce, personal communication, Rio de Janeiro, December 1990.

16. James Brooke, "Brazilian Moves to Rescue Tribe," *The New York Times*, March 27, 1990.

17. James Brooke, "Brazil Evicting Miners in Amazon To Reclaim Land for the Indians," *The New York Times*, March 8, 1993.

18. Cezar de Andrade, Brascan Brazil, written correspondence, Dec. 3, 1991.

19. For the quote, see note 17.

20. James Miller, Freeport McMoRan, personal communication, April 10, 1991.

21. See note 11, p. 9.

22. "Report on EDF/Freeport McMoRan Meeting on 1/17/91," internal memorandum, Environmental Defense Fund, Washington, D.C., February 1991.

23. Excerpt of June 3, 1992, letter from Freeport McMoRan to Rainforest Action Network, reprinted in *World Rainforest Report*, Rainforest Action Network, January/March 1993, p. 7.

24. See the article cited in note 23.

25. See note 11, p. 10.

26. David Hyndman, "Ok Tedi: New Guinea's Disaster Mine," *The Ecologist*, Vol. 18, No. 1, 1988.

27. Press release, Torres Strait Island Co-Ordinating Council, Nov. 8, 1989.

28. Executive Summary, Independent Evaluation of Ok Tedi Mining Limited Sixth Supplemental Agreement Environmental Study, University of Papua New Guinea, July 31, 1989.

29. Decision of the International Water Tribunal, Amsterdam, The Netherlands, regarding Ok Tedi Mining Ltd., Papua New Guinea, Feb. 19, 1991.

30. "Guidelines for a Good Mine," Mineral Policy Center, Washington, D.C., April 1991.

31. Marcelo Vianna, Alcoa Alumunia SA, "Environmental Management Tools," presentation at the Second World Conference on Environmental Management, Rotterdam, The Netherlands, April 10-12, 1991.

32. Donald Williams, "Rehabilitation of Mined Bauxite Lands at Pocos de Caldas," Minas Gerais State, Brazil, unpublished paper, 1986.

33. See note 12, p. 15.

34. Robert McGreebey, Amoco, written correspondence with the Securities and Exchange Commission, Washington, D.C., Dec. 19, 1990.

35. For the quote, see Mark A. Kubisz and Karen Williams, "The Activities of Canadian Mining Companies in Brazil: Brascan, Alcan and Inco," Probe International, Toronto, unpublished paper, May 1990, p. 48.

36. Ghillean Prance, "Give the Multinationals a Break!," *New Scientist*, Sept. 23, 1989.

37. Carol Saint-Laurent, "Mission to Brazil: A Case Study," Pollution Probe, Toronto, Canada, June 1990.

38. See note 35, p. 50.

39. R.P. Cezar de Andrade, Brascan, personal communication, December 1991.

40. "The Killing Fields," _London Sunday Times_, June 18, 1989; and BP response, "Brazil Rain Forest: Sunday Times Article," June 23, 1989.
41. David Fennell, Golden Star Resources, personal communication, November 1991.
42. Marcus Colchester, "Sacking Guyana," _Multinational Monitor_, September 1991.
43. Scott Hand, Inco, personal communication, October 1991.
44. Henry Brehaut, Placer Dome, personal communication, July 1991.
45. Robert Reed, Alcoa, personal communication, June 1993.
46. Antonio Miguel Marques, Billiton, personal communication, October 1991.
47. Lucia Andrade, Comisao Pro Indio, personal communication, November 1991.
48. See note 2.
49. Dorothy Harris, RTZ, personal communication, July 1991.

Chapter 6: Agribusiness in the Tropics

1. Arnold Newman, _Tropical Rainforest_, Facts on File Inc., New York, 1990, p. 220.
2. H. Jeffrey Leonard, _Natural Resources and Economic Development in Central America_, Transaction Books, Brunswick, N.J., 1987, p. 78.
3. Douglas R. Shane, "Hoofprints on the Forest: An Inquiry Into the Beef Cattle Industry In the Tropical Forest Areas of Latin America," prepared for the U.S. Department of State, Washington, D.C., 1980, p. 117 (unpublished).
4. For the quote, see note 2, p. 75.
5. Tom Barry and Deb Preusch, _The Central America Fact Book_, Grove Press, New York, N.Y., 1986, pp. 151-152.
6. Leslie Crawford, "Panama Offered Banana Investment," _Financial Times_, Feb. 15, 1991.
7. _Ibid._
8. _Ibid._
9. For the quote, see Christopher van Arsdale, "Banana Development in Costa Rica," _Multinational Monitor_, January/February 1991, p. 18.
10. _Ibid._
11. For the quote, see note 9, p. 17.
12. _Ibid._
13. Rocio Lopez, Environmental Association of Sarapiqui, personal communication, November 1991.
14. Carole Douglis, "Banana Split," _World Watch_, January/February 1993, p. 6.
15. See note 13.
16. Gabriela Mena, Chiquita Brands, personal communication, October 1991.
17. "Forestry Officials Probe Disputed Logging," _Tico Times_, San Jose, Costa Rica, July 17, 1992.
18. See note 14, p. 6.
19. _Ibid._, pp. 5-6.
20. John Myrick Ashley, "The Social and Environmental Effects of the Palm Oil Industry in the Oriente of Ecuador," printed manuscript, Oct. 1987, p. 6.
21. Simon Chapman, "Tobacco Control in the Third World," International Organization of Consumer Unions, Penang, Malaysia, 1990, p. 57.
22. _Ibid._, p. 58.
23. _Ibid._

24. *Ibid.*, p. 207.
25. *Ibid.*, p. 58.
26. *Ibid.*, p. 62.
27. Mark Collins, editor, *The Last Rain Forests: A World Conservation Atlas*, Oxford University Press, New York, N.Y., 1990, p. 42.
28. Richard Bourne, *Assault on the Amazon*, Victor Gallancz Ltd., London, U.K., 1978.
29. *Ibid.*, p. 148.
30. "Memorandum on the Responsibility of the Federal Republic of Germany for the Destruction of Tropical Rainforests and Her Obligation to Take Action for Their Protection," ARA, Bielefeld, Germany, 1989, p. 15. Also see note 32, p. 150.
31. "Herbicides: Agent Orange May Go to the South Americans," *Science*, April 6, 1973, p. 43.
32. Norman Myers, "The Hamburger Connection: How Central America's Forests Become North America's Hamburgers," *Ambio*, Vol. 10, No. 1, 1981.
33. See note 3.
34. Christopher Uhl, Pennsylvania State University, personal communication, December 1990.
35. *Ibid.*, and Daniel Nepstad *et al.*, "Surmounting Barriers to Forest Regeneration in Abandoned, Highly Degraded Pastures: A Case Study from Paragominas, Para, Brazil," in *Alternatives to Deforestation: Steps Toward Sustainable Use of the Amazon Rain Forest*, Anthony Anderson, editor, Columbia University Press, New York, N.Y., 1990.
36. See note 3, p. 113.
37. Mary Ann Lederer, McDonald's Corp., personal communication, July 1991.
38. Michelle Beale, Coca-Cola Foods, personal communication, June 1991.
39. See note 16.
40. Decision of the International Water Tribunal, "Association for the Defense of the Sarapiqui and Clean Waters vs. Standard Fruit Co. USA," Amsterdam, The Netherlands, Feb. 21, 1992.
41. Lori Ann Thrupp, "Sterilization of Workers from Pesticide Exposure: Causes and Consequences of DBCP-Induced Damage in Costa Rica & Beyond," World Resources Institute, December 1990 (unpublished).
42. Julie Gozan, "Poisoning Honduras," *Multinational Monitor*, October 1992, p. 4.
43. Judy Kosmo, Goodyear Tire & Rubber, personal communication, October 1991.
44. See note 21.
45. *Ibid.*
46. Geest annual report, Spaulding, Lancashire, U.K., 1991.

Box 6A: The Environmentally Friendly Banana Project

1a. Diane Jukofsky, Rainforest Alliance, personal communication, March 1993.
2a. Chris Wille, Rainforest Alliance, personal communication, March 1993.
3a. Lenin Corrales, Banano Amigo, personal communication, February 1993.
4a. Eduardo Augilar, Corbana, personal communication, February 1993.

Box 6B: The Hamburger Connection

1a. James Brooke, "Peruvian Farmers Razing Rain Forest to Sow Drug Crops," *The New York Times*, Aug. 13, 1989.

Chapter 7: Nontimber Forest Products and Ecotourism

1. Jorge Neves, State Planning and Development Agency research director, Rio Branco, Brazil, personal communication, November 1990.
2. Anthony Dixon, Hannah Roditi and Lee Silverman, "From Forest to Market: A Feasibility Study of the Development of Selected Nontimber Forest Products from Borneo for the U.S. Market," Project Borneo, Cambridge, Mass., 1991, p. 135-6.
3. Robert Repetto and Malcolm Gillis, *Public Policies and the Misuse of Forest Resources*, Cambridge University Press, Cambridge, U.K., 1988.
4. Charles M. Peters, Alwyn H. Gentry and Robert O. Mendelsohn, "Valuation of an Amazonian Rainforest," *Nature*, June 29, 1989, p. 655.
5. Walter V. Reid *et al.*, *Biodiversity Prospecting: Using Genetic Resources for Sustainable Development*, World Resources Institute, Washington, D.C., 1993, p. 12.
6. Norman H. Farnsworth, "Screening Plants for New Medicines," *Biodiversity*, E.O. Wilson, editor, National Academy Press, Washington, D.C., 1988, p. 83.
7. See note 5, p. 15; and David Lenderts, "Plants that Give Life," Rainforest Alliance, New York, N.Y., undated pamphlet.
8. Steven King, Shaman Pharmaceuticals, personal communication, August 1991.
9. Constance Holden, "Saving Forests with Their Own Medicine," *Science*, April 17, 1992. (The original research article appeared in the March 1992 issue of *Conservation Biology*.)
10. Varro Taylor, "Plant Drugs in the Twenty-First Century," *Economic Botany*, Vol. 40, 1986.
11. See note 5, p. 16; and "Ancient Remedies Provide Clues In Search for 'New' Medicines," *Chemecology*, June 1992, p. 10.
12. Sarah Laird, Rainforest Alliance, personal communication, September 1991.
13. See note 5, p. 2; and note 6.
14. Christina Findeisen, "Natural Products Research and the Potential Role of the Pharmaceutical Industry in Tropical Forest Conservation," Rainforest Alliance, New York, N.Y., July 1991.
15. Anne Newman, "Shaman's IPO Success Sets Example for Biotech Firms," *The Wall Street Journal*, Jan. 28, 1993.
16. "Eli Lilly & Co. Investing In Rain-Forest Research," *The Wall Street Journal*, Oct. 23, 1992.
17. See note 15.
18. Thomas Eisner, quoted in a Cornell University press release announcing the Merck-Inbio agreement, Sept. 20, 1991.
19. Leslie Roberts, "Chemical Prospecting: Hope for Vanishing Ecosystems?", *Science*, May 22, 1992.
20. World Resources Institute, World Conservation Union and the United Nations Environment Programme, *Global Biodiversity Strategy*, Washington, D.C., 1992.
21. Elissa Blum, "Making Biodiversity Conservation Profitable," *Environment*, May 1993.
22. For the quote, see Robin Eisner, "Botanists Ply Trade in Tropics, Seeking Plant-Based Medicinals," *The Scientist*, June 10, 1991.
23. Darrell Posey, remarks at conference on "Planning for Amazonia," Yale University, New Haven, Conn., April 1991.
24. See note 5, p. 19.
25. For the quote, see Timothy B. Wheeler, "Deal Shows Biodiversity's Possibilities," *The Baltimore Sun*, June 16, 1992.

26. See note 21.
27. See note 4.
28. See note 2.
29. Nels Johnson and Bruce Cabarle, *Surviving the Cut: Natural Forest Management in the Humid Tropics*, World Resources Institute, Washington, D.C., February 1993, *op. cit.*
30. For more on the life of Chico Mendes and the rubber tappers' movement, see Mary Helena Allegretti and Stephan Schwartzman, "Extractive Production in the Amazon and the Rubber Tappers' Movement," Environmental Defense Fund, Washington, D.C., May 28, 1987; Andrew Revkin, *The Burning Season*, Houghton Mifflin Co., Boston, Mass., 1991; and Alex Shoumatoff, *The World is Burning*, Little Brown and Co., Boston, Mass., 1991.
31. Philip M. Fearnside, "Extractive Reserves in Brazilian Amazonia," *BioScience*, June 1989.
32. Marguerite Holloway, "Sustaining the Amazon," *Scientific American*, July 1993, p. 93.
33. Alfredo Homma, "The Future of Extractive Economies in Amazonia" (in Portuguese), Belem, Brazil, unpublished paper.
34. See note 21.
35. Jason Clay, Cultural Survival, personal communication, August 1991.
36. Phillip Talbot, The Body Shop, personal communication, August 1991.
37. Anthony Anderson, "The Value of the Rainforest: Economic Strategies of Forest Extractivists in the Amazon Estuary," oral presentation at the conference, "Planning for Amazonia: Incorporating Indigenous Peoples' Knowledge into Land Use," Yale University, New Haven, Conn., April 20, 1991.
38. Christopher Uhl et al., "Heart of Palm Extraction in the Amazon Estuary," Institute of Man and the Environment, Belem, Brazil, 1990.
39. Karen Ziffer, Conservation International, personal communication, August 1991.
40. Paul Tebbel, Patagonia Corp., personal comunication, March 1992.
41. Arnold Newman, "Tropical Rainforest," *Facts on File*, New York, N.Y., 1990, p. 207.
42. Robert Winterbottom and Peter Hazlewood, "Agroforestry and Sustainable Development: Making the Connection, *Ambio*, Vol. 16, No. 2-3, 1987.
43. "Indonesia: Java Social Forestry," project profile, Winrock International, Morrilton, Ark., October 1988.
44. Frances J. Seymour, "Social Forestry on Public Lands in Indonesia: A Blurring of Means and Ends?", *Social Forestry: Communal and Private Management Strategies Compared*, The Johns Hopkins School of Advanced International Studies, Washington, D.C., Feb. 14, 1991.
45. Elizabeth Boo, "Ecotourism: The Potentials and Pitfalls," World Wildlife Fund, Washington, D.C., 1990.
46. Bruce Stutz, "Buying Time for Nature with the Tourist Dollar," *The Washington Post*, Dec. 30, 1990.
47. Susanne Frueh, "Report to World Wildlife Fund on Tourism to Protected Areas," Washington, D.C., 1988.
48. See note 46.
49. Inez Gallegos, Costa Rica National Parks Foundation, personal communication, November 1990.
50. Carole Hill, "The Paradox of Tourism in Costa Rica," *Cultural Survival Quarterly*, Vol. 14, No. 1, 1990.
51. Mac Chapin, "The Silent Jungle: Ecotourism among the Kuna Indians of Panama," *Cultural Survival Quarterly*, Vol. 14, No. 1, 1990.
52. Kathleen M. Adams, "Cultural Commoditization in Tana Toraja, Indonesia," *Cultural Survival Quarterly*, Vol. 14, No. 1, 1990.

Box 7A: Iguanas: Chicken of the Forest

1a. Lindsey Gruson, "A Plan to Save Iguanas, and Rain Forests in the Balance," *The New York Times,* Aug. 22, 1989.

Chapter 8: Innovative Investment in the Rain Forest

1. For the quote, see Dena Leibman, "Default or Deliver," *Sierra,* September/October 1990.
2. Bruce Rich, "The Emperor's New Clothes: The World Bank and Environmental Reform," *World Policy Journal,* Spring 1990.
3. *Ibid.*
4. Virginia Luling and Damien Lewis, "Cameroon's Road to Ruin," *Multinational Monitor,* September 1992, p. 12.
5. Marguerite Holloway, "The Big Nada?", *Scientific American,* July 1993, p. 21.
6. Korinna Horta, Environmental Defense Fund, press release, Washington, D.C., Nov. 22, 1991.
7. See note 5.
8. Korinna Horta, Environmental Defense Fund, press release, Washington, D.C., Aug. 20, 1991.
9. James Hester, U.S. Agency for International Development, personal communication, June 1991.
10. Randall K. Curtis and Francisco A. Tourreilles, "Debt-for-Nature Swaps: Reassessing the Role of a Maturing Financial Instrument," The Nature Conservancy, Washington, D.C., January 1992, unpublished paper; updated with personal communication in January 1993.
11. William A. Orne Jr., "The Greening of Latin Debt," *Latin Finance,* April 1990, p. 58.
12. For the quote, see note 9.
13. For the quote, see the article by Stephen G. Greene, "Second Thoughts About Debt Swaps," *Chronicle of Philanthropy,* Nov. 5, 1991.
14. For the quote, see "Debt for Nature: Dirty Deals?", *Mother Jones,* July/August 1990.
15. Randall Hayes, Rainforest Action Network, personal communication, November 1991.
16. See note 7.
17. More information on global warming is in the book by Douglas G. Cogan, *The Greenhouse Gambit: Business and Investment Responses to Climate Change,* Investor Responsibility Research Center, Washington, D.C., 1992.
18. Roger A. Sedjo, "Forests: A Tool to Moderate Global Warming?", *Environment,* January/February 1989, p. 14.
19. Mark Trexler *et al.,* "Forestry as a Response to Global Warming," World Resources Institute, Washington, D.C., June 1989.
20. Sheryl Sturges, "AES Carbon Offset Programs: 1991 and 1992 Summer Updates," AES Corp., Arlington, Va., undated manuscripts.
21. Sheryl Sturges, "The Oxfam America-AES Amazon Program Summary," AES Corp., Arlington, Va., undated manuscript.
22. David Stipp, "New England Firm Plans to Help Save Trees in Malaysia," *The Wall Street Journal,* Aug. 4, 1992.
23. Clive Marsh, Copec, personal communication, Oct. 9, 1992.

24. Francis Putz and Michelle Pinard, University of Florida, personal communication, Jan. 13, 1993.
25. Hans Verwey, Forestry Against Carbon Dioxide Emissions, personal communication, August 1991.
26. Mark Adams, Los Angeles Department of Water & Power, personal communication, November 1991.
27. Mark Trexler, World Resources Institute, personal communication, April 1990.
28. See note 20.
29. Kirsten Johnson, CARE-Guatemela, personal communication, May 1990.
30. Sheryl Sturges, AES Corp., personal communication, June 1990.
31. Peter Hazelwood, CARE, personal communication, May 1990.

Company Index